NOTES
on Bible Readings
1989

INTERNATIONAL BIBLE READING ASSOCIATION
Robert Denholm House, Nutfield
Redhill, Surrey, RH1 4HW, England

© 1988 International Bible Reading Association

ISSN 0140-8275
ISBN 0-7197-0586-X

Cover picture: Dead Sea shore at En-gedi
Photograph by Maurice Thompson, Bible Scene Slide Tours

Typeset by Avonset, Midsomer Norton, Bath, Avon
Printed and bound by Hazell Watson & Viney Limited,
Member of the BPCC Group, Aylesbury, Bucks

CONTENTS

International Bible Reading Association

Dear Friends,

Peter said, 'I now realise that it is true that God treats everyone on the same basis' (**Acts 10.34 – 35**, GNB). He had learnt an important lesson. Like many other Jewish Christians in the early Church, he had thought that people had to become Jews, like him, before they could relate to God. Peter's vision and his encounter with Cornelius convinced him that he was wrong.

It is easy for us to fall into the same trap. We can be tempted to believe that everyone ought to think and act in the same way as we do – that everyone should interpret the Bible as we do, worship in our way and have our experience of God's love. We would really like all Christians to be made in our image! The moment we put it so bluntly we can see how wrong this is. Our aim should not be to make other people become like us, but that everyone should become more Christlike.

Early in 1988 I spent five weeks in India, and learnt a great deal from Christians there. I gained new perspectives on the faith and on the mission of the Church. In some cases, their cultures and situations were very different from those with which I am familiar. In spite of this, we still have much to say to each other, for we share a common humanity and a faith in the same Jesus Christ.

The IBRA can help us to become the people God wants us to be, wherever we live. In the Bible we can all find vision, encouragement and support. Through the daily Bible readings in *Notes on Bible Readings* we can draw on the resources God offers to us. The words of the notewriters enable us to share understandings and experiences which may be different from our own. As we use this book, let us pray with all God's people that we can 'understand how broad and long, how high and deep, is Christ's love . . . and so be completely filled with the very nature of God' (part of **Ephesians 3.18 – 19**, GNB).

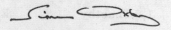

IBRA Staff: Simon J. Oxley (General Secretary)
Joy R. Standen (Editor)

INTRODUCTORY NOTES

These notes may be used with any version of the Bible. However, for convenience, the versions on which the authors have based their notes are named in the introduction to each section. Quotations are from this version unless otherwise stated. Abbreviations used in this book are given below. Sometimes it is suggested that you read the Bible passage after reading some of the notes and this is indicated by the symbol ▶. Each day there is a short prayer or an idea for meditation and these are marked by the symbol ✳. After each Saturday's notes a question is given for personal thought or for discussion in a group. These are not necessarily the work of the authors of the notes. Help and information on the questions is given in *Bible Study Handbook*, and more details about this are to be found on page 77.

ABBREVIATIONS AND ACKNOWLEDGEMENTS

We are grateful for permission to quote from the following Bible versions:

AV   *Authorised Version*

GNB   *Good News Bible* (The Bible Societies/Collins Publishers) – Old Testament © American Bible Society 1976; New Testament © American Bible Society 1966, 1971, 1976;

JB   *Jerusalem Bible* (Darton, Longman & Todd Ltd);

JBP   *The New Testament in Modern English* by J. B. Phillips (Collins Publishers);

LB   *The Living Bible* (Coverdale House Publishers Ltd);

NEB   *New English Bible* (Oxford and Cambridge University Presses) © 1970;

NIV   *The Holy Bible, New International Version* (Hodder and Stoughton) © 1973, 1978 International Bible Society;

RSV   *Revised Standard Version* © 1946 and 1952 Division of Christian Education, National Council of Churches of Christ in USA.

WB   *The New Testament*, a new translation by William Barclay (Collins Publishers).

We are also grateful to quote from:

The Methodist Service Book (Methodist Publishing House) on March 16;

The hymn 'God has spoken – by his prophets' by George W. Briggs (by permission of the Hymn Society of America) on July 8.

IBRA BOOKS for adults 1989 UK prices

NOTES on Bible Readings	**£2.00**
LIGHT FOR OUR PATH	**£2.00**
BIBLE STUDY HANDBOOK – for group leaders (see page 77)	**£1.70**
PREACHERS' HANDBOOK – sermon outlines (see page 87)	**£1.70**
LOOKING AT THE CROSS (see below)	**£2.00**
EVERYDAY PRAYERS **MORE EVERYDAY PRAYERS** **FURTHER EVERYDAY PRAYERS** (see page 162)	**£2.40** each book
BASICS for new Christians (see page 101)	**60p**

All these books may be ordered through your IBRA group secretary or from the appropriate address on the back cover.

LOOKING AT THE CROSS

This book focuses on the last few hours of Jesus' life on earth. Primarily a Bible study, examining the differences in the four Gospel narratives, it is about Good Friday – a day to pray, to wait, to wonder . . . to look at the cross.

● *UK price:* **£2.00**

KNOWING GOD

Notes by the Revd Michael Walker, BD, MTh, PhD

Michael Walker is tutor in Christian Doctrine at the South Wales Baptist College and University College, Cardiff. He has previously held pastorates in Beckenham (Kent), London and Edinburgh, and is one of the contributors to three books in the 'Everyday Prayers' series.

The notes in this section are based on the New English Bible.

Although God is the great and final mystery of our lives, he has surrounded us with 'signs' that point to his existence and that help us to know him. In the Bible, **knowing God** is more than an intellectual exercise; it is an encounter that is characterised by awe, faith, love, surprise and self-knowledge. We come to know God by;

- discerning him within the signs he has given us;
- by following, in obedience, the path he sets before us.

In this section we shall be looking at some of those signs and what they tell us about the nature of God. Central to all those signs is God's greatest sign of his love – Jesus Christ, the Word who became flesh and dwelt among us.

Suggestions for further reading

Picturing God by W. Norman Pittenger (SCM Press Ltd);
The Power of Symbols by F. W. Dillistone (SCM Press Ltd).

Sunday January 1

OUR FLAWED KNOWLEDGE

What does it mean to know God? We can learn about him from the Bible, and our knowledge of him may be increased by a study of theology, but this is not **knowing** him in the deepest sense. This should not surprise us. Think of the ways in which we know others. Our knowledge of them is not increased by making them the subject of academic study. Rather, we know others by sharing our lives with them, by speaking and listening to them and, above all, through loving and being loved. Adam and Eve knew God in this way.

▶ Read **Genesis 3.1–12.**

Adam and Eve were at home in God and shared the world with him. All this was marred when the serpent seduced them into listening to him and accepting his recipe for a better life. Instead, far from improving things, they lost what they had. They became frightened and ashamed of each other and, when God came looking for them in the garden, they hid from him.

This is a story about ourselves. Coming to know God is not an intellectual exercise; it is looking for a lost home, coming to terms with our fear and shame, accepting that God loves us and learning how to love him.

✳ *Lord, may our knowledge of you increase as our love increases.*

Monday January 2
THE SIGN OF THE BURNING BUSH

Yesterday's reading described the human situation as one in which we are no longer at home with God and see him as a stranger. Today, we shall look at the first of many **signs** that God has provided for us in order that we might find our way back to him and know him, no longer as a stranger, but as our Father. **Signs** are important in our pilgrimage. They point the way; they reveal something of the God who is hidden from our sight, and they interpret the world in which we live.

▶ Read **Exodus 3.1−12.**

The burning bush is the sign of God's passionate love, aflame in his heart, always alive and never coming to an end. It is because God is love that he looks on the anguish of his people and resolves to rescue them from their sorrow and captivity (see verses 7−8). Love is central to the character of God. It is the mainspring of his actions and it shapes the destiny towards which he is leading the whole human race.

We can see signs of the divine love in the roses of summer and the red berries of winter. They are present reminders of the loving purposes that lie behind everything.

✳ *Lord, may every tree aflame with life speak to me of your saving love.*

Tuesday January 3
THE SIGN OF THE PASSOVER

As with the burning bush, so the Passover is a sign of God's redeeming activity. Throughout Judaism, in every generation, Passover celebrates the birth of Israel and her deliverance from the bitterness of slavery. From the beginning of Israel's history, God revealed himself as a God who makes freedom possible, opening the doors that have held men and women in captivity. In the darkness of the night, God did his strange work, compelling Pharaoh to release the Jews.

▶ Read **Exodus 12.21–34.**

The Passover reminds us that God's redeeming work has a social and political dimension. It intruded into the economic plans of the Egyptians; it set in motion the migration of a vast community from one land to another, and it forged a diverse company of former slaves into a strong and deeply religious nation.

We must never lose sight of that social dimension of salvation. Like the Jews, Christians believe that, in redeeming us, God makes us part of a community. There is always the temptation to make our Christian faith private and divorce it from its social setting. The sign of the Passover will not permit us to retreat into private worlds of our own making.

✱ *Pray for those who are captives in today's world, that prison doors may be opened for them too.*

Wednesday January 4   **Exodus 19.17 to 20.6**

THE SIGN OF THE LAW

The circumstances under which the law was given to Moses (verses 17–19) can give the mistaken impression that the law itself is a threat to human happiness. We think of the law in negative terms: as a restriction on our freedom; as an impossible standard that burdens us with guilt when we fail to live up to it.

Yet it is 'freedom' wrongly understood, not the law, that is limiting and could destroy us. God reveals himself in the law as one who provides structures of morality and systems of values that enable us to grow to maturity. Without those structures and systems, we would be like people, without map or compass to guide us, living in a moral wilderness and becoming something less than human.

The Jews have always recognised the value of the law, which they call *Torah*. This is at the centre of their faith. Far from being burdened by it, they rejoice in it. Every year, in the feast of *Simchat Torah*, they carry the scrolls of the law around the synagogues, singing and dancing. It is a cause for great joy that God gives us his law and enables us to know him through the pursuit of goodness.

✳ *Lord, help me to love your holy laws and, with the aid of the Holy Spirit, to keep them.*

Thursday January 5   1 Kings 19.1–12
THE SIGN OF THE STILL, SMALL VOICE

Wind, earthquake and fire are familiar signs of God's presence. When Moses was given the law on Mount Sinai, the whole mountain resounded with the power of God's presence. When the Holy Spirit came on the day of Pentecost, his coming was heralded by the sound of rushing wind and affirmed by the tongues of fire that rested above the head of each of the disciples.

But here is another, very different, sign. It is the sign of stillness and silence. In some ways it is more disturbing and difficult to handle than the dramatic signs. In the silence God searches our conscience and asks us questions that are not easy for us to answer. Faced with the earthquake, wind and fire, we can externalise what is happening and hide the true state of our souls from others and from ourselves. In the silence, there is no place to hide.

Silence and listening should always form part of our prayers. Only then can we truly find God and God find us.

✳ *Breathe through the heats of our desire*
    Thy coolness and thy balm;
  Let sense be dumb, let flesh retire;
  Speak through the earthquake, wind, and fire,
    O still small voice of calm!   *John Greenleaf Whittier*

Friday January 6   Hosea 11.1–9
THE SIGN OF THE LOVER

As we draw on our experience, we find conflicting evidence in the ways in which God deals with our lives. There can be harshness in life that seems to point to a God who punishes wrong and reacts severely to our rebellion (verses 5–7). Yet there is also constant evidence of a patient and tenacious love that will not let us go or surrender us to the worst possibilities (verses 1, 4, 8).

Our knowledge of God derives from holding these conflicting experiences in balance. We cannot hide from what is harsh and difficult to bear, pretending it is not there. Nor do such experiences speak the final word about God. The final word is always love: behind everything that comes to us in life is the God who has loved us from the beginning and who will not let us go.

God's love is not a single attribute to be numbered among the rest, nor an aspect of his character to be counterbalanced by others. Love determines all God's attributes and is revealed in every aspect of his character. To know him is to know that we are loved by him, and to be loved by him is to love him.

✳ *Lord, help me to see beyond the dark and fretful experiences that dismay me, to that undying love that governs all things.*

Saturday January 7   Isaiah 10.33 to 11.9
THE SIGN OF THE CHILD

Beyond the turbulent times in which he lived, Isaiah looked to the coming of a child, 'a shoot . . . from the stock of Jesse' (verse 1). In a world where people were motivated by the quest for power and were indifferent to justice, this child would act and speak in a different way (verses 2–5). He would bring into being a new society in which the child would be a sign of the changed order of things, not intimidated by, but leading, the predatory wolf, leopard and young lion; not seduced by, but challenging, the power of the cobra; not threatened by, but dancing over, the viper's nest (verses 6, 8).

Jesus, too, set a child in the midst of his hearers and made him the sign of the kingdom (Matthew 18.1–3). Within the men and women we become, there is the child that we once were. Always challenging our worldly-wise sophistication, our compromises, our fading dreams, is the child we were – the child who believed in endless possibilities, had not then learned to be afraid and was yet to be disillusioned by the world and its ways.

We do not recover that child by regressing into childishness. The child is the sign of hope in a world grown old. Here is the sign of vision. When we become as children, we dare again to believe in the endless possibilities of a world in which God is present.

11

* *Lord, renew within me a childlike spirit, that I may trust, hope and believe in a world in which God is present.*

For group discussion and personal thought

What does it mean to know God? How did you come to know God? Consider what influence other people's beliefs had on you. What else influenced you? How can we increase our knowledge of God?

Sunday January 8   **Daniel 7.2–14**

THE SIGN OF THE MAN

In today's world, oppressive governments and terrorist movements are capable of killing and maiming without any remorse. There are tyrants who seem invincible, their armoury impenetrable and their cruelty boundless. By distancing themselves from human pain, they are unable to feel in themselves the agony they inflict on others. Regrettably, such cruelty seems to confirm our worst fears about the human condition and tempts us to lose faith in humankind.

Daniel was surrounded by nations whose policies towards others were characterised by barbarism. In his visions, they lumbered out of primeval depths like terrible beasts. Yet, he rightly saw that such cruelty bore no semblance of humanity. It was a denial of the human, not an expression of it.

Daniel never lost his faith in the final ascendancy of the human over the barbaric. The hope for the future lay with one 'like a man coming with the clouds of heaven' (verse 13). The one for whom Daniel waited came at last in the perfect humanity of Jesus Christ. He and those who, in their humanity, become like him, are signs of God's gracious presence in a harsh world.

* *Lord, we pray for men and women who choose the way of peace, whose humanity is a sign of the grace and love that hold sway over everything.*

Monday January 9   **Isaiah 40.18–31**

THE SIGN OF THE NATURAL ORDER

The natural order is full of contrasts. There is the contrast of

time. The world into which we are born has existed for countless ages and, after we have died, it may well go on for ages to come. Against the immensity of that time-scale, our own lifetime is little more than the blinking of an eye (verse 24).

Secondly, there is the contrast of **space**. Far more than the prophet could, we are able to see our own planet in the context of its universe and, beyond that, other vast universes. For us, it is even more marvellous that God should know all the stars by name and their movements (verse 26).

The sheer magnitude of time and space intimidates us. Yet the prophet paints his picture of the world not to frighten but to reassure us. The God who numbers the passing of the centuries, knows us in our youth and our age, in our running and our walking. He watches over our lives and, when our strength runs out, he lifts us on eagle's wings.

Our own time is as important to God as all other times. As Jesus said, God knows us just as he knows the fall of every sparrow (Matthew 10.29).

✳ *To thee, from whom we all derive*
Our life, our gifts, our power to give!
O may we ever with thee live,
Who givest all!   *Christopher Wordsworth*

Tuesday January 10   **Zechariah 8.14 – 23**

A SIGN FOR MANY PEOPLES

A true knowledge of God always seems to be for the few rather than for the many. God chose the small nation of Israel to reveal himself. Jesus chose twelve apostles from among the people who were around him. The Church has, at many times and in many places, been a minority. And even within the Church, just as within Israel, it has often seemed that only a small group has fully grasped the meaning of belief in God and its implications for life in the world.

However, God's dealings with small communities serve a far wider purpose. Zechariah saw Israel and the city of Jerusalem itself as a focus of salvation for all humankind. To this nation and this place, 'great nations and mighty peoples' would come in search of God (verse 22). In Zechariah's striking pun, they would 'pluck up courage' and 'pluck the robe of a Jew', following him to where God was to be found (verse 23).

13

God chooses small communities to fulfil his will, not with the aim of excluding the majority, but as a means of bringing them within his loving purposes.

✱ *Lord, may your blessing rest upon our church communities, that they may be signs that point the many towards you and provide them with a way of finding you.*

Wednesday January 11   John 3.1–16

THE SIGN OF THE CROSS

Martin Luther described the ways in which God shows himself to us as 'veils'. They are transparent enough to let through the light but, at the same time, they conceal what lies behind them so that our perception of it is imperfect. There is one place, he said, where God is profoundly hidden from us and yet most perfectly revealed. It is the cross of Christ. Here, in this place of darkness and suffering, God is present with us and shows himself to be love acting on our behalf.

Jesus speaks of that sign that is to be lifted up (verses 14–15). It is the sign that draws people to him and assures us that God loves us (verse 16).

Sometimes we speculate about the nature of God. We try to imagine what God is like and, even when we speak of God the Father, it is as if we imagine another, different reality beyond the God who reveals himself in Jesus. But there is no other God than the God revealed in Christ. There is not a distant God in contrast to the one who is near to us in the darkness of Calvary. There is not a vengeful God in contrast to the God of mercy seen at the cross. There is not a God of justice in heaven who somehow has to be reconciled with the God of love revealed on earth in Jesus.

✱ *Lord, I thank you that I see you at the cross where, concealed in pain, you show me your great love.*

Thursday January 12   John 17.1–12

KNOWING GOD THROUGH CHRIST

For Christians, the chief sign through which we know God is Jesus Christ. He is the key to all the other signs. He is the person in whom we see humanity most perfectly expressed. It is through him that we know eternal life (verse 3). Also, through Christ we know God, and the gifts that he has given

14

us. We know with certainty that Christ comes to us from the Father (verses 6 – 8).

The person of Christ has always been a profound mystery which the Church has endeavoured to explain in its creeds and its doctrines. Important as those creedal statements are for our understanding, nevertheless our ultimate conviction of who Christ is comes to us through our encounter with him. In him we know that we are face to face with a reality that we meet nowhere else. Through Christ we know ourselves to be in the presence of God himself.

✳ *In thee most perfectly expressed*
The Father's glories shine;
Of the full deity possessed,
Eternally divine:
Worthy, O Lamb of God, art thou,
That every knee to thee should bow.   *Josiah Conder*

Friday January 13   Acts 2.42 to 3.10
THE SIGNS OF THE CHURCH

In some sections of the contemporary Church, there has been a good deal of debate on the subject of 'signs and wonders'. Some believe that the life of the Church should be constantly characterised by miracles such as that recorded in today's reading in the healing of the man at the Beautiful Gate of the temple. Happenings such as this are believed to be the signs through which we come to a deeper knowledge of God.

This reading also contains reference to other signs, however, and on these there is little debate among Christians. They are the signs of apostolic teaching, the shared life of the Christian community, the Lord's Supper and prayers (verse 42).

Sometimes, in the quest for a more miraculous or dramatic manifestation of God's presence among us, we undervalue fellowship, word, sacrament and prayer. Yet, whether miracles happen or not, these remain signs through which God is surely known. As long as we listen to his word, look for and find Christ in one another, come to the Holy Table with expectation and joy, and open ourselves to the encounter of prayer, there will be no lack of evidence of Christ among us, nor of the means to know him more deeply.

✳ *Lord, may we value the signs of fellowship, word, sacrament and prayer above all others.*

Saturday January 14

THE END OF OUR KNOWLEDGE

All the 'signs' that speak to us of God are temporal:

- The signs of him that we see **in nature** belong to an order that constantly passes through a process of birth, growth, decay, death and rebirth.
- The **language** we use is subject to change – words alter their meaning and ideas their significance.
- The **materials** we use in the sacraments are temporary and finite.
- The **people** who, in love and faith, are signs to us of God's goodness are only our companions for a while.

However, although the signs are transient and part of this passing order, what they signify is eternal and imperishable.

▶ Read **2 Corinthians 4.16 to 5.10.**

Here Paul speaks of a truth – a reality at the heart of all things yet unseen – that is the goal of all our journeying (verses 16–18).

The truth given to us in words, the grace communicated to us in the sacraments, the love invested in us by our friends and families, the goodness glimpsed time and again in human actions – all these are realities that will last into eternity, far beyond the earthly and material medium through which they are conveyed to us.

✳ *Lord, you have filled the world with the evidence of your presence. We know you in things that we hear, see, touch and feel. May we cherish earthly things where they are the messengers of your grace. May we grow more and more to know that love which lasts for ever.*

For group discussion and personal thought

God continues to reveal himself to us in many ways. In what **new** ways have you come to know more about God in the past year? Now read again **2 Corinthians 4.16–18.** How do these verses help us to continue growing in our knowledge of God?

- The weekly questions in *Notes on Bible Readings* are not necessarily the work of the authors of the notes. *Bible Study Handbook* gives helpful material on these questions both for leaders of groups and for personal use (see page 77).

JESUS – TEACHER AND HEALER

Luke's Gospel 2–9

Notes by the Revd A. Gordon Jones, BD

Gordon Jones is an active supernumerary Methodist minister in East London. Previously, he has worked with the Richmond Fellowship for Moral Welfare and Rehabilitation.

The notes in this section are based on the New English Bible.

During this year there will be three sections of readings from **Luke's Gospel**. This first section begins with an incident in Jesus' boyhood and then tells of his ministry in Galilee up to the time when he set out to go to Jerusalem to face his final challenge. We shall read of Jesus' teachings and healings, of the success he had, and of the opposition he aroused. All through our readings we shall be aware of his integrity, his sense of purpose, his fearlessness and his great love.

Although it is not known for certain who wrote this Gospel, many have attributed it to Luke, a doctor and friend of Paul. The author is certainly a person of wide and humane sympathies. He clearly shows Jesus' care for all people – non-Jews as well as Jews, social outcasts and women. He saw Jesus as the Saviour of the world.

Suggestions for further reading

The Gospel of Luke by William Barclay, Daily Study Bible (Saint Andrew Press);

The Gospel of St Luke by George B. Caird, Pelican Gospel Commentaries (Penguin Books);

The Gospel of Luke by E. Earle Ellis, New Century Bible Commentaries (Marshall, Morgan and Scott);

The Gospel According to St Luke by Leon Morris, New Testament Commentaries (Inter-Varsity Press).

Sunday January 15   Luke 2.41–52

Parents often delight in recalling incidents from the

childhood of their grown-up children. We can imagine Mary telling the Gospel-writer: 'Even when Jesus was a boy, he had a strangely deep understanding of religious matters. That time when we lost him after the Passover festival – and found him in the temple – do you know what he called the temple? He called it, "My Father's House"! And he said he just had to be there. He felt like that about God even then. I was bewildered – he was growing away from us.'

By twelve years of age Jesus had recognised his unique relationship with God. Although for a while he continued to live under the authority of Mary and Joseph, the time did come when he had to make a choice between the claims of family and the claims of God (see Luke 8.19 – 21). He loved his family, but he had to be in his 'Father's house' and about his 'Father's business' (verse 49, AV).

This choice is not an uncommon one for those who have heard the call of God and know they must obey, even if it means turning away from family, friends, country and culture. It is a time of anguish, but in the end the will of the Father must be done.

✷ *Father, when I experience conflicting loyalties, show me what it means to be truly loyal to you, and give me courage to obey.*

Monday January 16   Luke 3.1–14

John came from a devout priest's family. How much of his zeal he must have owed to his parents! But he was to break through the boundaries of the conventional religion of his time. He was like Jeremiah before him, and like John Wesley after him – sons of priests who became prophets!

John saw his work as calling people to **repentance** – true turning to God – so that they were ready to receive the coming Messiah. 'Repentance' for John was not just to be declared in words – pious prayers of penitence were not enough. Neither was repentance to be a means by which the people affirmed their tradition – an escape into a false sense of security because they held the faith of Abraham. It was to be a personal experience for each individual, shown in a change of life.

Most of us say a prayer of confession at least once a week, on Sundays; and the forgiveness of our sins is declared by the one leading worship. But what difference does that make? None at all – unless it is accompanied by a determination to put right

18

the wrong things in our daily living. It is not the prayers of confession which we say on Sunday but the practical outworking of them, in our actions at work or at home each day of the week, that shows the reality of our repentance.

✴ *Lord, when I turn towards you, help me also to move closer to you.*

Tuesday January 17   Luke 3.15 – 38

We shall turn our attention to five things in this reading:

- **John's humility.** When the people began to think that John was the Messiah, he pointed beyond himself to the only true Saviour.
- **John's message.** Repentance was to be only the beginning; baptism with water was merely a sign of turning to God. The real baptism Jesus would bring would be an inner experience − devastating and life-giving. Baptism means nothing unless confirmed by our acceptance of the Spirit of God in Christ.
- **John's courage.** He was not afraid to preach his message even to the rich and powerful, whatever the consequences.
- **Jesus' identification with his people's hopes.** Why did Jesus undergo baptism of repentance when, as we believe, he was sinless? In being baptised Jesus was showing that he was one with the people in their longing for the coming of the kingdom of God.
- **Jesus' identification with the whole human race.** Verses 23 – 38 may seem dull and uninteresting to read, but they remind us that Jesus was human with forbears like the rest of us. This list goes right back to Adam, thus showing that Jesus is truly one with all humankind.

✴ *Give thanks that Christ has come into our human life that we may share his glory.*

Wednesday January 18   Luke 4.1 – 13

Luke's Gospel has been called 'The Gospel of the Spirit'. Yesterday we read how the Holy Spirit came upon Jesus at his baptism (3.22). Today we read how the Spirit led Jesus into the wilderness for forty days, during which time he worked out his calling. After his temptations, Jesus began his public ministry 'armed with the power of the Spirit' (4.14). When

19

Jesus finally left his friends, he promised them that they would be armed with the same power (24.49).

The Holy Spirit is God speaking to us and working in us, but there is a part of us which resists him. Paul called this our 'lower nature', and he wrote of the conflict between this and the Spirit (see Galatians 5.17). Jesus faced that conflict in the desert. He was tempted to win people by material gifts, compromise and spectacular acts, but he rejected all these means – and won his battle.

The Christian life has been described in many attractive ways, but we must not forget that it is also a life of **conflict** between God's will and our 'lower nature'. However, the Spirit, who empowered Jesus in the wilderness, is the same Spirit who can arm and protect us.

✳ *Pray for the Holy Spirit to come into your life.*

January 18–25 is the Week of Prayer for Christian Unity

During these eight days, pray that the Spirit of God may break down the barriers which, in our fear and pride, we are tempted to erect against each other.

✓ **Thursday January 19**   Luke 4.14–20

We have seen that Jesus identified himself with his nation in his baptism, and was identified with the whole human race through his genealogy (see January 17). However, at the beginning of his ministry Jesus identified with his immediate relations and friends. He did not make some great public declaration of his gospel on a mountain-top or in the capital city. Rather, he made it in his home town of Nazareth, in his usual place of worship and to the people who had watched him grow up from a child.

The gospel of Jesus is indeed of cosmic proportions – it is a message for all time, and for the whole earth; but it is also for **us** in our small, personal environments. It begins just where we are. Christ rules the universe, but he wants to enter **our** homes, **our** churches, **our** hearts.

To the people in his home town synagogue Jesus read a familiar passage from Isaiah 61.1–2, which contained

Israel's greatest hopes of salvation for the poor, the imprisoned, the blind and the broken. No wonder all eyes were fixed on him after he had read those words. Did he really fulfil these hopes? The good news – the gospel – is that he did, and that he continues to fulfil them today. Read verses 18–19 again as you think about the desperate material and spiritual situation of millions in the world today.

✷ *Lord God, out of the depths millions cry to you today for help. May they find the answer to their cries in Christ.*

Friday January 20   Luke 4.21–30

Jesus claimed that in him, through his ministry, the fulfilment of Isaiah's hopes were being expressed. There was immediate joy and admiration, but then doubt began to creep in: 'We know this man and his family,' they said. Jesus gently reminded them that familiarity breeds contempt. When he clearly illustrated that this good news was not to be limited to them, as Jews (verses 24–27), their admiration turned to anger.

What had happened to change the people's attitude? It seemed that they had interpreted the words from **Isaiah** in a different way from Jesus. For them, the words applied to their own nation only and thus excluded Gentiles. They spoke not so much of the universal love of God, as of their specialness and their superiority as Jews. Perhaps their hopes were founded on the verses which followed those that Jesus read (Isaiah 61.5–6).

Is our acceptance of the gospel based on self-centred wishes? Or is it because our eyes have been opened to the needs of others? Do we long to hear the gospel proclaimed not just for our own sakes, but also for the sake of those less fortunate than ourselves?

✷ *Lord Jesus Christ, may the love we discover in your gospel show itself in the love we show to others.*

Saturday January 21   Luke 4.31–44

Jesus' authority was different from that of the scribes and Pharisees to whom authority was given because of their position in society. Jesus had no such status. However, what he said and did carried a deeper kind of authority which convinced people that here was someone who was in touch with truth and reality. This is illustrated in the story of the devil-possessed man whose shriek indicated that the powers of 'illness' in him recognised in Jesus a power greater than themselves.

Do we still believe in devils today? Perhaps not in the naïve way people once did. But, if we believe that all illnesses are against God's will, then they can and should be seen as aspects of evil to be overcome. A missionary doctor, in attempting to explain to an African villager that a particular disease was caused not by devil-possession but by a virus, showed him a slide of the virus in his microscope. 'That is what caused the illness,' said the missionary. 'Yes, I know,' the villager replied, 'but the devil sent it!' Sickness is an enemy – God's will is that it shall be destroyed.

* *Pray for those engaged in the work of bringing health where there is sickness – researchers, medical and psychiatric doctors, nurses and counsellors.*

For group discussion and personal thought
Look again at the words Jesus read in **Luke 4.18–19.** Who are the 'poor', 'blind' and 'oppressed' in the world today? Discuss ways in which the Church can bring (a) 'good news to the poor', (b) 'sight to the blind' and (c) freedom 'to the oppressed'.

Sunday January 22   **Luke 5.1–11**
The setting for today's reading is the Lake of Gennesaret, which was another name for the Sea of Galilee – an inland lake about thirteen miles (20km) long and eight miles (12km) wide. It was here that Jesus called Simon and his companions to follow him.

In **Luke** there is no 'formal' call of the disciples as in **Matthew** and **Mark**. Rather, we read of Jesus helping some men with their fishing. Jesus, using play on words, suggested that Simon and his colleagues could put their fishing skills to even greater use by 'catching' people – drawing them into God's kingdom. They got the point.

When Christ calls us to share in his work, he often speaks to us in our own familiar sphere, calling us to use our skills to further the work of his kingdom. Day school teachers may be called to teach or preach in church, musicians to enrich the worship by playing or singing, and those who work with their hands to help and advise the elderly and handicapped. For example: a skilled engineer, together with a group of doctors, is giving much of his time to invent and create special equipment to help disabled people to cope better with their individual disabilities. What are your particular gifts? Maybe Christ is calling you to offer them to him.

✳ *Reflect on these words of Paul: 'There are varieties of gifts but the same Spirit. There are varieties of service, but the same Lord.' (1 Corinthians 12.4 – 5)*

Monday January 23

In the time of Jesus, people who had leprosy were treated as social outcasts. It has been the same in more recent times. In a certain West African town those with leprosy lived in a separate colony. Their isolation was a worse burden than their illness. How gladly they welcomed some students from a nearby college who visited them regularly and came to take services for them!

▶ Read **Luke 5.12 – 16.**

This man was sure that Jesus could heal him, but he wondered if he actually would. Jesus did heal him – and then told him to observe the laws regarding a person who had been cured of a skin-disease (see Leviticus 14.1 – 9).

Who are the people in our time who are avoided socially? Are they the mentally ill? Are they those who appear to have brought trouble upon themselves – such as alcoholics and drug addicts? Are they sufferers from AIDS? Are they perhaps the bereaved? And to what extent are people avoided because of class snobbery and racism? With his healing touch, Jesus went to the despised, the feared, the sinful, those suffering through their own fault or through no fault of their own. Do we, his followers, do the same?

✳ *Forgive us, Father, for fearing and avoiding those who are in great need of love. Help us to follow the example of Jesus and help the outcasts of our society today.*

Tuesday January 24   Luke 5.17 – 26

Today, if you felt ill and, upon consulting your doctor, were told: 'Your sins are forgiven you', you would no doubt be very surprised! However, if you lived in a time when most people firmly believed that all illnesses were a punishment for sins, these words would indeed be good news, for they would be clearing the way for a recovery. It was the general understanding among Jews that sickness was God's punishment. Jesus did not hold that view, but the paralysed man probably did. He was given hope when Jesus assured him that he was a forgiven man. Jesus dealt with the paralysed man's underlying fears and anxieties before healing his outward symptoms.

We know that a person's illness is not usually the result of sin. Yet guilt can lead to, or worsen, physical ill-health. The removal of our guilt, by the assurance that we are forgiven children of God, then becomes an integral part of our cure.

Christ is the healer – he gives us wholeness and reunites us with the love of God. Whether or not a physical cure is evident, we are made whole by his word of forgiveness.

✳ *Lord, we pray for wholeness, so that whether or not we are cured, we may have victory over our sufferings and be enabled to live full and joyous lives.*

Wednesday January 25   Luke 5.27 – 39

In today's reading there are three challenges which were addressed to those regarded as the most religious in Jesus' time. Are they addressed to us, too?

- The challenge to **respectability** (verses 27 – 32). Jesus called Levi, a dishonest tax-gatherer, to be one of his disciples and then shared in a party with his associates. Do we distance ourselves from those who do not share our church life, or are not among our accustomed circle of friends?
- The challenge to a **joyless religion** (verses 33 – 35). There is a deeply serious note in our faith. But if this hides from us, and from others, the basic joy that Christ brings – the joy of forgiveness, in the presence of the risen Lord – are we not distorting the whole meaning of Christianity?
- The challenge to **old ways of thinking** (verses 36 – 39). The faith of our fathers is our faith, too. However, the ways in which they expressed it, their dated language and pictures, may no longer fit the thinking, needs and opportunities of today's world. All too often we refuse to listen to those who are re-thinking the faith. We fear to move forward. But our God is always on the move – are we with him?

✳ *O Breath of life, come sweeping through us,*
  Revive your Church with life and power;
O Breath of life, come, cleanse, renew us,
  And fit your Church to meet this hour. Bessie P. Head

Thursday January 26   Luke 6.1 – 11

Rules are necessary, but they can limit genuine goodness. The
ten commandments were splendid principles; but, by the time
of Jesus, they had been expanded into hundreds of detailed
regulations. Jesus said that there were only two basic rules –
love God, and love your neighbour (see Matthew 22.36 – 40).
Every other regulation should be looked at in the light of
these. Unnecessary work was forbidden on the Sabbath. That
was a good principle, for we need a day of rest. But suppose
this meant human beings suffering unnecessarily as a
consequence? The hungry disciples were seen to be reaping
corn – and reaping was forbidden on the Sabbath. Jesus
responded to the Pharisees' criticisms by quoting an example
of how one rule was waived because of human need in David's
time (1 Samuel 21.1 – 6).

On another Sabbath, Jesus was faced with the possibility of
healing a man's withered arm. Would this be seen as
breaking the 'no work' rule? Jesus got in first, and challenged
the Pharisees to say whether doing harm – for that is what not
helping the suffering man would have been – was allowed on
the Sabbath.

Throughout his ministry Jesus continued to challenge the
rigidity, lifelessness and inhumanity of the official religion of
his time. Likewise, he challenges us today. He does not ask us,
'Are you keeping the rules?', but 'Do you love one another?'

✳ *Lord, help me not to be rigid, as the Pharisees were, but to*
  live each day, guided by your love and wisdom.

Friday January 27   Luke 6.12 – 19

In Luke we often read of Jesus spending time in prayer (for
example, see 3.21; 5.16; 9.18,29; 11.1 and 22.41). In today's
reading we see how Jesus prayed all night before choosing the
twelve **apostles** – 'those sent out'. Jesus did not follow his
human ambitions, but what he discerned to be the will of his
Father. This is a thought to be borne in mind by all Christians
and churches who are making decisions or future plans.

The gospel was spread not by individuals each working on their own, but by a group working as a team. Jesus had many disciples and from these he selected twelve to be trained as apostles. What a mixed bunch they were – fishermen, a tax-gatherer, one who had belonged to a rebel group! These men loved him and he entrusted to them the continuance of his work.

There is a story told about Jesus meeting the angel Gabriel after he had finished his work on earth. 'Lord,' Gabriel said to Jesus, 'you have done a wonderful work on earth, what plans have you made for carrying on that work?' 'I have given the message to Peter and John and to the other disciples,' replied Jesus. 'But supposing they let you down, what other plans have you made?' Gabriel asked. 'I have no other plans,' Jesus said quietly, 'I am depending on them.'

✳ *Lord, we constantly fail you; yet we love you. Give us deeper love and stronger faith, and use us in your kingdom.*

Saturday January 28   Luke 6.20–26

Jesus' teaching here may seem absurd to many people today. 'Surely,' they say, 'the happy ones are those who have plenty, eat well, enjoy life and are popular.' But are they right? In a world dedicated to such aims we find fear, division, racism and war. Jesus turned the world's values upside-down. We shall look at two main things that today's verses have to say to us:

● It is not those who are well-endowed with this world's goods who are dear to God, but those who are in need or in distress. We are challenged to have special concern for the oppressed: for example, for starving children, and victims of political struggles and injustice. We are called to be God's agents of loving response to their cries of need.

● People who suffer through oppression are likely to long for something better – in fact, to reach out towards God. On the other hand, those who are materially comfortable and regard this world as the only world, may miss the offer of entering God's kingdom. Jesus said, 'How hard it is for the wealthy to enter the kingdom of God!' (Luke 18.24).

✳ *Father God, help us to long not for wealth, prestige and ease, but for love, humility and compassion, so that we may become true followers of Christ. Give us the mind that was in him.*

For group discussion and personal thought

Read again **Luke 5.12–13**. In Jesus' time, people who had skin-diseases (leprosy) were considered to be 'unclean' and were avoided by everyone. Who are the people in our time who are avoided socially? In what ways can we show them the kind of acceptance and love which Jesus showed to social outcasts?

Sunday January 29   **Luke 6.27–36**

Many people say, 'Love my enemies — that is ridiculous! Surely the only thing to do with enemies is to destroy them — either physically or with words — or ignore them and so cut them out of one's life. Why should we love them?' Jesus' answer is that if we love them then they are no longer our enemies. We must endeavour to turn our enemies into our friends, and so become a part of God's family (verse 35).

In Ephesians 2.14–16, we are reminded that, when we were God's enemies, he did not set about to destroy us. Rather, he set about to destroy the things that make us his enemies and enemies of one another. In Christ, it was not the enemies that were destroyed, but the *enmity*.

Jesus hated sin but he loved sinners. He was able to see the good in them. When we begin to see good in our enemies, then we shall find that we can love them, and the enmity between us and them will begin to be healed. If we are not willing to forgive those who hurt us, and continue to nurse bitter and revengeful feelings against them, then we are damaged. Only as we allow love to flow through us to others can we be spiritually whole.

✳ *Pray by name for those you are tempted to regard as enemies.*

Monday January 30

There is a West African proverb that says: 'When you point a finger at anyone, three fingers point back at you.' When we judge another person, it is likely that our own prejudices and failings will be revealed. For example, if I say of someone, 'That person talks too much,' I am probably indicating my own unease because I do not have any clear opinions of my own.

There is obviously a place in our personal and social relationships for judgements to be made, but only in a spirit of humility and compassion. To those who wanted to stone a woman who had been caught in the act of adultery, Jesus said: 'That one of you who is faultless shall throw the first stone' (John 8.7) – but no one dared to do it.

▶ Now read **Luke 6.37 – 42.**

Here Jesus teaches that only those who have learned the art of self-criticism are fit to give true judgements.

Our readings for the past three days (Luke 6.20 – 42) have all had the same basic theme: the greedy, the unforgiving and the judgemental are out of touch with the reality of God's kingdom of selflessness, love and humility. Only those who have understood and grasped these values are truly part of God's family.

✳ *Help me, Lord, to see others and myself as you see us.*

Tuesday January 31   Luke 6.43 – 49

On festive occasions a tree may be decorated with imitation fruit. It looks very attractive, but everyone knows that the fruit is not edible. For example, a Christmas tree can never produce real oranges, apples or figs. A tree is only able to produce the fruit which originates from within its own cells.

In the same way, despite appearances to the contrary, a person's words and actions are the consequences of what is inside the heart. Pretence is useless. It is what is in a person that makes that person. To say, 'Lord, Lord,' but have no genuine desire to obey the Lord's commands, will soon sound hollow. As Christians we have been called to bear fruit – the fruit of the Spirit spoken of in Galatians 5.22 – 23a, which is 'love, joy, peace, patience, kindness, goodness, fidelity, gentleness, and self-control'.

Many people have refused to accept the Spirit of Jesus, and have rejected his attitudes and values. Sooner or later, bitter and harmful fruits begin to appear in their lives.

Jesus used another example from everyday life – the story of two houses (verses 48 – 49) – to illustrate the importance of a person's inner life. Unless the foundation of our life is Christ, then our self-confidence will soon collapse and our life will fall apart. There is only one true way – the way of Christ.

✳ *Lord, may your Spirit dwell in me so that I may grow more like you.*

A Roman centurion had considerable power and responsibility in a country which was under the rule of Rome. The centurion in today's reading was unusual in that he was popular with the Jews and had built them a synagogue. He was one of those rare persons who wielded power and yet possessed humility. Familiar with military authority, he recognised a greater kind of authority in Jesus and was willing to submit to it. Jesus interpreted that ability to accept an authority greater than his own, as evidence of his faith (verse 9).

Many people so value their independence that they become proud of their own unaided ability to run their lives. Such pride is dangerous. We are all fallible – liable to error and sin. If we humbly realise this and seek God as our authority, then we are putting our faith in the only true power.

In one of her plays, Dorothy Sayers imagines that this centurion was the one who was responsible for overseeing Jesus' crucifixion. If so, imagine his feelings of sadness, and yet wonder, as he saw his benefactor still somehow exercising authority – the authority of love – even in his dying. His faith deepened. He could only whisper, 'Truly this man was a son of God' (Mark 15.39).

✳ *Lord Christ, help me to recognise your authority and, in simple faith, to submit myself entirely to you.*

In the Gospels there are three stories of Jesus bringing the dead back to life – the young man in today's reading, Jairus' daughter (Luke 8.40 – 56) and Lazarus (John 11.1 – 44). They all show Jesus' deep compassion for the close relatives whose loss was especially hard and distressing – a widow who had lost her son; parents who had lost their only daughter; two sisters who had lost the brother on whom they relied. However we may interpret these stories, they demonstrate the deep understanding and compassion of Christ. They tell us that God is not apathetic to our situations. He, with all his strengthening love, shares our sorrows as well as our joys.

When the onlookers saw Jesus bring this man back to life, they were reminded of the time when Elijah had compassion on a widow and earnestly prayed that God would give life back to her dead son (see 1 Kings 17.17 – 24). In Jesus, the people recognised a likeness to Elijah – 'a great prophet'; but Jesus was more than a prophet. He was the Christ – the Messiah – the one who authoritatively declared the love of God in words and actions. He was the one who defeated the powers of death.

✱ *In your prayers remember those who mourn the death of someone they love, asking that they may experience the peace and hope that comes from a compassionate God.*

Friday February 3

John the Baptist had courageously preached in the wilderness, calling people to repent in readiness for the coming of the Messiah. Perhaps he imagined that Jesus would bring about a great revolution in the life of the nation. But now John was in prison, and nothing seemed to be happening – no overthrow of Roman dominion, no messianic triumph. So he sent messengers to Jesus to question him.

▶ Read **Luke 7.18 – 23**.

In his reply to John, Jesus was saying in effect, 'I have not come to set up a militant, material kingdom. I have come to show countless individuals the loving care and mercy of God – new life for the disabled and new hope for the oppressed. This is what the kingdom of God means.'

Christ brings us the assurance of the love of God in all situations and circumstances. He offers us a wholeness of life which is far more than a cure of our physical illnesses or a release from literal imprisonment. He brings light to those who are in spiritual darkness and freedom to those who are imprisoned by sin, fear or anxiety. Jesus never promised his followers material ease – rather he promised the opposite (Mark 13.9) – but he did promise us the presence and the love of God with us always.

✱ *Think about the ways in which God's kingdom is present today.*

Saturday February 4   Luke 7.24 – 35

What a wonderful testimonial Jesus gave John! John was no weakling, no soft, effeminate courtier in expensive clothes – he was a **prophet**. And more than that, he was the herald or forerunner of the Messiah. Jesus pointed to John's greatness by saying that the words of the prophet Malachi (3.1) applied to him.

However, despite all this, John belonged to the old dispensation, to BC rather than AD, to the era of the Old Testament rather than to the New Testament. John was the last of the pre-Christian prophets and he had the privilege of announcing the coming of the new age. But the kingdom Jesus established was so much greater than all that had gone before that the humblest member of it is greater than John.

John did not point people to himself but to Jesus, for he knew that it was Jesus who held the key to a full life. Jesus and his gospel were greater than John because:

- John preached repentance, but Jesus offered forgiveness.
- John alerted people to their need, but Jesus was able to satisfy their need.

It is the same with those who proclaim Christ today. We must leave our hearers admiring not us, but Christ. Our lives must lead others to seek the secret of life in Christ.

✳ *Father, we thank you for those who have led us to Christ. Help us to lead others to him.*

For group discussion and personal thought

Discuss Jesus' teaching, in **Luke 6.27 – 36**, about our reaction towards those who would harm us. In what ways does non-retaliation condone or encourage wrongdoing? Think of some specific situations today (personal, social or international) in which there is enmity, and consider what our reactions should be in the light of Jesus' teaching.

Sunday February 5   Luke 7.36 – 50

This story of a sinful woman, who anointed Jesus' feet, vividly illustrates the close relationship between love and forgiveness. When forgiveness is experienced and guilt removed, the grateful recipient responds with love. The parable which Jesus told to Simon (verses 41 – 42) suggests that the more we experience forgiveness, the greater our response of love will be.

A warm-hearted person is more ready to forgive and open to receive forgiveness than a cold, self-righteous person is. People who think they are in no need of forgiveness are often hard, insensitive and forbidding. They do not realise that their cold attitude hinders them from giving and receiving love, both to God and to other people. However, truly loving people – people of compassion who withhold harsh judgements – are those who know they have received from God more compassion and understanding than they ever deserve. When we lovingly contemplate the cross of Christ, we not only realise our need of forgiveness, but also we know that we are forgiven; our pride is dissolved and we become truly loving people.

✴ *When I survey the wondrous cross,*
  On which the Prince of glory died,
  My richest gain I count but loss,
  And pour contempt on all my pride.   *Isaac Watts*

Monday February 6

▶ First, read **Luke 8.1–3.**

What a mixed company travelled with Jesus! His friends and disciples did not belong to one social class or sex. Women, as well as men, followed him. Joanna was connected with the royal household, and Mary Magdalene is traditionally believed to have been a prostitute. The call of Christ crosses all boundaries.

▶ Now read **Luke 8.4–10.**

Jesus' parable of the sower contains both a challenging and an encouraging message. He knew that his disciples – and, in fact, all who would follow him – would be despondent at times because of lack of response and opposition to their preaching. In this parable he indicated that this was to be expected, and encouraged his followers to believe that there would be a harvest – that the seed does bear fruit.

Jesus often taught in parables. Those who were eager to know the truth quickly understood their deeper meaning, while to others they were just stories until they were ready to go further. God never forces himself on anyone – he leaves them free to choose for themselves. We must not become overwhelmed with despair because so many reject Christianity. Rather, let us remember the millions who have accepted it.

✴ *Lord, give me receptive ears to hear your word, and the courage to speak it to others.*

What prevents people from accepting Christ and following his way? Three things are suggested in the explanation of the parable of the sower:

● The first is a **shut mind**, a mind which refuses to listen to any new teaching or idea.

● The second is **superficiality**. A person may get caught up in the emotionalism of following Jesus, but have not considered what this really means in terms of Christian living. Such religion is only 'skin-deep'.

● The third is allowing oneself to become so **busy** with other things that Christ gets crowded out.

In contrast with these three types of 'soil', there is the good 'soil'. This stands for those who hear God's word, accept it with complete sincerity, keep it in their hearts and minds, consider what it means for them and seek to let it bear fruit in their lives. In following Christ we shall experience setbacks and times of discouragement, but we must never despair for the 'harvest' is sure. We are called to work patiently to spread God's kingdom.

✳ *Father, may I always be open to your word, ready to listen to and understand whatever you have to say to me, and willing to respond to your call.*

Ash Wednesday, February 8

Jesus did not dismiss the natural family as being of no significance. Remember how he restored a young man to his widowed mother (see February 2), how he spoke sternly to those Pharisees who evaded the commandment to honour their parents (Matthew 15.4 – 6), and how from the cross he commended his mother into John's care (John 19.26 – 27). Nevertheless, Jesus put family love in the right perspective.

▶ Read **Luke 8.19 – 21**.

'Charity begins at home,' we say – but it does not stop there. In the intimacy of the family we learn to love, but that love must extend to the wider world. Our natural family, our nation or race, even our church, can actually limit love. Only commitment to Christ, first and foremost, can safeguard us from this. Sometimes we may have to resist the pull of family ties if our loyalty to God clashes with their demands. A happy, human family is a centre of love, but it must never be an enslaving love.

▶ Now read **Luke 8.22 – 25**.

Coping with conflicts of loyalty between God and our family can be very distressing. But it is comforting to know that, in all the stresses and storms of life, Christ is with us and he will not let them overwhelm us.

✳ *Lord Jesus Christ, as we begin the season of Lent and seek to follow you on your way to Calvary, help us to give our ultimate loyalty to the Father, as you did, whatever the cost.*

✓Thursday February 9   Luke 8.26 – 39

The country of the Gergesenes (or Gerasenes or Gadarenes) was most likely Gentile territory. The madman had given himself, or been given, the name of 'Legion' – he felt as if a legion of soldiers were attacking him. His first reaction to Jesus was fear. The challenge that complete sanity presents to insanity often produces an initial panic and hostility.

In the time of Jesus, it was widely believed that mad people were possessed by devils. If the devils were got rid of in some clearly-seen way, then the madness would be gone for ever. Therefore, when the pigs charged into the lake, probably disturbed by the madman's shouts and screams, Jesus saw this as an opportunity to convince the man that he was cured.

All this frightened and angered the local inhabitants. They had lost their pigs – but surely that was a small cost for the healing of a tormented human being? They asked Jesus to go away and leave them alone. Sometimes we treat Jesus in a similar way for we would rather be 'safe' with our familiar, dull lives than risk experiencing a new and exciting way of living.

Jesus often called people to come with him. However, he told this man to go back to his home town and tell people of the wonderful things God had done for him.

✳ *Lord, when you say to us in our need, 'Come'; help us not to be afraid to respond. When you say to us, 'Go'; give us the desire and the courage to obey.*

✓Friday February 10   Luke 8.40 – 48

In this reading we have the story of two **daughters**. One was the only daughter of loving parents; the other was a woman whose illness had made her ceremonially unclean and left her feeling alone and unwanted. Jesus restored her to the human

family with his gentle words, 'My daughter' (verse 48).
Today's verses are also the story of two '12-year-olds'. One had
lived for only twelve years and Jesus was asked to give her
more years; the other had endured twelve years of living
death – ostracism – and Jesus gave her new life and a sense of
belonging again.

We know that Jesus possessed wonderful healing powers,
but we know little about how they worked. What we do know
is that they were not just easy acts of magic – Jesus actually
felt power go out of him and afterwards felt drained of energy.
That leads us to think how little we know of what it means to
Christ when he heals **our** fears and distresses, our sins and
selfishness.

Jesus is very much involved with our healing inasmuch as
he suffers with us in our suffering. It is as if he releases us
from our cross, by yet again taking up his own cross. He is
truly God's suffering servant – his longing to heal broken
humanity led him to the knowledge that he must die.

✴ *Read and meditate upon Isaiah 53.4–5.*

✓ **Saturday February 11**　　　　　　　　　**Luke 8.49 – 56**

There are times when pride and prejudice – the barriers we
put up against people we do not like – come tumbling down.
Desperate need forces us to look beyond our prejudices and
recognise that those people are the ones who can truly help us.
Perhaps this was the case with Jairus. He may have shared
with other synagogue rulers a suspicion of Jesus and his
outspoken teaching. However, in his distress, he knew that
Jesus was the only one who could possibly help him. Humbly,
he asked for help (verse 41) – and Jesus responded. He did not
treat Jairus as a humbled opponent but as a grieving father,
encouraging his faith and going with him to his house.

Do we sometimes have doubts about Christ and feel we
cannot accept all his teachings? We may even oppose him in
our mind. Then, a crisis comes in our life – a time of great fear,
burdening guilt, or extreme loss – and we **know**, deep within
us, that only Christ can meet our need as he offers us the
forgiving, healing love of God. Hesitatingly – perhaps because
of our past unfaithfulness – we come to Jesus, and gladly he
welcomes us and responds to our need.

✴ *O Saviour, I have nought to plead,*
　In earth beneath or heaven above,

35

But just my own exceeding need,
And thy exceeding love.   *Jane Crewdson*

For group discussion and personal thought

Women feature prominently in several of this week's
readings. Look again at these, and consider how they show
that Jesus' attitude to women was different from the
conventional attitudes of his time. Today we hear much about
the rights of women in society and in the Church. What do you
think Jesus would say to those who are opposed to women
holding positions of leadership?

1st Sunday in Lent, February 12   Luke 9.1–9

In this reading we have the account of Jesus sending out the
twelve apostles. Let us look at four aspects from this account
and apply them to the Church today:

- The apostles' **right and ability to do their task came**,
  not from themselves, but **from Christ**. Whilst we believe
  that it is our duty to proclaim the Christian message, there
  is a danger of the Church claiming an authority beyond
  what Christ has given it. Not all declarations that the
  Church has made have been from God. Only a truly
  humble church can speak the authentic words of God.

- The apostles' **task was to deliver a message in words
  and also in deeds**. Preaching and practice must go
  together. This means that the Church should be actively
  involved in political, economic and social issues.

- The apostles were to be **free from anything which might
  hinder their work**. There must be a flexibility in Church
  organisation and action so that its work is not confined to
  church buildings and it does not become static and
  moribund.

- The apostles were **not to be discouraged by opposition**.
  The scepticism and materialism of the modern world
  inevitably mean that the Christian message is often
  opposed and rejected. This does not disprove the truth of
  the gospel but, rather, indicates that it is affecting people's
  lives.

✳ *Lord Jesus Christ, help us to be faithful, free and fearless as
we seek to preach and do your will.*

Today's reading vividly shows the compassion of Jesus for
hungry people and his ability to satisfy them. Some people
interpret this story by saying that Jesus' concern moved those
who had food to share generously with those who had none.
Whatever interpretation we accept, it was the miracle of
Christ's presence that enabled the people to be fed. There is
much that we can learn from this story. Let us look at just two
points:

● It should stir the conscience of all of us who have more than
  enough while millions are starving to death. Experts
  assure us that there is enough food in the world to feed
  everyone adequately. Therefore, if the way of Christ were
  seriously adopted and his compassion really at work
  within us, then we should be able to ensure a fair
  distribution of food throughout the world.

● Look again at verses 14–17. There is a eucharistic feel
  about the language here. The people are arranged in
  orderly groups, and there is the blessing followed by the
  breaking of the bread and its distribution by the disciples.
  Is there a hint here of a sacramental meal – a feeding on
  the broken body of Christ? Sharing in the **bread of life** is
  our greatest nourishment.

✳ *Bread of the world, in mercy broken;*
   . . . by thy grace our souls are fed.   *Reginald Heber*

As Jesus' words and deeds became more widely known, people
began to ask, 'Who is this?' Jesus knew that the climax of his
ministry was drawing near and he wanted to be sure that his
close followers knew who he really was. So he questioned
them. Peter voiced their convictions: 'You are God's Messiah.'

They were sure – but they were told to keep quiet about
their conviction for a while. People were not yet ready to
accept the type of Messiah that Jesus was. He was not the
military leader whom they were expecting to come and free
them from Roman rule, but one who would suffer, be rejected
and killed. Further, the disciples had to understand that those
who claimed Jesus as Messiah would also have to suffer and
be rejected. Look at Mark 8.32–33 to see how hard Peter
found it to accept all this.

The Christian way is the way of the cross – of loving

enemies, returning good for evil, and non-retaliation. Jesus did not come to bully, destroy or take revenge, but to encourage, forgive and bear the suffering others would inflict on him. What a challenge this is to us, his followers! The way of Christ is indeed a hard way – but how rewarding it is!

✳ *Help us, Lord Jesus, to follow the way of the cross, seeking only to love those who hate us.*

Wednesday February 15

Peter had boldly declared that Jesus was the Messiah, and then Jesus had told the disciples of his forthcoming sufferings and death. How bewildered they must have been! Together, they must have discussed what it all meant. Then came the experience which we usually refer to as the **Transfiguration**.

▶ Read **Luke 9.28 – 36**.

Jesus wanted reassurance – he wanted to be sure that the way he was taking was the right way. All that had been unclear before, became clear to him on the hills as he prayed in the presence of his disciples. He saw his ministry in the full light of his people's history – Moses the liberator and lawgiver was there, and so was Elijah, the first great prophet. They spoke to him about the fulfilment of God's plan through his death. Through his suffering, Jesus was to save humankind from fear, sin and despair. He was ready to go to Jerusalem.

The disciples, Peter, James and John, saw Jesus in his full glory. They were shown that his death would not be a tragic defeat but a glorious victory. Although they did not fully understand the meaning of Christ's transfiguration until after his resurrection, this experience enabled them to have a glimpse of the glory that was to be his.

✳ *Lord Jesus Christ, may the glory of your transfiguration shine into the dark places of our lives, showing us the meaning, challenges and triumph of life in your kingdom.*

Thursday February 16   Luke 9.37 – 43a

Jesus came down with Peter, James and John from the glorious serenity of the hills to be confronted by a large, helpless crowd. On the hilltop Jesus had become assured of the power of God and the mission committed to him and to his disciples. But here were the rest of his disciples seeming as powerless to deal with the epileptic boy as everyone else.

Jesus' outburst (verse 41) may seem somewhat unfair, but it was the frustration of one who longed for others to share the certainty of his own faith. Our everyday life is not lived on the spiritual mountain-tops, but in the hurly-burly of the plains. The glory of God is certainly revealed to us on the 'mountain'. However, if we do not take this experience with us into our day-to-day living, then it becomes meaningless.

We may love our church and find true peace, assurance and strong faith in the environment of worship there, but what effect does this have on our daily life and struggle? Does our sense of the glory of God diminish as we resume our daily tasks? Does our certainty of his presence dwindle when we come face to face with our everyday problems?

✳ *Pray that you may have eyes which not only see God's glory on the 'mountain', but are also able to discern him on the 'plain'.*

Friday February 17

After Jesus had cured the epileptic boy (see yesterday), he turned his attention towards his disciples.

▶ Read **Luke 9.43b – 50**.

The disciples still did not fully understand the true meaning of Jesus' messiahship. Once again he told them that the Son of Man – this object of their wonder and admiration – must be given up into the power of men. They did not seem to hear. Rather, as if the kingdom was about to arrive, they excitedly started arguing about who among them was the greatest and so would be entitled to the best positions in it. Jesus patiently redirected them to God's way of humility.

Can we ever really understand the mind of Christ? It seems to involve both forcefulness and humble submission. Why did Jesus so often adopt an attitude both of assertiveness **and** self-denial? Was it because he was engaged in a kind of 'war' – overcoming evil with goodness, destroying hatred with love, and conquering death with life?

✳   *May the mind of Christ my Saviour*
        Live in me from day to day,
      By his love and power controlling
          All I do or say.   *Kate B. Wilkinson*

Saturday February 18

We end this section of readings from **Luke** on a note of tremendous challenge – the challenge to learn from Jesus and the cost of following him.

▶ Read **Luke 9.51–62**.

It was time for Jesus to go to Jerusalem and resolutely face his death, but there was still so much for his disciples to learn. Even James and John, two of his closest friends, had not fully learnt the way of Jesus. Perhaps they were still filled with the awe of 'seeing' Moses and Elijah (verses 30–33), and remembered that Elijah had called down fire on an unfriendly company of soldiers (2 Kings 1.10). But seeking revenge was not Jesus' way of dealing with rejection.

Jesus showed his followers a completely new way of living. However, to follow this way was costly. Look again at Jesus' words to the would-be followers in verses 57–62. Those who follow Jesus must always put his claims first and be resolute in their discipleship.

When Jesus says to us, 'Follow me', it is a call to great joy but it involves the carrying of a cross.

✳ *Jesus calls us! By thy mercies,*
   Saviour, may we hear thy call,
 Give our hearts to thine obedience,
   Love and serve thee best of all.

Cecil Frances Alexander

For group discussion and personal thought
Read the story of the transfiguration in **Luke 9.28–36**. What do you think was the meaning of this experience (a) for Jesus and (b) for the disciples? What does it mean for us today?

● Have you ordered your copy of **Looking at the Cross** (see page 6)?

1 SAMUEL 17–2 SAMUEL 1

Notes by the Revd John H. Atkinson, MA

John Atkinson is a Methodist minister in Lincolnshire. He has been a tutor in the West Indies, the General Secretary of British Methodism's Division of Social Responsibility, and Chairman of its West Yorkshire District.

The notes in this section are based on the New International Version.

Saul was Israel's first king, and the early years of his reign were successful ones. Our readings from the latter part of **1 Samuel** trace the decline and final disaster of Saul which resulted from his disobedience to God. These chapters also record the rise of David, the shepherd boy who conquered the giant Goliath, won the friendship of Jonathan, the son of King Saul, married the princess Michal, and gained great popularity among the people.

Old Testament history was written to show that obedience to God brought success, while rebellion against him led to disaster. Life is perhaps not quite as simple as that but the underlying theme, that God is above all earthly rulers and kings, is emphatically true.

Suggestions for further reading

First Book of Samuel by Peter R. Ackroyd, Cambridge Bible Commentaries on the New English Bible (Cambridge University Press);

Samuel by David F. Payne, Daily Study Bible (Saint Andrew Press).

2nd Sunday in Lent, February 19

One of Saul's main tasks as Israel's first king was to beat off the frequent attacks of the Philistines. Like the Israelites, they had come from outside Canaan. They had settled in the southern coastal plain and were trying to push north-eastwards at Israel's expense.

Meanwhile, the prophet Samuel had already anointed in private the one who, in due course, would succeed Saul as king. Surprisingly, this was a shepherd boy — David. It was during one of the most dangerous raids of the Philistines that David appeared for the first time before the king and the people of Israel.

▶ Read **1 Samuel 17.1−25**.

A nine-foot (three-metre) giant in heavy armour and with massive weapons would strike terror into anyone's heart. No wonder the Israelites ran away from him (verse 24)!

We, too, have our 'giants' to face — for example, fear, loneliness, insecurity, anxiety and sin. It is no use running away from them. We must remember that God is infinitely greater than any 'giant'. If we trust him and do what he says, our 'giants' will take to their heels.

✳ *What 'giants' trouble you? Ask God to help you defeat them.*

Monday February 20   1 Samuel 17.26−51

God is constantly using the most unlikely people to carry out his plans. David was 'only a boy' (verse 33); how could he possibly defeat a giant warrior in hand-to-hand combat? Indeed, David made his task seem more hopeless by refusing protective armour and a sword. Yet the utterly improbable happened and the boy saved Israel by defeating the giant.

God often works in this way, As Paul wrote: 'God purposely chose what the world considers nonsense in order to shame the wise, and he chose what the world considers weak in order to shame the powerful. He chose what the world looks down on and despises, and thinks is nothing, in order to destroy what the world thinks is important' (1 Corinthians 1.27−28, GNB).

We may think that we are nothing — unable to do great things for God as evangelists, reformers or leaders. We may think that we could never win someone else for Christ. We may think that these things — and many more — are utterly impossible as far as we are concerned. But God may well be planning to use us to do for him the very things we firmly regard as impossible. Be a 'David' — tackle them!

✳ *Ask God to tell you what improbable plans he has for you.*

Tuesday February 21

After David had killed Goliath, the Israelites drove the Philistines away. Saul then sent for the young hero.

▶ Read **1 Samuel 18.1−16**.

David was now much more than the boy who killed the giant. He had become a senior army officer and the close friend of the king's son. Above all, David's successes had made him so popular that Saul was insanely jealous of him.

Before we condemn Saul, we ought to take a close look at how well we cope with other people's success. Are we really glad for them? Or does jealousy sour our relationships? Sometimes we can rejoice with other people when their successes do not threaten our own standing. Saul was jealous because he knew that David's popularity was rapidly driving him into second place. Are we any better than Saul at making way for those who have more to offer than we have?

At home, at work, among friends, and — not least — in church, we must shun jealousy, share the joy of those who succeed where we may have failed, and make way for those whose gifts are greater than ours.

✳ *Lord, I know I should shun jealousy, but sometimes it is very hard. Help me to have the right spirit always.*

Wednesday February 22

Jonathan, King Saul's son, was David's closest friend. Michal, the king's daughter, had fallen in love with David and they had married. However, increasingly it seemed that their father meant to kill David.

▶ Read **1 Samuel 19.1–18**.

Jonathan and Michal did all they could to protect David and warn him of the danger he was in. Jonathan spoke up for David and persuaded his father not to kill David and to give him back his old place at court. When Saul's soldiers were sent to kill David, Michal organised and concealed her husband's escape.

From time to time, we may find ourselves caught in disputes and estrangements within our families and the circle of our friends. The actions of Jonathan and Michal give us useful pointers in handling these problems:
- Make sure that any danger in the situation is recognised.
- Speak up for anyone who has been unfairly treated.
- Aim at reconciliation.
- If reconciliation fails, try to minimise the damage which may then result.

✳ *Pray for those who have to deal with quarrels among their families or friends.*

Jonathan's first thought was to save David from any hurt which his father, Saul, might try to do to him. However, Jonathan also realised that if, despite his endeavour to protect David, Saul did harm his friend he, too, would be in great danger. David enjoyed God's favour and God would no doubt avenge any evil done to him. Therefore, Jonathan begged David to promise solemnly to be merciful to him and his family if the worst happened.

This promise was made in the form of a covenant. The two men bound themselves in faithfulness to one another, just as God and the Israelites were bound together in the great covenant he had made with them. Jonathan pointed to the essential nature of that covenant when he entreated David, 'Show me unfailing kindness like that of the Lord' (verse 14).

In the Old Testament, the real meaning of God's 'mercy' is his 'constant loving-kindness'. This is the covenant love which God steadfastly showered on his people. Jonathan and David confirmed the faithfulness of their friendship by promising to act towards one another as God acted towards them.

✶ *Praise God for his constant loving-kindness to you. Commit yourself in similar faithfulness to those you love.*

Saul was angry with Jonathan because his loyalty to David had made him push aside his obligations to his father the king. By protecting David, Jonathan was sheltering the very person who would prevent any of Saul's family succeeding him. In his anger, Saul nearly murdered his son.

Jonathan realised the sacrifices he would have to make. If he loved David, he must send him away where he would be safe from Saul. As a result, he might never see him again. (In fact, they did meet again, but only briefly.) By protecting David, Jonathan was dooming himself in two other ways:

● As his father had warned him, he was sparing the one who would become king instead of himself.
● He was tying himself to his father's fate – which proved to be death in battle against the Philistines.

The moving story of the parting of Jonathan and David is made even more poignant by the extent of the sacrifices which Jonathan was making for his friend.

✻ *How much have we sacrificed for our friends? What sacrifices ought we to make now? What sacrifices ought we to be ready to make in the future, if necessary? Think and pray about these questions.*

Saturday February 25   1 Samuel 24.1–19

David threw away a golden opportunity to kill Saul. If he had killed him, he would have become a king instead of a fugitive. He could have stopped running and started ruling. But David would not stoop to such an act. Saul might be his enemy, bent on killing him, but he was still the one who had been anointed king at God's command.

There are times when we all have the chance to get our own back on people who have wronged us. We may have the chance to start or to support a rumour which would turn other people against them. We may be able to prevent them securing some position which they would like to have at work, in the community or in church. We may be able to get the better of them in some business deal or in some other way.

● Why should we not seize these opportunities?
● Or at least, make sure, as David did, that when we are generous to our enemies, we draw attention to the fact?

Is the answer to the first question that Jesus told us to love our enemies? And is the answer to the second that Jesus wants us to be generous without seeking credit for our kindness?

✻ *Lord, help me to follow David's example of showing mercy and kindness to my enemies.*

For group discussion and personal thought.

Saul became jealous of David (see **1 Samuel 18.6–9** and the notes for **February 21**). Why? What kind of things make us feel jealous? Why is jealousy harmful and wrong? How can we prevent ourselves becoming jealous of others?

3rd Sunday in Lent, February 26

When David was a wandering fugitive, he was accompanied by a small army of supporters. Usually such roving bands lived by robbery, raiding and violence. David's men, however, made themselves useful by protecting the large flocks of a rich man, Nabal, and the shepherds who looked after them.

▶ Read **1 Samuel 25.2–19, 23–28a**.

Nabal was an ill-natured, ungrateful, inhospitable man. Fortunately for him, his wife was very different in her attitude. She saw that Nabal's rudeness to David and his men was not only dangerous, but also grossly unfair and mean. She used her common sense and took practical steps to make sure that Nabal did not suffer the punishment he deserved for his surly behaviour.

Are there times when we are inclined to be ungrateful or inhospitable? How can we avoid being mean like Nabal? Have we friends or members of our family whose ill-nature is likely to get them – and others – into trouble? What can we do to stave off this deserved result of their pettiness?

✳ *Lord, give me a generous spirit. Save me from meanness and surliness. Show me how to react helpfully when others are ungrateful or churlish.*

Monday February 27   1 Samuel 26.1–12

On a previous occasion when David had spared Saul's life (see the reading and notes on February 25), his reason had been that Saul was the anointed king of Israel. This time, David had a further reason for refusing to kill the king. God himself would punish Saul for his misdeeds (verse 10). Behind this simple – and not entirely charitable – belief lie some important truths.

Often evil seems to flourish and good people suffer. However, violence, self-indulgence, recklessness and many other wrongs frequently rebound on those who practise them. To a certain extent, evils carry their own punishment. This is not surprising if we believe that God made the world, that he knows best how we should live in it, and that flouting the Maker's guidance is likely to bring trouble upon us.

Of course, not every sin is punished and goodness sometimes seems unprotected and unrewarded. But the degree to which some wrongdoing brings its own doom on itself, even on earth, lends strong support to the biblical view that in eternity goodness will be vindicated and evil ended.

✳ *Justice and truth from his sceptre shall spring;*
Wrong shall be ended when Jesus is King.
                                                    Charles S. Horne

46

Jesus endorsed a simple pattern for right living which was so wise that it is often called the 'Golden Rule': 'Do to others what you would have them do to you' (Matthew 7.12). David had an interesting variation on this: 'Do to others what you would have God do to you.' This is surely the significance of his belief that, if he valued and spared Saul's life, God would value his life and deliver him from trouble (verse 24). This is a rule worth following. It is echoed in Jesus' words:

● 'Blessed are the merciful, for they will be shown mercy' (Matthew 5.7);
● 'Forgive us our debts, as we also have forgiven our debtors' (Matthew 6.12).

Doing to others what we want God to do to us is one way of growing more like him – and that is what the Christian life is all about.

✳ *Help me, Father, always to do to others*
   what I would like them to do to me –
   for that will make me more human.
   And help me to do to others
   what I would like you to do to me –
   for that will make me a little more like you.

Wednesday March 1

When David once more spared his life, Saul promised never to harm him again (26.21). David, however, had many narrow escapes from the king's unpredictable anger and felt he could not rely on Saul's promise.

▶ Read **1 Samuel 27.1 to 28.2**.

Quite apart from a natural human desire to save his own skin, David could not possibly forget how God had sent his prophet Samuel to anoint him as the next king of Israel. If he was to fulfil God's command, he had to find some way in which to stay alive until he was called to the throne. He felt himself forced into a desperate and dangerous double-game, pretending to be an ally of the Philistines without bringing any harm on Israel. We may well be appalled at some of the incidents which resulted from David's difficult situation (for example, verse 9 will offend many readers).

David's predicament may lead us to consider the fearful dilemmas which face many Christians today. Confronted with persecution, they may be driven to desperate measures to avoid betraying their fellow-Christians. In trying to rid their land of oppressors, they may be driven into the company of those who use violence. These people need our prayers.

❋ *Pray for Christians facing oppression and persecution, that God will guide them as difficult decisions are forced upon them.*

Thursday March 2

✔ When men and women are in great danger, their true nature is often revealed. Some prove to be heroes and saints; others are shown to be cowards and devils.

Saul was terrified at the sight of the Philistine army and did not know where to turn for help. He had driven David away, and Samuel the prophet was dead. He had rejected God and so, not surprisingly, he received no answer through the usual means of hearing God speak in dreams and by the 'Urim' – the casting of lots.

In despair, Saul went in disguise to see a medium, thus directly disobeying one of God's oldest commandments (see Deuteronomy 18.10 – 12). Saul knew this; and earlier in his reign he had banished mediums and spiritists. No good came now from consulting one – it never does.

▶ Read **1 Samuel 28.3 – 19**.

This story is a strong reminder to us, at a time when witchcraft, spiritism, and an interest in the occult is increasing, to have nothing to do with these 'detestable' things.

❋ *Think about the dangers of dabbling in the occult, and pray that God will deliver those now in its grasp.*

✔Friday March 3   1 Samuel 30.1 – 24

David was fortunate in rescuing all the people and recovering the possessions he had carelessly left unprotected in Ziklag when he and his men had gone on campaign with the Philistines. The exciting story in today's reading reveals not only David's good fortune, but also his deep faith in God.

At the critical moment, when he realised that Ziklag had been sacked and all its people abducted, David turned to God for strength and guidance (verses 6 – 8). Then, when he had defeated the Amalekites and taken a great deal of plunder, he regarded this as wealth that God had given to him and his men (verse 23). They had not won it by their own strength, and so it was to be shared not just among those who had fought the Amalekites, but also with those who had stayed with the supplies.

We can follow David's example by:
- turning to God for strength and guidance when we face difficulties;
- recognising that anything we achieve or receive is God's gift and not merely a result of our own success.

✳ **Prayer for (Women's) World Day of Prayer**

Teach us, Lord, how to pray. Fill our hearts with love and faith so that we may praise you for your goodness, trust you to hear us and, in your mercy, to answer us.

✓ **Saturday March 4**

David's defeat of the Amalekites was immediately followed by the battle of Mount Gilboa in which the Philistines defeated the Israelites. Saul and Jonathan were both killed. It took three days for the news to reach David.

▶ Read **2 Samuel 1.1–12**.

Jonathan's death must have been a profound loss to David; Saul's might have been a relief. However, David grieved over them both.

▶ Read **2 Samuel 1.23–26**.

David's generous tribute to Saul was consistent with his attitude to the king during his lifetime. Often Saul had tried to kill David. Twice David had spared the king when he could have killed him easily. While Saul lived, David had acted generously to him. Now he was dead, David's words about him were equally generous. He was not guilty of hypocrisy.

This graciousness of spirit is one of David's most attractive characteristics. Let it be one of ours, too.

✳ *Lord, give me a generous spirit always – even to those who are ungracious or unfriendly to me.*

For group discussion and personal thought.

Read, in **1 Samuel 28.3–19**, how Saul consulted a medium (a woman 'with a familiar spirit'). Why do people today still dabble in witchcraft and the occult? In what ways, and why, is this dangerous and wrong? Why should Christians never become involved with anything to do with the occult?

THE KING AND THE CROSS

Readings from Luke 19–24 and Acts 1–2

Based on notes by the Revd Iain M. Roy

Iain Roy is a Church of Scotland Minister at Stevenston in Ayrshire, and is also an industrial chaplain. He was formerly Moderator and Clerk of the Presbytery of Ardrossan.

The notes in this section are based on the Good News Bible.

In this, our second section of readings from **Luke's Gospel**, we shall be looking at the events in the last week of Jesus' life, and the days and weeks immediately following. We shall read about the way in which Jesus met his death and consider what this means for those who believe in him. His death on the cross was not the end!

Suggestions for further reading – see page 17.

✓ **4th Sunday in Lent, March 5**　　　　　　**Luke 19.28–40**

Jesus was near Jerusalem and the confrontation that awaited him there. He could have stayed in comparative safety in Galilee, but knew that the time had come for him to face his strongest and final challenge. He approached the city as the servant Messiah on a humble beast of burden – not as a great and mighty warrior in the way many of his contemporaries hoped. Nevertheless, most of the crowd acclaimed him and praised him – except some of the Pharisees, whose hostile silence was only broken by protest (verse 39).

There is a time for silence – the silence of awe and wonder. Our worship of Jesus need not always be in shouts of loud acclamation, but we have to be sure that our silences are of the right kind, not born of hostility or fear.

During the next two weeks, as we read about the last days of Jesus' earthly ministry, let us take time to think about the words he spoke and his determination to complete the task to which he was called.

✳ *Ride on! ride on in majesty!*
  Hark! all the tribes 'Hosanna!' cry . . .
  O Christ, thy triumphs now begin
  O'er captive death and conquered sin.

Henry H. Milman

Monday March 6

▶ First, read **Luke 19.41–44**.

What Jesus saw at close quarters in the city of Jerusalem moved him to tears. Sometimes we are uncomfortable in the presence of emotion; but these verses remind us that emotion is an essential part of life, both human and divine.

Christ is never an objective bystander of the human scene. His tears over Jerusalem showed that he was involved in the human predicament. He cried because there was such ignorance of what could lead to real peace for the city.

▶ Now read **Luke 19.45–48**.

The buying and selling, which were taking place in the precincts of the temple, reflected the people's misplaced trust not only in material things but also in religious ritual. This was indicative of shallow spirituality. Jesus looks for a deeper spirituality which has its expression in prayer. That is why prayer has to be at the heart of our corporate and individual life as Christians.

For the moment Jesus was still safe despite his provocation of the temple officials. People were still listening to him, eager not to miss a single word. Soon the listening would stop and he would be rejected. Listening is an essential part of prayer.

✳ *Lord, may I continue to listen to you so that I may be drawn closer to you and reflect your values in my life.*

Tuesday March 7   Luke 20.1–8

The priests, teachers of the law and elders had a problem concerning Jesus' authority because he posed a threat to their position and power. They failed to see that his authority came from God. When they questioned the source of Jesus' authority, he did not attempt to justify himself. Rather he posed a counter-question – one which perhaps challenged the authority of the Jewish religious leaders.

Jesus' authority is a matter of crucial importance for **us**. It is not just a past historical issue; and it is more than a legal argument, as today's reading shows. These are the questions that we must try to answer:

● What authority does Jesus have in **our** lives?
● What weight do **we** give to his words?
● What place to **we** give to his teaching, and what respect to his presence and love?
● Is Jesus **our** Lord and Master, whose authority and demands upon our lives we recognise as paramount every day?

✴ *Lord Jesus, rule over my life in every part.*

Wednesday March 8   Luke 20.9–18

Why did Jesus tell this parable in Jerusalem, at this particular time? Did he do so to tell his opponents that, although he knew what they were planning to do, he was not intimidated? Or was it to give them a last chance to look at themselves and repent? Whatever Jesus' reason, the meaning of the parable was clear to the Jewish leaders. The vineyard stood for Israel and the tenants were the rulers into whose hands the nation had been entrusted. The messengers were the prophets and the son was Jesus himself.

This parable also has a message for us today. We can think of the **Church as the vineyard**. In the same way that God was patient with the nation of Israel, sending them one prophet after another, he has sent prophets to the Church – the new Israel. These prophets have pointed out the various errors into which Christians have fallen. However, since its beginning, the Church has often persecuted and even killed some of God's prophets.

In most countries today we may not actively or intentionally persecute our prophets, but do we always pay attention to what they have to say – and act accordingly?

✴ *Pray that we may all recognise the prophets of our age and listen to them – even when their words make us feel uncomfortable.*

Thursday March 9   Luke 20.19–26

These verses are among the most important, not just in **Luke's Gospel**, but in the whole New Testament. The relationship between the spiritual and the political is often an uneasy one, and some see these as two entirely separate worlds. Christians, who do so, often use today's verses as justification for their point of view. When this happens Christianity is being limited to the state of our souls.

By his teaching and his way of life Jesus clearly showed that the spiritual side of life cannot be separated from the rest. What we believe will affect what we do — our faith will inevitably be reflected in our actions. Further, we will be unable to deal adequately with important social and political issues (for example: justice, racial equality, unemployment) unless we see faith as related to the whole of life.

However, merely knowing that faith is related to life is not enough. Although we may give God's truth and love the place they claim and deserve in our lives, there is always the possibility of a clash between what we believe we owe to God and what we owe to the state in terms of loyalty and obedience. Therefore, let us pray for the kind of wisdom Jesus had in dealing with these matters.

✳ *Help us, Father, to have the wisdom and the mind of Christ.*

Friday March 10

There are some questions to which we have no answer. Many of those about life after death come into this category. I once knew a man who wanted to know how there would be enough room for everyone in heaven! This type of question reflects some nineteenth-century hymns which describe heaven in spatial terms.

▶ Read **Luke 20.27 – 40**.

In these verses Jesus showed that our concepts in this life are very different from those in the life hereafter. Heaven is not just a continuation of this world.

When the Sadducees tried to trap Jesus with their question about the next world, he directed their attention to the realities of this world (verse 38). He did this because the Sadducees were always quoting from the law of Moses which was intended to deal with the practicalities of living in this world. The law which they quoted to Jesus (see Deuteronomy 25.5 – 6) showed continuing care for a dead man's widow and also assured that the memory of the person be retained by carrying on the family line.

Jesus affirmed the classical Jewish view of God as the God of the living and not of the dead. He is indeed the God of living, personal relationships. It is only in a growing, living relationship with God that our own personalities have meaning in this life and in the life hereafter.

✳ *Lord Jesus, help me to live now to your glory, to honour you in this world and to trust you for the next.*

Saturday March 11   Luke 20.41 to 21.4

The last part of this reading leaves us in no doubt that status, wealth and power are not the currency of the kingdom of God. The teachers of the law tried to win favour with God by completely the wrong methods. Their ostentatiousness (verses 46 – 47) may have impressed people but Jesus saw that this was really an expression of their selfish ambition and pride.

On the other hand, the widow with her small copper coins could not compete with rich people who lavishly put their large gifts in the temple treasury. Yet, in the eyes of Jesus, she rated very highly – she gave '**all** she had to live on' (verse 4).

The spirit of our giving is far more important than what we give. Therefore, we have no excuse for miserly giving nor for false pride in generous giving. Whatever we give is small compared with what God has given us.

Often giving to God is thought of only in terms of money, but Christian stewardship involves much more than that. In considering what we can give to God we must take into account our time and talents as well as our money. All that we give should be given in a generous and thankful spirit.

✳ *Lord, help me to give generously of my time, talents and money to you, always remembering what you have so freely given to me.*

For group discussion and personal thought

Read **Luke 19.28 – 40**, and consider the significance of this event (a) for Jesus, (b) for those who witnessed it. How do you celebrate this event in your church? In what ways could your celebration become more meaningful to you and the community in which you live?

When my wife and I were on holiday in Yugoslavia, we visited the Museum of Hostages in Begunje. During the Second World War this building imprisoned some 12,000 men, women and children. It was a place of torture and death, and is now a stark reminder to us of people's inhumanity to one another.

▶ Read **Luke 21.5–19**, which tells of similar inhumanity.

Some scholars believe that Jesus did not actually say all of this, but that the author of this Gospel inserted into his story a description of the persecution which occurred at a later date. There is a sense in which this does not really matter because such things have happened throughout the history of the Christian Church and still happen today.

Jesus does not offer his followers exemption from persecution nor from the stress in human relationships which may result from commitment to him. However, he assures us that no matter what happens there is one relationship which will remain steadfast – his relationship to us. That is why we can take courage; that is why we know that even the bad times can be opportunities for spreading the gospel. The crucified Christ speaks to us of the final victory of love and truth over the inhumanity of humankind.

✳ *Lord God, give us courage, both in favourable and unfavourable conditions, to witness to the truth we know and the love we have received in Christ.*

Monday March 13   Luke 21.20–29

If we were intent on proving that Jesus was a prophet, today's reading would be a passage we could quote. It has all the marks of Old Testament prophecy:

● the foretelling of the future, not as in newspaper horoscopes, but as the declaration of the inevitable outcome of certain events;

● a reminder that the outcome is God's punishment for sin;

● advice on what to do in certain circumstances.

However, Jesus was far more than a prophet. In him God was revealed directly; also in him word and action were combined. By the time Jesus spoke the words in today's reading he had already set out upon that course which would lead to the salvation of humankind. So he was able to speak with an authority that exceeded that of the prophets. He gave each fearful heart the encouragement that 'salvation is near' (verse 28).

Like Jesus we must not forget the fear that can often lie in human hearts. We must speak encouraging words to those Christians who are fearful. Further, in all circumstances we should pray that God will remove our fears and help us to trust in him, always remembering that nothing can separate us from his love.

✳ *Lord, may I remember to trust in you always because 'salvation' is near.*

✓ Tuesday March 14

The cosmic events which we have read about in Luke 21 have given, and no doubt will continue to give, ample cause for speculation about the end of the world. However, speculation is no ground for faith. We can rest firmly on the truth and enduring nature of Jesus' words.

▶ Read **Luke 21.29 – 36**.

The history of Christianity shows, to some extent, the history of the ebb and flow of attention and importance given to the teaching of Jesus. Periods of revival and witness have invariably centred around the rediscovery of the truths Jesus taught. This indestructible quality of everything he saw and did can really give us increased confidence to trust his words today.

Nevertheless, most of us would have to admit that we neglect Jesus' teaching in our lives. Jesus' words remind us to be on our guard against this neglect. Every day we are called to live the kind of life which bears witness to the things we believe, the love we know, and the truths we have learned from him.

✳ *Lord, revive your truth within me and keep me faithful to you day by day.*

✓ Wednesday March 15

▶ First read **Luke 21.37 – 38**.

The loneliness of men and women who are at the centre of great events is rarely realised. Those of us on the fringe forget that responsibility is essentially a lonely burden. Reading that Jesus retreated to the Mount of Olives at the end of each day reminds us that he too was carrying such a burden. However, we can also see that his answer to this was found in spending a prolonged time of quiet with God in prayer and meditation.

▶ Now read **Luke 22.1−6**.

While Jesus was strengthening himself in solitude, Judas Iscariot was making plans to betray him. Many reasons have been put forward for Judas' action. One rather unconvincing suggestion is that he did it for the money. A more interesting viewpoint is that Judas was attempting to force Jesus' hand − to manipulate him so that he would be in a position where he would have to declare himself as the nationalistic leader Judas believed him to be.

We may denounce what Judas did, but are we so very different from him? How often are we tempted to do things our own way! Perhaps without realising it we are manipulating Jesus and his truths to reflect our will and not his.

✳ *Lord Jesus, in all I do or say, may I seek to do your will and not mine.*

Thursday March 16 Luke 22.7−13

The main point to note about today's reading is that Jesus and his disciples were preparing to share together in the Jewish Passover meal. Christianity is deeply rooted in Judaism. Jesus was a Jew and we need constantly to remind ourselves of this fact. He did not set out to establish a new faith. Rather, Christianity developed because many Jews rejected Jesus and his teaching.

Therefore, we must never forget the debt we owe to Judaism. The New Testament concepts of deliverance and salvation derive from the Judaism of the Old Testament. The Passover proclaims these ideas for Jews just as the Holy Communion proclaims them for Christians. Jesus came, as he himself said, not to reject the laws and teachings of Judaism but to fulfil them (see Matthew 5.17). In the Passover celebrations a lamb from the field was sacrificed. For the Christian, Christ himself is the Passover lamb − the Lamb of God. In the Holy Communion we celebrate his sacrifice on the cross and remember that he came to take away the sin of the world so that we may be brought closer to him.

✳ *Lord Jesus Christ, only Son of the Father,*
Lord God, Lamb of God,

you take away the sin of the world:
have mercy on us.   *(From the Gloria)*

Friday March 17   Luke 22.14 – 23

In today's reading we have the account of Jesus' last supper
with his disciples. In many branches of the Christian Church
the regular celebration of this event continues to have a very
important place in worship.

As a minister of the Scottish Presbyterian Church, where
traditionally preaching has been considered so important, I
find it strangely reassuring to administer the sacrament of
Holy Communion. I know that no words of mine are really
necessary, for the symbols of bread and wine speak for
themselves. When I have worshipped in another country
whose language is unknown to me I have found that the
symbols of the Communion have still spoken clearly to me.

However, this sacrament is more than significant symbols
to those who share in its mystery. Its symbols point to reality
– the reality of the love of God for us and our response to that
love. When we participate in the Communion we are sharing
in the sacrifice of Christ, and in response we offer to him our
praise and thanksgiving. After receiving the bread and the
wine we are commissioned to go out in peace, to live and serve
in the world.

✱ *Father, remind us that there was no other way and no other
one by whom we could be saved, except your own Son. In
that knowledge may we serve you sacrificially.*

Saturday March 18   Luke 22.24 – 38

It should hardly surprise us that Jesus' disciples were
concerned about status. The world has never been without its
men and women of ambition, and there are those who say that
ambition is a good thing. Certainly we need people with
purpose and drive in life – both in the world at large and in the
Church. However, Jesus taught his disciples that the really
essential driving-force of life was service.

We may call Jesus our Master and Lord, but he said that he
had come to be our servant (see verse 27b). It is not because of
who he is, but because of what he did for us, that Jesus calls
for our obedience. He desires to teach us and the world a better
way to live. Too often, both within the Church and outside it,

we seek to assert our influence from a position of strength and status. We forget that Christ has shown us that his strategy is to influence from a position of weakness and service. The Church more effectively commends its truths to people in places where it serves rather than where it rules.

✳ *O Jesus, I have promised*
   To serve thee to the end:
   O give me grace to follow,
   My Master and my Friend.   *John E. Bode*

For group discussion and personal thought

Study **Luke 22.3 – 6**. Judas 'may have betrayed Jesus with the intention of compelling Jesus to act' (William Barclay). Do you agree? What other reasons may Judas have had for betraying Jesus? In what ways and for what reasons do we betray Jesus today?

Palm Sunday, March 19   Luke 22.39 – 53

Verses 41 – 44 are crucial to our understanding of the depth of Jesus' inner struggle as he faced the thought of death. It is comparatively easy to picture the physical struggle of Jesus on the cross — the nails, pierced hands and crown of thorns — but what of his state of mind in the hours before his crucifixion? He was not a puppet, but the Son of his Father, God. In Gethsemane he prayed, 'Not my will, but your will be done' (verse 42).

This great prayer shows us that Jesus accepted the necessity of his sacrifice, but he did not embrace it without the realisation of its cost in physical, mental and spiritual terms. At the beginning of Holy Week, let us meditate upon Jesus' total suffering. Let us never underestimate the cost of his death on the cross. Our awareness of his inner, as well as his outer, anguish may lead us to a deeper sense of gratitude for our salvation and to a deeper commitment to his service.

✳ *On this Palm Sunday think about these lines:*
   Ride on! ride on in majesty!
   Thy last and fiercest strife is nigh . . .
   Bow thy meek head to mortal pain,
   Then take, O God, thy power, and reign.
                                        Henry H. Milman

Accents betray us. They pin-point our place of origin and reveal something of our background. Sometimes they can be a point of ridicule. Peter's accent placed him in a position of danger. He was a Galilean and, to those in the courtyard, that marked him out as an associate of Jesus.

Danger in turn causes fear, and fear rouses in us our sense of self-preservation. Peter's earlier vow of loyalty (see verse 33) evaporated when the pressure of the situation made him think more about himself that about Jesus.

Invariably it is the pressures of life which expose our weaknesses and which lead to our betrayals of Christ. In the calm peace of worship it is easy to commit ourselves to faith and obedience. But the real test of our loyalty comes in the midst of life – in the tensions of our work situation, difficult decision-making, pressing problems, disagreeable confrontations. Peter's testing experience taught him the uselessness of relying on his own resources. However, it was not long before he learnt that he could always rely on Christ.

✳ *Lord, help me not to trust in my own resources but in you, that in the time of testing I may stand and not fall.*

The Jewish Council of elders, chief priests and teachers of the law, had found Jesus guilty of blasphemy (Luke 22.66 – 71) which, in Jewish law, was punishable by death. However, the death sentence had to be ratified by the Roman governor, Pilate. This meant that the Jewish Council needed to present their accusations against Jesus in political terms (verses 2, 5).

Pilate had a difficult job to do – he had to keep law and order and, at the same time, maintain a good working relationship with the Jewish authorities. He was unable to find Jesus guilty of any crime but he was trapped by the manipulative Jewish leaders. Not even sending Jesus to Herod could solve Pilate's problem and, to this day, his is the name in Christian creeds associated with the crucifixion of Jesus.

Certainly Pilate and Herod were weak men, but it was the nameless Jewish leaders – the leaders whose jealousy and outrage drove them to plot against Jesus – that brought pressure to bear on the powers of Rome. We often criticise those who rule our nation – our 'Pilates' – but let us remember the enormous pressures to which they are subjected.

✳ *Pray for political leaders, that they may have the strength,*
wisdom and courage to stand up for what is right, even
when they are pressurised to act unjustly.

Wednesday March 22   Luke 23.13 – 25

Yesterday we considered the part played by the Jewish
Council in the death of Jesus. Today's reading shows how the
responsibility extended to the crowd – to the ordinary person
'in the street'.

Pilate was afraid that there would be a riot if he did not
appease the crowd, and this would have jeopardised his
position as governor. At the Passover festival 'Pilate was in
the habit of setting free any one prisoner the people asked for'
(Mark 15.6) – he hoped they would ask for Jesus. But the more
Pilate tried to sway the crowd, the louder they cried out for
Jesus to be crucified.

Were the crowd being incited by the supporters of Barabbas
or the chief priests? Were they attempting to revolt against
Rome, or were they just being carried away by mindless
emotion? Whatever it was, in calling for Barabbas they were
choosing a path of hatred and violence, rather than the way of
love and peace as taught by Jesus.

Each of us has the capacity to be violent and to hate – each
of us could have been members of that crowd. Jesus was
sentenced to death by **our** sins.

✳ *Guilty, vile and helpless we;*
Spotless Lamb of God was he.   *Philipp Bliss*

Thursday March 23

He was despised and rejected by men;
a man of sorrows, and acquainted with grief.

(Isaiah 53.3, RSV)

▶ Read **Luke 23.26 – 37** looking particularly at the reactions
of some of those who saw Jesus struggling with the heavy
cross and were there at his crucifixion.

● **Simon of Cyrene** gave **support** to Jesus. He was forced to
carry the cross and we have no way of knowing the extent
of his compassion. However, it is likely that later he
became well-known in the Christian community. This
experience of carrying Jesus' cross no doubt had a profound
effect upon him.

- The **women** wept — their reaction was deep **sorrow**. However, their tears were but a dim reflection of the compassion and sorrow that Jesus felt for them.
- The **Jewish leaders** jeered at Jesus and treated him with **scorn**. They despised him and gave full vent to their contempt.

What is our reaction to the suffering, crucified Christ — to the Christ who still suffers today?

✳ *O sacred Head, sore wounded,*
   With grief and pain weighed down . . .
   How pale art thou with anguish,
      With sore abuse and scorn!   *Paul Gerhardt*

Good Friday, March 24   Luke 23.38 – 49

According to **Luke's Gospel**, the last words spoken by Jesus in the depth of his anguish were: 'Father! In your hands I place my spirit!' (verse 46). These words are from Psalm 31.5, with one added word — 'Father'. They were words from a prayer which Jewish mothers taught their children to say last thing at night. Even in his agony on the cross, Jesus had such a deep trust in God that he could die 'like a child falling asleep in his father's arms' (William Barclay).

God did not come to rescue Jesus in his agony on the cross, but suffered with him in the blackness of his dying hours. 'God loved the world so much that he gave his only Son' (John 3.16a). And Jesus trusted his Father completely throughout the whole tortuous ordeal.

Can we, too, trust God through the dark times in our life? Can we trust him in our anguish?

✳ *With silence in our hearts, on this Good Friday, let us stand at the foot of Jesus' cross, waiting with him in his agony.*

Saturday March 25   Luke 23.50 – 56

How often we lump people together in groups and accuse them of the same faults! But, in every group of men and women, there are always exceptions — those who have an independent outlook and spirit. Joseph of Arimathea was one such person. He was a member of the Jewish Council who had condemned Jesus. Although he was unable to save Jesus from death, he had disagreed with the Council's decision and later offered a burial-place for Jesus. This was a very bold thing to do, and he had to act quickly as the Sabbath was about to begin.

The bodies of those who were crucified were often left for the wild dogs and vultures. Jesus' body did not suffer this indignity. He was given a proper place of burial — perhaps it was the place Joseph had prepared for his own burial.

Because it was the Sabbath the women were not able to anoint Jesus' body immediately with spices and perfumes. They had to wait until the Sunday morning. The waiting-time is often the hardest time during a period of mourning — for example, waiting for a funeral service. The thirty-six hours of waiting must have been anxious ones for those women. They were unaware of what they would eventually find when they went to the tomb. If they had been, they would have waited with joyous expectation. They did not know that the great truth of the resurrection was about to break into their lives.

✳ *As we wait expectantly for Easter Day pray for those people who have not yet discovered the hope of the resurrection.*

For group discussion and personal thought
Read again **Luke 22.39 – 42**. How do we decide when God is calling us to tread a hard or difficult path, and when he is calling us to pleasant things? Is it always possible, or right, to accept hardship automatically as God's will? How does prayer help us to answer these questions?

Easter Sunday, March 26   **Luke 24.1–12**

How often we have heard this story! But do the tensions and feelings it contains penetrate our lives with renewed meaning each time we think about it?

This account of the empty tomb — the most significant discovery for Christians — is very 'human'. There is no immediate jubilation — only bewilderment, fear, awe, disbelief and amazement. Joy had not yet come to these first followers of Jesus.

The women had come early to the tomb, eager to anoint the dead body of their beloved Lord and Master. The disciples and 'all the rest' were presumably together — grieving. Even Peter was with them — Peter who had denied his Lord three times. Then, overcoming his shame and cowardice, he was the first to rush out to see for himself if the women's story could possibly be true. In his remorse, had he been thinking about the time when he had confidently declared that Jesus was the Messiah (Luke 9.20)? Yet even Peter, in discovering that the tomb was empty, was merely, 'amazed at what had happened'.

Looking back at the first Easter, we can understand all these very 'human' reactions. However, **we** can rejoice in the resurrection of Jesus, knowing that the power of God has overcome death and that this victory can be ours, too, through Jesus Christ.

✱ *Christ the Lord is risen today: Hallelujah!*
  Raise your joys and triumphs high: Hallelujah!

Charles Wesley

Monday March 27   Luke 24.13 – 24

These two followers of Jesus were filled with despair. They had hoped that Jesus was the one who would free Israel from the Romans; but, when he died on the cross, their hopes had been dashed.

As they talked together, Jesus appeared alongside them as an ordinary traveller. He walked with them and asked them questions which enabled them to share with him their frustration and despair. But they had not recognised who he was.

There are many times when we feel despair. Followers of Jesus today are not exempt from despair, nor indeed from any other ill. When we are feeling low, it is important to talk about it to someone who will really understand and listen. If we do not unburden ourselves we may become isolated in our need.

Of course we can always take our needs directly to our Lord in prayer and he will lift us out of our despair. But there are times when Christ comes to help us through the lives of ordinary people. It is important that we learn to recognise his presence and love in others.

✱ *Remind me, Lord, that your ear is ever open to my cry, but help me also to see you in the lives of ordinary people.*

Tuesday March 28

Jesus first **listened** to the two people walking home along the Emmaus Road, and then he **spoke** to them – explaining things so that they saw him in a different light. He enabled them to make sense of what had happened and eased their confusion and despair. However, words alone were not sufficient to help them to recognise the true identity of the stranger who had joined them.

▶ Read **Luke 24.25 – 35**.

It was only when Jesus broke the bread and gave it to them – familiar acts – that these two followers recognised him. Thus assured that he was alive, they no longer needed to see his physical form and so 'he disappeared from their sight' (verse 31).

Often words are not enough for us to recognise the presence of Jesus – we, too, need to experience him in 'the breaking of bread'. This happens in the sacrament of Holy Communion. The sharing of this symbolic meal affirms within us that Christ is present in our lives. He is alive and at work in us, filling us with his healing love and peace and lifting our confusion and despair.

✷ *Lord, help me to recognise your living presence with me in all the experiences of life.*

Wednesday March 29   Luke 24.36 – 49

Although the resurrection of Jesus remains a mystery to us, it was indeed a physical and historical reality. In today's reading it is described in terms both of time and space. The fact that Jesus had risen from the dead – he was alive – is clearly emphasised.

In showing himself to this group of disciples, Jesus confirmed that he was no hallucination or ghost. They could touch him and share a meal with him. His appearance demonstrated that life after death had reality, and there was nothing his disciples need fear. His death was in fact the beginning of a new life which would be available to all humankind.

Because it is difficult for us to understand Jesus' resurrection, we can easily become trapped into centring our thoughts only on Jesus' suffering and death. We emphasise his identification with people in their suffering, but fail to give sufficient emphasis to the victorious message of the resurrection – victory over death and hope for the life to come.

✷ *Lo! Jesus meets us, risen from the tomb;*
Lovingly he greets us, scatters fear and gloom;

Let the Church with gladness hymns of triumph sing,
For her Lord now liveth; death hath lost its sting.

Edmond L. Budry

Thursday March 30

Saying goodbye to people you love is usually a sad occasion. It is never easy, especially when the parting is going to be prolonged or even permanent.

▶ Read **Luke 24.50 – 53** and **Acts 1.6 – 11**.

The departure of Jesus from his disciples and friends was not a sad, but a joyous, occasion. It heralded the dawn of a new era of history – an era in which the power of the Spirit of God would be felt throughout the whole world. Acts 1.8 summarises all that was to follow – the empowering by the Spirit, the work of witnessing and the extension of God's kingdom from Jerusalem to the ends of the earth.

However, despite this wonderful promise of the coming of the Spirit, this parting from Jesus could not have been easy for the disciples. As they stood, staring up into the empty sky, they were assured by two men that the parting would not be permanent. In fact there was a sense in which Jesus would never leave them. He had gone from their sight but he would always be by their side. Jesus is by **our** side today and we can always rejoice in his presence with us.

✳ *Jesus said; 'Be assured, I am with you always, to the end of time.' (Matthew 28.20, NEB)*

Friday March 31

▶ First read **Acts 1.12 – 14**.

After Jesus ascended (see yesterday's reading), his disciples frequently gathered with Jesus' family and other friends to pray together. It was important for them to meet in this way so that they could support one another and share their faith. In our Christian life it is essential that we gather together with our fellow-Christians to worship and pray together. Our faith becomes impoverished if we do not share it with others.

▶ Now read **Acts 1.15 – 26**.

At one of their meetings together the followers of Jesus prayerfully decided to find a replacement for Judas, who had betrayed Jesus and then committed suicide. The number **twelve** was important. In the Old Testament days there had been twelve tribes of Israel. Jesus had come to start a new kingdom – the new 'Israel' – based on his love. This new 'Israel' was to have twelve leaders just as the old Israel had twelve tribes.

We may be surprised that they drew lots to decide who the new apostle should be. However, this was a device often used in Old Testament times but never mentioned again after the Holy Spirit came to the apostles at Pentecost. With the guidance of the Holy Spirit, Christians had a better way of discovering what God wanted them to do.

✳ *Do I always ask the Holy Spirit to guide me when making decisions?*

Saturday April 1   Acts 2.1–13

The second chapter of **Acts** must be one of the most exciting in the Bible. During the past four weeks we have read about the traumas and sufferings experienced by Jesus and his disciples in the days prior to the crucifixion. We have read about the great joy of the resurrection and the way in which the disciples were reunited with their risen Lord, who told them to wait for the coming of the Holy Spirit.

On the day of Pentecost, the waiting days were over. In a most dramatic way, the disciples experienced the power of the Holy Spirit entering their lives. They were enabled to speak boldly and intelligibly about their faith to the large crowd which had gathered.

This marked the birthday of the Church and confirmed the universality of the gospel, which is for all people and all nations. God's love transcends the barriers of communication and language. His Spirit empowers and makes us one.

✳ *Come Holy Spirit,*
   fill the hearts of your people with the fire of your love;
   kindle in them the power to proclaim your word
   in all the world.

For group discussion and personal thought

Two of Jesus' followers recognised him as he broke the bread (see **Luke 24.30 – 33**). In what everyday situations and places do you find it easiest to recognise the risen Jesus? Are there people who seem to be able to make him more real to you?

JOB

Notes by the Revd Donald H. Hilton, BA

Donald Hilton is Moderator of the Yorkshire Province of the United Reformed Church in the United Kingdom. He has previously served as a minister in London, Hampshire and Norfolk, and was also Youth and Children's Secretary of the Congregational Church in England and Wales. He has written and compiled several books published by the NCEC.

The notes in this section are based on the New English Bible.

Why do good people suffer? Shouldn't God give special protection to believers? These are questions with which people have struggled down through the ages. At the time when the book of **Job** was written, popular belief would have given a firm 'Yes' to the second question. Most people believed that only the wicked suffered – in fact, they considered that suffering was proof of wickedness.

The author of **Job** wanted to show that this was a shallow understanding of human experience and expressed a false relationship with God. He did this by telling the story of a man who lives a blameless life but, nevertheless, enters a period of great suffering. Three friends, following the popular belief, tell him to repent of the sin he must have committed. But Job argues with them, asserting that sin and suffering are not linked in such a simple way.

The book is written like a four-act play in which Job and his friends appear on the stage to argue it out. The notes in this section will comment on each of the acts of the play and the conversation that takes place within them. You will get most from the book of **Job** if you allow your own experiences to shed light on the conversation on the 'stage'.

Suggestions for further reading

Job by Francis I. Anderson, Tyndale Commentaries (Inter-Varsity Press);

Job by John C.L.Gibson, Daily Study Bible (Saint Andrew Press).

The first two chapters of **Job** can be regarded as a **Prologue** to the drama. They tell of an upright, blameless man who is both rich and the head of a happy, united family. This caring father is so scrupulous in his religion that he makes extra sacrifices on behalf of his children in case they have sinned secretly.

Then this happy situation is disturbed. Satan organises a series of calamitous events in which, one by one, Job's cattle, sheep, camels, and children are destroyed. Satan is sure that Job will lose his faith and will curse God for his misfortune.

The story thus becomes relevant to everyone in every age. What is the relationship between material prosperity and faith? Is it easier to be a believer when all is going well? How would our faith be affected if, one by one, we were robbed of our material possessions? Does affluence help or hinder our belief in God?

Job is held before us as the example of one whose confidence in God is unaffected by adversity.

✳ *Look back on your life. Can you see any link between changes in your personal fortune and your spiritual awareness?*

Satan now attacks Job at another level – the suffering becomes personal and physical when Job is inflicted with 'running sores from head to foot'. How will he react?

Experience suggests that it might be in several ways. Personal suffering can sometimes seem to deny our beliefs. How do we answer those who say:

● 'If God can't stop wars, I can't believe in him'?
● 'If God is powerful and loving, why doesn't he feed all the hungry, and heal the sick'?
● 'How can a God of love see a child suffer'?

However, there is another side to the coin. Many people have maintained their faith in the midst of great personal suffering:

● When Stephen was stoned he called out, 'Lord Jesus, receive my spirit', and prayed for his enemies (Acts 7.59 – 60).
● Some cancer victims have died with a radiant faith.

- Father Damien ministered to people with leprosy. When he contracted the disease himself, he could still praise God within his accepted illness.

The first step in understanding suffering is to recognise that our responses are complicated and diverse. There are no simple answers. Such humility may help us in our quest.

✳ *'God is often nearer to us, and more effectually present with us, in sickness than in health.'* (Brother Lawrence)

✓ Tuesday April 4   Job 3.1–2, 11–26

At the beginning of **Act 1** Job expresses utter helplessness before his fate; he would prefer death. This is an understandable response to acute personal suffering, for death would avoid suffering.

Job's despair, expresses in an acute form, the dilemma we all face. We can avoid suffering by avoiding life itself. In one of his novels, A.J.Cronin portrays a woman who cannot cope with human relationships. So, to avoid them, she goes to bed – permanently. Her husband waits on her; she meets no one else. We are left asking, 'But is she really alive?' We know that real life always carries risks and problems.

- When an infant makes his first faltering steps, he will often fall and hurt himself. Suffering is the price of growth.
- When a young girl falls in love, she may be rejected by the one she loves. Being hurt is the price of growing up.
- When a teenager embarks on an examination course, he knows he may fail. Risk is the price of personal development.

In his suffering, Job envies those 'in the quiet grave'. However, the price of being alive is to risk suffering and hurt.

✳   *Take thou our courage, for thy trumpets call us*
     On where new perils still our manhood greet.
                            Geoffrey Hoyland

✓ Wednesday April 5   Job 4.1, 6–9; 5.17–21; 6.1, 24–30

Three friends of Job have sat with him in silence for seven days (2.11–13). Now Eliphaz begins to speak. He offers two of the standard answers of his time to the problem of suffering:
- If Job is sinless, he really has nothing to worry about; the illness will be temporary.

- Suffering is a method God uses to discipline us. If we heed it, he will heal and help us.

Few would deny that suffering is sometimes a necessary corrective. A hangover rebukes drunkenness, and the pain of a broken relationship can remind us to foster tolerance in friendships. But this is not the whole truth.

Job pleads for realism. He has not sinned in any way that might invite the great misfortune that has befallen him. Eliphaz is using religion to comfort Job. That is splendid unless, as in this case, it obscures the reality of Job's experience. Religion can comfort but it must also help us to face up to the painful facts of life. Much suffering, like Job's, is real and undeserved. For example, poverty kills innocent children; drought and flood destroy good and bad alike. There is an indiscriminate aspect to life's pain. Religion should not cover it up, but give us the ability to face it.

✳   *Grant us wisdom,*
     Grant us courage,
For the facing of this hour.   *Harry Emerson Fosdick*

Thursday April 6   Job 8.1 – 7; 9.1, 15 – 24

The scene changes, and Bildad speaks. He argues that God is just, and therefore, if Job is suffering, then someone must have sinned. Perhaps it was Job's dead children. Job must now turn to God.

For Bildad, 'justice' is a pair of scales. As human sin goes on one side, God balances it with suffering on the other. In reply Job is forced to argue that, if this is true, then God is unjust or blind, or even malicious because Job's scales are out of balance; his suffering is in excess.

Job is not alone in wrestling with the terrifying possibility that the world is ruled by evil and not good. Only a devil would administer eternal justice so coldly. But 'judge' is only one picture we use to describe God; 'father' and 'lover' are others. God's nature can be understood, not only from pictures taken from a court of justice, but also from those of a loving home where justice and mercy walk hand in hand. Paul was convinced that there is 'nothing in all creation that can separate us from the love of God in Christ Jesus our Lord' (Romans 8.39).

✳ *What picture of God best interprets your own spiritual experience?*

71

Zophar, the third friend, now takes the centre of the stage. He chides Job for asking questions and advises him to accept that God's ways are a mystery. Job might have accepted such teaching except that Zophar spoils it by telling him that, if he changes his ways and prays more, then all his troubles will seem like nothing. What a thing to say to a man who has lost his wife, family, possessions and personal health!

'Pray more' can be a coward's way out of distress unless it is linked with action. The hunger of half the world needs sacrificial giving alongside prayer. Unemployment needs a change of government policy. A broken marriage needs patient counselling. Prayer is only one part of the process. A man died leaving a widow and young family. After the funeral service people gathered in a group and expressed their sympathy. Their sorrow was genuine. Then one man pushed to the centre, 'I'm sorry, too,' he said. 'I'm sorry £50. How much sorry are the rest of you?'

Prayer, like sympathy, has sometimes to be measured in hard cash, time sacrificially given, or physical effort.

✳ *Show me, Lord, in the circumstances of each day, how prayer and action may combine to serve you.*

Act 2 now begins. The three friends approach Job again. Eliphaz has become exasperated and tries to silence Job's questions by stressing his ignorance and youth. An important quality which Job displays is his willingness to question accepted truth. He is joined by a noble company including people like Paul and Galileo:

● **Paul** questioned the accepted belief that only Jews could be thought of as 'the people of God'. His questions helped to create the new community of the Christian Church.
● **Galileo** was attacked by the Church of his day for daring to suggest that the sun was the centre of our universe. Galileo was right – the Church was wrong.

Job questions the beliefs of his time. Throughout the book he asks, 'What is man? How do people relate to God? In what way are sin and suffering related?' To ask conscientious questions about serious subjects is an important part of the religious quest.

To what questions do you think people in your society too readily accept easy answers? What are the important questions you yourself are asking at the moment?

✱ *Grant me, O Lord, an open mind that seeks the truth with courage, and without prejudice.*

For group discussion and personal thought.
Look at what Job's three friends said to him, in **Job 4.6 – 9**; **8.2 – 7** and **11.13 – 19**. Now think of an occasion in your life which involved suffering; how did people react to you? What was most helpful? How does this enable you to bring true comfort to others who are suffering?

Sunday April 9   **Job 18.1 – 9; 19.1, 21 – 27**

The arguments in **Act 2** are more fierce than those in **Act 1**. Bildad accuses Job of attacking 'undeniable' truths. He repeats his one argument that only sinners suffer. Job's penetrating questions are answered by sarcasm rather than discussion. In reply, Job offers one of the most famous comments in the book (verse 25). In wanting his testimony to be 'engraved . . . with an iron tool and filled with lead' so as to be kept for ever, he is making a distinction between what seems to be God's harsh judgement now (his suffering) and God's eternal purpose. It is an appeal to the God of eternity against the partial view of God we now have. If that seems contradictory we must recognise that Job is trying to break out of a limited view of God to a bigger, broader perception of him.

J.B.Phillips wrote a book entitled *Your God is Too Small*. In this he suggested some of the narrow views of God we still hold including:

● God is a **policeman**, only concerned that we keep the law, and devoid of grace and mercy.
● God is a **doting parent**, ready to indulge our every whim.

Think of other pictures used of God. Does 'father' deny his motherly care? If we think of God as 'an old man in the sky', are we forgetting that he is active in the world? Can you identify your own false or partial pictures of God?

✱ *Lord God, grant us humility. We know you, and yet you are beyond our knowledge.*

Zophar has also run out of arguments and can only repeat himself, covering his inadequacy with the assertion that everybody knows that what he is saying is true. Job's answer is to ask him to widen his ideas. Are you sure that is what everybody knows? Ask travellers and examine your own experience. Realise that, in fact, innocent people sometimes suffer while wicked people get off scot-free.

It is easy to accept 'what everybody thinks'. However, great explorers and thinkers have been ready to question accepted ideas and push back the boundaries of human thought. Think big yourself.

- What new jobs should your church be doing in your area that no one has yet suggested?
- Should you be making new endeavours in your own life?
- Have you new and radical ideas about life to share with others?

In the eighteenth, and even in the nineteenth century, most people thought it impossible to end slavery. It seemed necessary to the economy and part of the natural order. A few pioneers dreamed of the impossible – and it happened. We now say, 'There will always be racism in the world.' Are there enough people ready to dream of equality?

✳ *Father, with our dreams we offer our service.*

Tuesday April 11

Chapters 22–27 form **Act 3** of the play. Here the same arguments as in **Acts 1** and **2** are repeated with a few additional ideas. Chapter 28 is like an interlude in a play, marking time for a change of scenery. In the first part (verses 1–11), human industry and exploration are praised. Even so, wisdom has not yet been discovered.

▶ Read **Job 28.12–28**.

In verses 12–22 it is acknowledged that wisdom cannot be bought even with the most precious metals. Then verses 23–27 affirm that wisdom is linked with God himself. He both created and understands it.

This wisdom is not cleverness. It is not even knowing a great deal or being highly educated. The wisdom this beautiful poem outlines is the ability to perceive God's purpose in creation, and most especially in humankind. The poet introduces the thought of divine wisdom as a partner with God in creation. In **John's Gospel** it is called 'the Word' and becomes flesh (1.1–14).

Spend a few moments looking at a single flower. What does it tell you about God? Recall times when you have gazed into the night sky. Was it just 'the sky' or 'God's sky'? Look at a baby. Do you sense God's eternal purpose?

✳ *Creator God, let me see you through the works of your creation.*

Wednesday April 12   Job 31. 16 – 18

Act 4 now begins. Job, as the main character, begins a process of self-examination and considers his relationship with people and God. Has he been obedient to God's law? He examines:

- his care of those less fortunate than himself (verses 16–20);
- his commitment to justice (verses 21–22);
- the possibility of greed (verses 24–25);
- the danger of false worship (verses 26–28).

Job believes himself to be innocent of these faults. One commentator has called this 'Job's last passionate outburst of innocence'. Another compares this message to that in Paul's New Testament letter to the **Romans**, because both Paul and the author of **Job** clearly understand God's demand for an obedience shown not only in actions but in inner conviction.

God does not ask us to make a list of good deeds which we can tick off as we do them to show how good we are. Rather, he asks that our hearts should be obedient. Actions will then follow naturally.

✳ *Father, help me to trust you with my heart, and work for you by what I do.*

Thursday April 13

In chapters 32–37 – probably written later than the rest of the book – a fourth friend, Elihu, appears. He has no new arguments but stresses the idea that suffering is God's discipline.

▶ Read **Job 38.1–18**.

God now speaks but Job does not get the answer he expected. He wanted to hear specific charges from God to explain his suffering and which he could then answer, or else a complete declaration of his innocence. Instead, God converses with Job in a series of questions which demonstrates that God is not aloof in some far-distant heaven but is present and active in his creation. These questions do not explain suffering any more than the cross of Jesus explains suffering. However, like the cross, they put all human experience, including suffering, in a new light.

In today's reading God speaks out of creation. Job is led from a limited understanding of God's power and might to a sense of awe at God's creative power. Job's sin is not paraded before him, which is what his friends did; instead, he is given a new humility.

What aspect of creation most gives you a sense of awe?

✳ *Creator of all things, we acknowledge your greatness, O God.*

Friday April 14   Job 39.19 – 30

God continues to speak to Job through a series of questions which require him to think rather than give immediate answers. A vivid word-picture of a horse in the field of battle is drawn and the three questions in verses 19 – 20 affirm that this splendid creature is all of God's making. Man has played no part in it. Of the hawk, God asks if Job knows how it makes its annual southerly migration; of the vulture, how it got its keen eyesight.

Each of us could continue the list of those creatures that speak to us of God's power and creative might – the communal sense of the ant; the instinct that takes the salmon back to its place of birth; the team-work of the beehive.

Recently, an impressive service was held in an English cathedral in the presence of many church dignitaries. The organ played magnificently and the congregation responded with full voice. Suddenly, in a moment of silence, a butterfly fluttered over the heads of the congregation and came to rest on the altar table. In the midst of this splendid human occasion, the sign of God was seen in a creature he had made.

✳ *Lord God, may the strength, the intricacy, and the beauty of your creation speak to me.*

Saturday April 15   Job 42.1 – 17

Before an **Epilogue** to round off the drama, Job responds to

God. He has not been given a neat and simple answer about human suffering. Within our limited human knowledge and perception no completely satisfying answer can be given. However, by seeing God afresh through creation Job has come to a new awareness of the breadth and harmony of God's world. Job sees himself as a small, though not unimportant, part of God's creation. It has led him to a personal relationship of trust in God – see verse 5.

Children often recognise that they do not fully understand a situation but trust their parents' wider knowledge. Now that Job is assured of an intimate relationship with God, he responds in this childlike way. Once we 'see' God with our own eyes – that is, know him as a friend – we can trust him no matter what life may bring to us. The final **Epilogue** (verses 7–17) may be interpreted as suggesting that, once we truly know God, then neither poverty nor affluence can rob us of our trust in a loving Father.

✴ *Lord, no matter what happens I trust in your almighty purposes of love for all your creation.*

For group discussion and personal thought

Consider how God became very real to Job in his sufferings (**Job 42.1–6**). In what circumstances has God become most real to you?

A **helpful book** for **group leaders** who use the weekly questions in *Notes on Bible Readings*. It contains useful information and guidance on discussion topics. Also helpful for personal guidance.

● *UK price:* **£1.70** for **1989**

IBRA *Order through your IBRA group secretary or from the appropriate address on the back cover.*

PRAYERS OF THE BIBLE

Notes by the Revd Michael Walker, BD, MTh, PhD

The notes in this section are based on the New English Bible.

Prayer is a deeply personal encounter with God. We learn to pray by praying. However, we can make progress in our journey by learning from others and the way in which they pray. But other people's prayers can never be a substitute for our own willingness to stand before God in the nakedness of our faith, as St John of the Cross described it, although they can throw light on prayer itself. In the first week of this section we shall look at some **Prayers of the Old Testament**. Then, in the second week, we shall turn to **The Lord's Prayer** and consider each line of this very familiar prayer.

Suggestions for further reading

Marked for Life: Prayer in the Easter Christ by Maria Boulding, Triangle Books (SPCK);

School for Prayer by Anthony Bloom, Librabooks (Darton, Longman & Todd).

✓PRAYERS OF THE OLD TESTAMENT

Sunday April 16   **1 Chronicles 29.10−19**

A PRAYER OF DAVID

These verses contain the prayer which David offered after telling the people that his son Solomon would carry out his plans for building a temple. It is a hymn of praise to God (verses 10−13) and a recognition that all we offer to him is a gift that he himself has given to us (verses 14−17).

Those two themes run constantly through prayer. The language that we use to express the nature of God is always a striving after a truth beyond our words. Worship − praising God for what he is in himself, quite apart from what he has given to us − is one of the most difficult aspects of prayer. That is why we often turn to the prayers of others, such as this prayer of David, rather than try to pray out of the resources of our own vocabulary. Sometimes, we do not need to use words at all but simply kneel in silence in God's presence.

However much we may strive to adore God for what he is in himself, it is difficult to separate worship from the acknowledgement of what he has given to us. He is known through his gifts. All prayer is a response to a God who has spoken to us, cared for us and, as Christians believe, come to be with us in Jesus Christ. In worship, we cannot help but realise that all we have is God's gift to us.

✳ *Lord, sometimes in words, sometimes in silence, we pray: but always we remember your love to us.*

Monday April 17   2 Chronicles 6.12–21
A PRAYER OF SOLOMON

Solomon's prayer was offered on completion of the building of the temple which, above all, was to be a place of prayer (verses 19–21). In many differing situations, and faced with a variety of needs, the people of Israel would turn to this place and pour out their prayers to God (see verses 22–42).

The house of God is still a **centre of prayer**. Much else may happen there – singing, preaching, discussion, teaching, celebration – but none of this should be allowed to overshadow the offering of prayer. In some of our modern attempts to enliven our services of worship we create a sort of busyness that crowds out prayer. Prayers can easily become hasty and self-centred, a means of whipping-up our enthusiasm rather than an opportunity for stillness and quiet adoration in God's presence, bringing to him human need.

The house of God is also a **sign of prayer**. Solomon remembered the men and women who would pray 'towards this place' (verse 20) and would derive from its very existence an assurance that God hears and answers prayer.

✳ *Remember the prayers that are offered by Christians all over the world, and pray that our churches may truly be places of prayer.*

Tuesday April 18   Psalm 23
A SHEPHERD'S PRAYER

Of all the prayers in the Bible, few have entered into people's imaginations, vocabulary and religious experience as much as has this one. The picture of the shepherd is a powerful one, even for men and women who live in towns and cities where they never see a shepherd at work.

79

Each verse of Psalm 23 describes God's constant, vigilant care. The Lord is portrayed as one who guides us, renews us and is with us, even in the darkest places of our lives. He is present with us when we are faced with enemies, and of his love we can finally be assured.

It is through prayer that we come to share the testimony of this psalmist. In prayer, God can lead us from turbulent days or arid periods to a place marked by its tranquillity and gentleness. In prayer, we discover that even life's darkest moments cannot separate us from God's protecting strength. These are truths not easily learned — we have to experience and prove them for ourselves. The continuing popularity of this psalm among Jews and Christians in every generation is evidence of people's experience of God's ceaseless providence.

✷ *Lord, wherever we are may we know you as the good shepherd. Even in the city, among the valleys of the tower blocks and by the streams of endless traffic, may we know your caring presence.*

Wednesday April 19   Psalm 84
A PRAYER FOR GOD'S HOUSE

This psalm was sung by pilgrims on their way to the temple in Jerusalem. The great festivals of the Jewish faith – the Day of Atonement, Passover, Tabernacles and Pentecost — drew people to the city in great numbers. For some, the journey was long and often dangerous. In it, they were sustained by the longing to reach Jerusalem where, with countless other pilgrims, they would join in the prayers and celebrations in the house of God.

For most of us today, the journey to the house of God is neither long nor dangerous. Yet there are sufficient deterrents: the pressures and busyness of modern life combine to stand in the way of our attendance at church. However, every Sunday is a high celebration, affirming that God has created the world and called us to inhabit it as his children. Furthermore, we celebrate the resurrection of Jesus, the beginning of a new world that is still to be completed.

The longing to share with our fellow-Christians the joy of creation and resurrection, can still draw us like a magnet. And, like our Jewish kinsfolk, with that longing in our hearts, we will let nothing stand between us and the joy of worship.

✷ *Lord, may love for Christ, and the world you have made, create in us a true love for your house.*

A PRAYER FOR THE GENERATIONS

The first two verses of this psalm are memorable because they
set our lives within the perspective of all the generations that
have gone before us and will follow after us. Further, those
generations are seen within the context of God's eternity.

This psalm also reminds us that we, ourselves, have only a
limited time span on this earth (verse 10). In consequence, we
are to make the wisest use of our time (verse 12) and to trust
God to establish 'the work of our hands' (verse 17, RSV).

In our prayers, it is good to acknowledge our debt to those
who have gone before us. We build upon what they have done.
While we may inherit the results of their follies, we have
received a legacy of beauty that others have created, freedoms
they have won, words they have composed and skills they
have discovered. During the span of our own lives, the world
continues to make progress and we are called to add to what
we have received, thus securing a legacy for those who will
follow after us. We shall do this if we live in continual
awareness of the God who is the ground of all our being, the
one who remains constant as generation follows generation.

✳   *Before the hills in order stood,*
      Or earth received her frame,
   From everlasting thou art God,
      To endless years the same.   *Isaac Watts*

A PRAYER OF TRUST

This prayer revolves around two themes, both of which relate
to the role of trust in our praying:
● God's knowledge of us (verse 14b–16);
● God's presence with us (verses 7–12).

First of all, there is the realisation that God knows me at a
depth that is far deeper than the knowledge I have of myself.
Self-understanding increases only slowly with the years.
There is no easy access to such wisdom — it is gained through
experience and an honest recognition of the motives, the
memories, the strengths and weaknesses, that go into making
us the people we are. Sometimes, in moments of insight, we
are appalled at what we discover inside us. Finding it hard to
accept ourselves, we wonder whether God can love us,
knowing us in the way that he does. But, in Christ, there is

the surest ground of all to believe that the God who knows us also accepts and loves us.

Secondly, no matter where we are, God is there and will hear our prayers. There are no God-forsaken ends of the earth — no depth of hell, no impenetrable darkness — where his presence is not to be found. We may have to live with what **seems** like his absence, and through moments when we are thrown back on the nakedness of faith; but, seen or unseen, God is there.

✴ *Lord, I believe you know me, you are with me, and that you never cease to love me.*

Saturday April 22 — Lamentations 1.17 – 22

A CRY OF THE HEART

Some prayers rise out of situations in which it seems that the world is falling apart. Good seems to have no victories, and evil many triumphs. It is out of such anguish that our hearts cry out to God. Such is the prayer in today's reading.

The writer was not wrestling with private and personal afflictions, but with the collapse of a very public world. A nation was falling around him and the cries of war and defeat were at his doorstep. Few of us live in such times of national ordeal. However, these words can be transposed into our world – the world of the personal and of the individual. The collapse of a private world may be no easier to cope with than the fall of a society. In some ways it may be more difficult, because we are alone in what happens to us.

Happenings such as the sudden loss of a job, the death of a loved one, the loss of love within a family, a disabling or debilitating illness can, almost overnight, leave us standing in the rubble of our dreams and the debris of what we had so carefully built up through the years. At such times, prayer is a cry — often without words. The only eloquence of these moments comes from our breaking hearts.

✴ *Pray for those who are living through times of affliction.*

For group discussion and personal thought

Which of this week's prayers from the Old Testament have you found the most helpful? Why? In what ways have you been able to relate them to your life?

THE LORD'S PRAYER

LORD, TEACH US TO PRAY

Even with the final doxology – 'For thine is the kingdom and the power and the glory, for ever. Amen' (see footnote to Matthew 6.13) – the **Lord's Prayer** seems a very short prayer indeed. In **Luke** the prayer is given in response to the disciples' request that Jesus should teach them how to pray. It must be one of the shortest lessons in history!

Does that brevity in itself teach us anything about prayer? Yes – it teaches us that we should not complicate what God has made simple. The advice and guidance of a revered teacher may help us to grow in the life of prayer, but the way into prayer needs no help or advice from anyone. In praying, we begin where we are. Speaking to God as Father, we can ask for daily needs, for help in sorting out our relationships through the way of forgiveness, and to be spared the worst that life can hand out to us.

There is a sense in which, as much as we grow in prayer, we do not grow beyond these beginnings. Prayer is a constant exploration of these basic themes – the nature of God, the provision of our natural needs, our human relationships and our survival.

✳ *Repeat the* **Lord's Prayer**, *pausing between each phrase.*

ABBA, FATHER

It is not easy for us to enter into the experience of Jesus in the garden of Gethsemane. Mark speaks of the 'horror and dismay' (verse 33) that came over him, and of his heart breaking with grief. Yet, even in that agonising crisis, Jesus called God by the intimate name of *Abba* – Father.

The name *Abba* is an expression of our ultimate trust in God, no matter what situation we are facing. Many people wish to include in that expression their experience of God's motherhood, as well as his fatherhood. Motherhood and fatherhood, together, embody for most of us our first experience of love. It is love experienced in a pre-reflective stage of our lives, love to which we had not then learned to give a name, love that filled the environment in which we

lived, love over which we had no control and which did not
depend upon the response we made to it.

The love of God – the fatherly and motherly love of God – is
like that first experience. It is an environment in which our
lives are lived. It is not one that we have made for ourselves,
but one which God has created for us.

✱ *Lord, may we know you in the fullness of your love to us,*
trusting you as a child trusts its father and mother, and
believing that your love surpasses every human experience
of love.

Tuesday April 25   John 17.13 – 26

THY KINGDOM COME

The kingdom of God is seen by those who have faith enough to
discern its presence in the midst of human life. In this prayer
for his disciples, Jesus describes two of its features.

First of all, it is to be found in people who seem to be
strangers to the world (verse 16). This does not mean that they
live in isolation from it, nor that they are in any way
indifferent to its welfare. Their 'strangeness' lies in the truths
by which they live and the values that they cherish. The
truth, to which Christ prayed we might be consecrated, is the
truth of the gospel that reverses all our notions of power,
status and achievement. The world might find those values
'strange' but they are the values of the kingdom.

The second sign of the kingdom is found in the unity of
Christ's disciples (verses 20 – 21), and we are still seeking the
fullness of that unity. Yet, our very search for it is a sign that
human wholeness lies in reconciliation, in healing the
wounds of division, and in drawing together the great variety
of human experience.

The coming of the kingdom lays great responsibility on our
shoulders. It will come as we live in obedience to its values
and overcome the barriers to its unity.

✱ *Lord, may we open our own lives to the coming of your*
kingdom. Give us the faith to live in obedience to your word
and to seek the unity of all Christians.

Wednesday April 26   Colossians 1.3 – 12

A PRAYER FOR DAILY LIVING

Verses 9 – 12 contain Paul's prayer for God's provision in the daily lives of the Christians at Colossae. Just as God gives us bread to eat, so he gives us the spiritual and mental resources for our daily living.

There is nothing that Paul hesitates to ask of God – wisdom and spiritual understanding, the fruit of active goodness in our lives, fortitude, patience and joy. Just as there is no limit to God's grace, so there is no limit to what we may ask of him.

In the **Lord's Prayer** we pray for 'daily bread'. Bread has to do with the staple diet of life – it is provided for our nurture and our growth. In today's reading Paul's prayer for his fellow-Christians is concerned with the basic necessities of their spiritual life, constant nurturing and growth to Christian maturity. Caviar is more exotic than bread, but it is not the basis of our development as healthy human beings. A longing for spiritual caviar, in preference to bread, denotes a wrong sense of values. Pray for what you need. Then leave it to God to give you more than you ever dreamed of.

✳ *Lord, give me that bread of life that will keep me strong and enable me to grow.*

Thursday April 27
FORGIVE US OUR SINS

Forgiveness is not an abstract concept in the Christian life. We learn to forgive through coming to terms with experiences that are painful and cause distress, anxiety and tears. As human beings, we have a great capacity for loving and enriching one another; that same capacity for good makes the ill we do to one another much harder to bear. In a perfect world, we would not cause one another pain, but the world is not perfect. In our sin, we cause God pain, as well as our families, friends and fellow-Christians.

▶ Read **2 Corinthians 2.1–11**.

Paul here asks his fellow-Christians to forgive someone who had caused them pain. The need to forgive and be forgiven is never far from our lives. That is why Jesus places that need so centrally in his prayer and in much of his teaching.

We need both to be forgiven by God and to forgive others the wrong they do to us. If we accept the first, but refuse the second, life is being lived with unhealed wounds and feeds on bitterness and anger. Worst of all, to lose the capacity to forgive is to lose the capacity to seek and accept forgiveness.

Forgiveness is central to our relationships with others. Not to seek it, or to refuse it to others, is to live without grace.

✳ *Lord, forgive the wrongs I have done and help me to forgive those who have wronged me. May there be no bitter legacy of unforgiven sins in my life.*

Friday April 28   Psalm 91

DELIVER US FROM EVIL

God cannot change the world for us in such a way that we never suffer, never face danger or are never imperilled by evil. The world is a dangerous place, as well as a joyous one, and we would be unwise to turn a blind eye to its potential for ill in our lives.

The greatest dangers, however, are those that threaten to destroy our souls. The physical ills that men and women are able to bear almost defy belief, but some people suffer evil of such magnitude that their will to survive is broken, their faith is blighted and they come to a place where they feel there is nothing left to hope for. It is from such terror that we pray to be delivered. We ask God that, finally, nothing will rob us of our faith, hope and love.

The psalmist offered his prayer in the face of pestilence, plague, disaster, calamity and snakes. These were the enemies that confronted him and over which, by God's grace, he triumphed. The secret of that victory and ours, is the 'shelter of the Most High' (verse 1) – the unfailing presence of God within which we are safe.

✳ *Lord, may no evil come that will take from me faith, hope or love.*

Saturday April 29

THINE IS THE KINGDOM, THE POWER AND THE GLORY

The final acclamation of the **Lord's Prayer** (see April 23) does not appear in the earliest manuscripts. It may be seen as a burst of praise added by the early Church to the original, simpler prayer of our Lord. It is an addition that has presentd its own dangers, for its language is the language of all earthly kingdoms. Far too often Christians have sought a kingdom, a power and a glory, that owed much to human ambition and little to Christian obedience.

We must not isolate the end of the **Lord's Prayer** from its beginning. The kingdom is the kingdom of the Father, and the power and the glory are the power of glory of heaven, not the blood-stained and discredited reflections we see on earth. It is the Father who reigns and holds all things in his hands, not some heavenly Caesar throwing his weight around the universe.

▶ Read **Revelation 5.6—14.**

In this reading, all heaven awaits the appearance of the Lion of Judah. However, it is not a Lion that makes its appearance in the midst of the throne, but a Lamb, the symbol of sacrificial love. The power and the glory of God are the power and the glory of unending love, and it is in that faith that we should offer our final doxology.

✱ *Lord God, Lamb of God, we adore you who, in love created all things, redeemed all things and will, one day, gather all things into your eternal kingdom.*

For group discussion and personal thought

Jesus gave the Lord's Prayer in response to his disciples' request to teach them to pray (**Luke 11.1—4**). How can we use this prayer as a guide to all our praying? In what ways is the familiarity of the Lord's Prayer a help or a hindrance when we say it?

Preachers' Handbook

Helpful book for **preachers**, containing sermon outlines for each Sunday of the year on texts from *Notes on Bible Readings.* Also includes sermon for Good Friday.

● *UK price:* £1.70 for **1989**

Order through your IBRA group secretary or from the appropriate address on the back cover.

1 CORINTHIANS

Notes by Edward J. Hughes, BA

Edward Hughes is on the staff of a printing firm in Leicester, and is a Methodist local preacher.

The notes in this section are based on the Good News Bible.

Corinth stood on a narrow isthmus linking southern and northern Greece. It was a prosperous commercial centre, so widely known for its immorality that 'to live like a Corinthian' became one of the gravest insults in the Greek language of the first century AD. Paul stayed there for about eighteen months (see Acts 18.1–18), and wrote this letter from Ephesus a few years later.

The aim of the letter was to reunite a divided church and to put right misunderstandings about Christian faith and conduct. Consequently Paul's words have a timeless quality which makes them as relevant today as when they were first written. Through his writing we discern the heart of a pastor who, with understanding and frankness, set about resolving the problems which afflicted the early Church. At the same time, Paul restated the basic principles of the Christian faith.

Suggestions for further reading

The Letters to the Corinthians by William Barclay, Daily Study Bible (Saint Andrew Press);
First Epistle of Paul to the Corinthians by Leon Morris, New Testament Commentaries (Inter-Varsity Press).

Sunday April 30   **1 Corinthians 1.1–9**

In verse 2, Paul makes two important statements about the Church. First, by referring to 'the church of God which is in Corinth', he emphasises the universal nature of the Christian church of which the congregation in Corinth is only a part. Paul deals with local problems in such a way that what he says may also be applied to 'all people everywhere who worship our Lord Jesus Christ'. Paul's vision of the Church is unlimited by time or space. There is **one** Church – there and then in Corinth, and here and now in our situation.

Its congregations are in every corner of the earth and in heaven.

Secondly, Paul describes the Church as 'all who are called to be God's holy people'. These words remind us of the Israelites who were different from other people because they belonged to God and were specially chosen for his service (Exodus 19.5 – 6). When applied to Christians, Paul's words mean that we are marked out, by the kind of people we are, as belonging to Jesus Christ. We are disciples – that is, men and women under the discipline of his redeeming love, called to be his serving hands and his loving heart for the people of our generation.

✳ *Ye seed of Israel's chosen race,*
   Ye ransomed of the fall,
 Hail him who saves you by his grace,
   And crown him Lord of all.   *Edward Perronet*

Monday May 1   1 Corinthians 1.10–17

When I was a boy I lived about six miles from a spot on the river Thames where the annual Oxford and Cambridge University Boat Race took place. None of the neighbourhood children had any connection with either university but, on the day of the race, we would all wear rosettes to show which crew we favoured.

Taking sides and expressing hostility to those on the other side seemed to be an integral part of our childhood. Unfortunately, there are people who carry this attitude with them into their adult lives. It is at the root of racial intolerance and fuels the violence at football matches or between rival gangs. Such a partisan attitude had begun to affect the Corinthian church. Groups were claiming allegiance to a particular leader rather than to Christ himself. As a result there was discord and rivalry in the congregation. It is this situation that earned Paul's rebuke.

If a particular denomination is more important to us than our devotion to Christ, then we merit the same rebuke. Our different traditions are part of the richness of the Church, but we need to guard against wearing them like a rosette.

✳ *Love, like death, has all destroyed,*
   Rendered all distinctions void;
 Names, and sects, and parties fall:
   Thou, O Christ, art all in all.   *Charles Wesley*

Notice how, in this reading, Paul bases his argument on three contrasting attitudes: those adopted by Greeks, by Jews and by believers in Christ.

The **Greeks** were the intellectuals of the ancient world. They were renowned for their great thinkers, their skill in debating and their use of logical argument. Their intellectual training had led them to believe that God was without emotion; and so the idea of a loving God was impossible. They believed also that God was utterly detached; and, therefore, to say that he had come into the world in Jesus was equally unacceptable to the Greeks.

The **Jews** were always looking for miracles to prove that God was active in history. They thought of the Messiah as one attested by striking manifestations of power. Couple this with the Jews' belief that anyone crucified was under God's curse (Galatians 3.13), and we can see how offensive the thought of a crucified Messiah must have been to them.

Those of us who **believe** in Christ, however, accept the cross as the saving power in our lives. We are not forever looking for miracles, nor seeking by argument, to prove that God is active on our behalf. The greatest miracle of all is that Jesus Christ died for our salvation.

✳ *O God our Father, we thank you that Christ's death on the cross, which the world considers foolishness, is the power by which we are saved.*

Wednesday May 3   **1 Corinthians 2.1 – 9**

The ancient Chinese merchants had a unique method of teaching an apprentice to recognise the value of jade. The apprentice had to sit in a circle of experienced merchants who wordlessly passed pieces of jade around. Sometimes they put a piece on one side to go into the reject box. At last the day came when the apprentice himself rejected a piece. When that happened, he had finished his apprenticeship. Years of experience had taught him what even the wisest words could not.

What is it that persuades the Christian believer of the truth of the gospel? Certainly not the force of logical argument; but rather, the experience of God's love for us. At times, actions speak much more eloquently than the finest words – the touch of a sympathetic hand, the nod of approval, the smile that bids us welcome or a kiss from someone we love. In the cross of Christ we see a loving God in action on our behalf. Even the greatest preacher can add nothing to this, the supreme moment in our salvation. The cross has no need of an interpreter. Through the Holy Spirit it commends itself to our hearts.

✳ *Inscribed upon the cross we see,*
   In shining letters, 'God is love';
   He bears our sins upon the tree;
   He brings us mercy from above.   *Thomas Kelly*

Ascension Day, May 4   1 Corinthians 3.1–9a

A hospital patient once told me, 'I have been saved by the London City Mission.' He was making, albeit rather clumsily, the same claim that Paul makes in today's reading – that God works through men and women. Paul and Apollos were not rivals, but colleagues striving, each in his own way, to proclaim the gospel. They were 'partners working together for God' (verse 9a) – that is, they were bound to each other by God in a common purpose. More important still, they were in partnership with God himself who was able to work through them.

It is hard to understand how God can choose people like us to be his partners, yet he does. A Christian in a factory once invited a workmate and his wife to go with him to a concert. As they talked together he began to speak to them about his faith in Jesus, and invited them to come to church with him. They came and, in course of time, they accepted Jesus Christ as their Lord and Saviour. What a privilege it is for all of us to be, with Paul and Apollos, God's fellow-workers!

✳ *Lord Jesus, we praise you that you have made a path for us through life's confusing maze, leading on to heaven, where you live and reign with God, your Father and ours.*

Friday May 5   1 Corinthians 4.1–7

In the court of law on the Greek island of Corfu, the witness stand is opposite the judge's bench above which is a picture of our Lord. It is a very potent reminder that our real judge is above the bench and not on it. The trouble with most of us, however, is that we put ourselves on the bench, turning our back to the picture and usurping the place of God. This is what the church at Corinth was doing in comparing Paul and Apollos. What really mattered was that they were both doing the job that God had entrusted to them. He alone was able to judge how well they performed their task.

One of the drawbacks of judgement being in the wrong hands is that it becomes corrupted and leads to sin. People in ethnic minority groups have been deprived of basic human rights because others have adjudged them to be inferior. Misguided men have robbed women of opportunities to develop their full potential as creative individuals with much to contribute to society by casting them exclusively in the role of home-maker. The Bible is right in insisting that judgement belongs to God; only he is capable of judging without prejudice.

✳ *Think about these words of Jesus: 'God will judge you in the same way as you judge others, and he will apply to you the same rules you apply to others.' (Matthew 7.2)*

Saturday May 6   1 Corinthians 4.8–16

An old story tells of the Holy Spirit meeting a man who was turning away from the door of a church. 'I am the town drunkard,' he said. 'I came here for help but they won't let me in.' 'No, nor me,' answered the Holy Spirit.

The Christians at Corinth had that kind of church. Concerned for their own status, they had become boastful and arrogant. They had lost their humility and forgotten that they were men and women under grace. They believed that their church life was the best that it could be and were so turned in on themselves that they had lost their sense of ministry.

In the light of their boasting Paul catalogues the deprivations and sufferings of the apostles. He is reminding this church that the cross is unavoidable if we are to fulfil the ministry to which Christ calls us. It is impossible for people like the Corinthians to accept authentic Christian ministry. Those who are prepared to let God's strength be made perfect in their weakness not only accept it, but enthusiastically embrace it. Letting the Holy Spirit into our lives can be a costly experience, but the prize is a crown of glory.

✳ *Ponder on Jesus' words: 'If anyone wants to come with me, he must forget self, carry his cross, and follow me.' (Mark 8.34b)*

For group discussion and personal thought

There were serious divisions in the Corinthian church (see
1 Corinthians 1.10 – 17 and the notes for **May 1**). What
divisions are there in the Church today? Why? What can we
do about them?

Sunday May 7   **1 Corinthians 5.1 – 13**

At Passover, Jews still recall the way God delivered them
from bondage in Egypt (Exodus 12). In the week before the
festival all the yeast and leavened bread is cleared from the
house and only unleavened bread is eaten. Passover is a
celebration of the believing community. In today's reading
Paul says that the absence of leaven is a sign of purity and
truth (verse 8). Christians, too, have to celebrate their
deliverance without compromising with those things from
which they have been set free. That is the reason for Paul's
strong reaction to the continued fellowship of the Corinthians
with a 'brother' who carries on sinning.

According to Paul there are two good reasons for the
expulsion of the sinner:

● that he may repent and be saved – that is, caring about him
   at the deepest level;
● for the good of the fellowship.

Today, in a moral climate of lowered standards, the Church
needs to be seen as a symbol of the kingdom of God in which
there is nothing corrupt. If there is no difference between its
standards and those of the world outside it, then it ceases to be
a place of refuge for the sinner. The Church must be seen to
take sin seriously, enjoy forgiveness fully and act lovingly at
all times.

✱ *O God of all grace, thank you for giving us your Church to
   be a refuge for repentant sinners, like me.*

Monday May 8   **1 Corinthians 6.1 – 11**

Paul makes it very clear in his letter to the church at Corinth
that there is a vast difference between the standards of the
Church and those of the world. The Corinthians had not
grasped this fact and were attempting to graft worldly values

93

on the Church with predictably disastrous consequences. We
have already witnessed two examples of this sad fact in their
partisanship and divisions, and in their tolerance of
immorality. Now Paul draws attention to a third. The Greeks
were a proud people, jealous of their rights. Going to law was
a common practice among them, but for one Christian to take
another Christian to court was clearly not in keeping with the
law of love which must govern the lives of Christ's flock.

As members of the Church we are bound to have different
standards from the world around us. The law which governs
us is based on caring and compassion. It has to do, not with our
rights, but with undeserved grace and unlimited forgiveness.
Consequently, we should not allow grievances to sour our
relationships with one another. Nor should we bear grudges
or harbour resentment against others, especially those of our
own fellowship, for 'we are ruled by the love of Christ'
(2 Corinthians 5.14a).

✱ *Pray for those whose relationships have become soured
because they are harbouring grievances.*

Tuesday May 9   **1 Corinthians 6.12 – 20**

The custom of sacral manumission was widely practised in
the ancient world. By it a slave could save money and
purchase his freedom. The money was paid to the temple of a
particular god who was then said to own the slave although,
for all practical purposes he was a free man. In their own
tradition the Jews had the figure of the *go-el* or redeemer who
would buy back any member of the tribe who had fallen into
slavery. These are the ideas Paul has in mind when he writes,
'You do not belong to yourselves but to God; he bought you for
a price' (verses 19 – 20).

It is clear from these verses that our social conduct ought to
arise out of our response to God's grace. The freedom we enjoy
as a result of Christ's death at Calvary has been bought for us
at a price far beyond our means. A most precious part of that
freedom is the power to say 'no' to those things which would
devalue us as the rightful property of God. All that we have
and are should be used to his glory.

✱ *Father, we praise you that you have always valued us even
more highly than we value ourselves. Give us grace to live
our lives in such a way that your name may be glorified.*

During World War II, Great Britain was often referred to as
'the home front' – meaning that the people at home were as
much a part of the battle as the forces engaged in the fighting.
The work of keeping the army supplied, feeding the nation,
and maintaining homes for servicemen and women to return
to were as important as being in the forefront of the battle.

In today's reading Paul is saying that everyone should be
willing to serve God in his or her own situation. Serving
Christ does not always mean dramatic changes in our lives.
Rather, true Christian living means allowing Christ to
change us from day to day just where we are.

Living out the gospel in our own situation is one of the finest
services we can render to Christ. Not everyone is called to
serve in the full-time ministry of the Church, nor are we all
bound to carry the good news to distant places, important as
these tasks are. But we are all called to serve Christ, each in
our own way, in our church life and in our daily living.

✸ *Heavenly Father, stir up in us the desire to know your will,
and give us the grace to obey your call.*

I was born into a family who, although full of love for one
another, was rarely seen in church. Once, when my mother
was ill, a young lady from the Salvation Army came to cook
and clean for us. I still have a vivid memory of her, bonnet and
jacket off, down on her knees scrubbing the floor. Her
wordless sermon on Christian love was a powerful means of
witness to a small boy. It was to bear fruit many years later.

Getting alongside people is one of Paul's themes in today's
reading. Becoming 'all things to all men' (verse 22) is not easy.
It has to be done without patronising people. It takes time and
patience and may mean being misunderstood and risking our
reputation. But we are servants of one who himself gave up
equality with God to get alongside us, who was prepared to be
misunderstood and risk his good name to bring sinners back
to God, and who even went to the cross for us.

Paul challenges us to take the gospel out of the cosiness of
our weekly meetings and hazard it, and ourselves, in the
secular culture of our local community.

✸ *Father, we give you thanks for those who, by their life and
witness, brought us to a knowledge of your eternal love.*

When Paul wrote this letter to the Christians at Corinth there were many pagan temples in the city. It was the custom for surplus meat from sacrificial worship to be sent to the meat market for sale to the public. Jews were forbidden to eat such meat and their custom of enquiring about its origin had been carried into the Corinthian church by Jewish Christians. Clearly, there had been criticism, both inside and outside the church, of Christians who ate with unbelievers. Paul, however, argues for Christian freedom, provided that it is used to help others and not to shock or offend them.

One obvious conclusion from today's reading is that our beliefs ought to govern all our actions. The world at large certainly expects that from us, as any newspaper report of a Christian's 'fall from grace' will prove. But there are good examples of people who have exercised Christian freedom to the glory of God: those who, as conscientious objectors, served and sometimes died in wartime ambulance units; those who refuse to buy goods from countries governed by oppressive regimes; and those who support and minister to prisoners of faith and conscience.

✳ *Whate'er I say or do,*
  Thy glory be my aim.   *Charles Wesley*

Today's reading contains the earliest written account of the Last Supper (verses 23 – 25). With it we have Paul's confirmation that the Lord's Supper had already become an important part of the worship of the early Church. At a fellowship meal someone would break the bread and bless the wine, following the example of our Lord at the Last Supper. However, what should have been the occasion of the deepest fellowship in the Corinthian church only served to highlight its divisions. Worse still, some of these Christians had such disregard for each other that, while some made it an occasion for over-indulgence, others went away hungry.

It must surely grieve the Holy Spirit that, despite all the moves towards Christian unity in recent years, the Lord's table is still the point at which we are most divided. However, the sacrificial death of Jesus should remind us that we are reconciled to God and united to one another. Even within our own congregation there may be those with whom we do not always agree. This should not sour our relationships. At the Lord's table there is the opportunity to examine ourselves to determine whether we are truly 'in love and charity with our neighbours'.

✳ *Many, and yet but one we are,*
   One undivided bread.   *Charles Wesley*

For group discussion and personal thought
Paul said that our bodies are 'the temple of the Holy Spirit' (1 Corinthians 6.19). What does this mean? Discuss the implications this has for our attitudes towards (a) health, (b) morality.

Whit Sunday, May 14   1 Corinthians 12.1–11

Whit Sunday or Pentecost is sometimes called the birthday of the Christian Church. *Charismata,* the word Paul uses for 'spiritual gifts', comes from a word which means 'birthday presents' in modern Greek. This serves to remind us that the Holy Spirit, who first gave life to the Church, regularly renews its life by continuing to shower gifts upon it.

The Corinthians tended to parade their own spiritual gifts, discounting those of others, but here Paul stresses the diversity of God's giving to those he has called. No gift is superior to any other. Different gifts are given to different people 'for the good of all' (verse 7).

An evangelist had a richly blessed ministry some years ago. Every campaign he undertook was borne up in prayer by a small group of people. Their gift was to pray and, through their prayers, the evangelist's work was wonderfully blessed. Some people's gifts are expressed in thrilling, often dramatic ways. But, if the things that we do in God's service are the quieter, often unnoticed, things, they are nonetheless valuable gifts of the Holy Spirit specially given to us to use to God's glory.

✳ *Merciful God, may we discover the gifts you have given us through your Spirit and help us to use them to your glory.*

Monday May 15   1 Corinthians 12.31b to 13.13
Paul now comes to the greatest gift of all – **love**. Without this

97

all the other gifts are meaningless and ineffectual. Look again
at verses 4–7: this is how Christ wants us to be. But we
cannot even begin to love like that unless the Holy Spirit lives
within us. Love is the greatest of all gifts because through it
Jesus is giving himself to us to live in our hearts and rule over
our lives.

It would be a useful exercise for every local church and
every individual Christian to measure themselves, from time
to time, against Paul's definition of love. We acknowledge the
truth of this, but honesty would force us to admit that we fail
to live by it. We are often impatient; we resent the success of
others; we are envious; we bear grudges; we are self-
important, and frequently inconsiderate. However, we are
blessed with two saving graces:

● the **love of God** who accepts us as we are;
● the **Holy Spirit** who works within us, like a lapidary with
  a precious gem, cutting and refining, until we are able to
  catch and reflect the love of Christ with every facet of our
  being.

✳ *Gracious Spirit, Holy Ghost,*
    Taught by thee, we covet most,
  Of thy gifts at Pentecost,
    Holy, heavenly love.   *Christopher Wordsworth*

Tuesday May 16   **1 Corinthians 14.1–12**

Speaking with tongues was considered to be at the 'top of a
league table' of spiritual gifts in Corinth. It was prestigious
for those who possessed the gift, but it was beginning to
overshadow all other gifts. The difficulty was that if no one
could interpret what was said, then worship was a
meaningless babel of sound and unhelpful to the
congregation. Throughout chapters 12–14 Paul's message to
this church is 'get your priorities right'. Love must be first.
Ecstatic language, which is unintelligible to others, is self-
indulgence: it ministers only to the one who utters it. On the
other hand, proclaiming God's message in words that can be
easily understood, arises out of a love for people and is meant
for their comfort and encouragement.

Not everyone is called to preach the gospel, but every
Christian can proclaim God's message. To help others less
fortunate than ourselves without patronising them, to be
'there' when someone needs a friend, to share another's
burden, to wipe away the tears – all these things proclaim

that God is love. Moreover, they testify to the love which is at
the centre of our lives and makes us what we are.

✳ *I long to know, and to make known,*
   The heights and depths of love divine.   Charles Wesley

Wednesday May 17   **1 Corinthians 15.1–11**

The Greeks had believed in the immortality of the soul for
centuries, but the Corinthians were clearly in doubt about the
resurrection of the body. Paul sets out to remove that doubt in
this superb fifteenth chapter. In so doing, he throws light on
the theme of Christ's resurrection and our own.

The evidence of the eye-witnesses to the risen Lord Jesus is
impressive. That some were still alive and, therefore, able to
be consulted is important for two reasons:
● It confirms the resurrection as an historical fact.
● It shows that Paul's letter was written within living
  memory of the events recorded in the Gospels.

Three witnesses are singled out: **Peter**, who had denied
Jesus (Matthew 26.69–75); **James**, our Lord's brother, who
misunderstood him (John 7.5); and **Paul**, the chief persecutor
of the Church (Acts 9.1–2). What a comfort to all who have
failed Jesus—and that means all of us at some time or another
—to have this assurance of forgiveness and reconcilation, and
the hope of new life now and in heaven!

✳ *I know that my Redeemer lives—*
   What joy the blest assurance gives!   Samuel Medley

Thursday May 18   **1 Corinthians 15.12–22**

The resurrection of Christ may be said to be the foundation-
stone of the Christian gospel. In denying its truth, the
Corinthians were really denying the distinctive message of
the gospel which speaks of God's power enabling men and
women to die to sin and be raised to new life in Christ.
Without the resurrection there could also be no hope of
eternal glory and the Christian would, indeed, 'deserve more
pity than anyone else in the world' (verse 19).

Notice how many times Paul uses 'Christ has been raised' in
today's reading. The Greek tense he uses is that for a
completed action which has a **continuing** state. The
significance is that, although Christ was raised once long ago,
his rising has a continuing effect. Just like a stone thrown

into a lake, whose ripples spread outwards in ever-greater circles, so the power of the risen Christ spreads through all the world, even to your life and mine. Because of this continuous character, salvation has an ongoing effect, changing us from glory to glory (see 2 Corinthians 3.18), until we attain the perfect life of heaven.

✳ *Heavenly Father, we thank you that, through the power of the resurrection, Jesus Christ is able to live in us, changing and renewing our lives.*

Friday May 19   1 Corinthians 15.35 – 44

Some parts of the river Nile are so murky that many fish cannot survive there. They are unable to see their food or any enemies who wait to destroy them. The Nile pike is different. Unable to see, it transmits about 400 electrical impulses a minute which sense where its food is and where danger lurks. Thus God, our Creator, has given it a body perfectly fitted to its environment. Paul's argument in today's reading is precisely that. His answer to the question, 'What kind of body will they have?' (verse 35), is that it will be as perfectly in keeping with the life of heaven as our earthly bodies are with our environment now.

The Corinthians' question reveals the fear shared by many people that, even if there is a resurrection, the body we shall then have may not be recognisable. In his glorified body, Mary mistook our risen Lord for the gardener, but he spoke her name and she knew him. The disciples on the Emmaus road knew him when he broke the bread. Our heavenly bodies will be different, too, because we shall have shed the imperfections of this life, but those who love us will know us again in the glory of God's everlasting kingdom.

✳   *Then shall I see, and hear, and know*
     All I desired and wished below;
       And every power find sweet employ
       In that eternal world of joy.   *Isaac Watts*

Saturday May 20   1 Corinthians 16.1 – 4, 13 – 24

At the time when Paul wrote to the Corinthians, the church in Jerusalem was in need. Famine had struck Judaea (Acts 11.27 – 30), a far from wealthy area. The Jerusalem congregation, probably suffering the after-effects of the sharing of possessions practised in earlier days (Acts 4.32–35), was in difficulties. Paul was deeply concerned and asked the Gentile churches to help the mother church. In so doing, he shows that there was already a measure of interdependence in the scattered congregations of the Church as early as twenty to twenty-five years after the resurrection. Moreover, it was a gracious act which helped to cement relationships between the Jewish and Gentile Christians.

Regular and systematic sharing of our resources is a charge laid upon every Christian. Sometimes the need is on our doorstep, such as allowing another denomination to share our premises. Or, we may hear of the needs of Christians in other lands imprisoned for their faith, or of countries where there is no money to buy Bibles or obtain medicine for the sick. If all our work is done in love (verse 14), then calls for help from our fellow-believers will not go unanswered.

✷　*In sickness, sorrow, want, or care,*
　　Whate'er it be, 'tis ours to share;
　　May we, where help is needed, there
　　　　Give help as unto thee.　　　　　*Godfrey Thring*

For group discussion and personal thought
Read **1 Corinthians 12.1–11, 31b; 13.1–13.** Paul said that love is the greatest of the Holy Spirit's gifts. What does this 'love' really involve? Why are other spiritual gifts invalid and ineffective without it? What difference does it make when love is added to the other gifts?

BASICS
by David Weeks

This small book has been written for new Christians, especially those recently received into church membership.

● *UK price:* **60 pence**

Order through your IBRA group secretary or from the appropriate address on the back cover.

GENESIS 12–35

Notes by Adrian G. Hudson, MA

Adrian Hudson is a Methodist local preacher living in North Devon. He has worked as a probation officer in various parts of England; and, for ten years prior to his retirement, was Deputy Chief Probation Officer for West Yorkshire.

The notes in this section are based on the New International Version.

Genesis 12–35 covers the lives of the three patriarchs: Abraham, Isaac and Jacob. Other lesser characters – wives, sons, daughters, servants and so on – are involved as well. Interesting as these are, our readings will concentrate on the fulfilment of God's purposes through the three main characters. When God revealed himself to Moses, he told him to say to the people, 'The Lord – the God of Abraham, the God of Isaac and the God of Jacob – has sent me to you' (Exodus 3.15). The covenant promises made to the patriarchs were the first steps in establishing the nation of Israel.

The Bible is the book of God's covenant relationship, first with individuals, then with a nation and, finally in the New Testament, with his Church. Thus, in looking at God's promise and the reactions of Abraham, Isaac and Jacob to it, we are seeing the beginnings of what God does for us today. As Paul pointed out (Romans 8.17), we are also heirs to God's promises.

Suggestions for further reading

Genesis II by John C. L. Gibson, Daily Study Bible (Saint Andrew Press);

Genesis by Derek Kidner, Old Testament Commentaries (Inter-Varsity Press).

Sunday May 21   **Genesis 12.1–9**

Abram, whose name later became Abraham, had been born in Ur of the Chaldees, but had then moved with his father Terah to Haran where the family had settled. Here God's word came to Abram. There are two parts to it — a command and a promise of blessing.

- The **command** was to move (verse 1). For Abram the stability afforded by his country, his kindred and his home had to be left behind, so that he could journey to a promised, but unknown, land. How often does God have to unsettle us, requiring us to move first before he can do anything else with us?
- The **promise** (verses 2 – 3) was for the future. It was to be realised in future generations. In fact, it was not so much that Abram would be blessed as that he would be a source of blessing.

Although he was old, Abram responded, uprooting his family and setting out in faith. For many of us today retirement comes at an age less than that at which Abram set out. Then, our freedom from the routine of daily work may be God's challenge to us to move on to new activities and explore the wide territory of voluntary service.

✻ *O God of our fathers, when we are too settled call us to venture out in faith, that you may bless us and make us a blessing to others.*

Monday May 22   **Genesis 13.3 – 18**

The conflict, that arose when Lot's and Abram's herdsmen disputed over grazing rights, has modern parallels. All too often a solution is sought by use of force, the stronger tribes or nations dispossessing the weaker. How many leaders of today would follow Abram's example in giving first choice to their rivals? The person of faith, who trusts God for his needs, can afford to act more generously than those who believe only in their own power and resources.

With hindsight we can see that Lot, in choosing the most fertile land, did not make the best choice. Abram on the less fertile, higher land would have had to keep moving to find sufficient pasture. This played its part in keeping him alert and active and preventing complacency. Facing the challenge, he knew he had God with him and the promise was renewed (verses 14 – 16). Today God challenges us to choose, not the easy way, but **his** way.

✻ *Jesus said, 'Whoever wants to save his life will lose it, but whoever loses his life for me will save it.' (Luke 9.24)*

Tuesday May 23

A small girl was delighted with the news that she was to be bridesmaid at her cousin's wedding. Her mother promised her that she would make her a new dress to wear, just like the other bridesmaids. As the days went by she began to fret, not knowing that her mother was making the dress at night so that it would be a surprise. One day she burst out, 'I shall never get my dress in time,' but she was reassured when reminded, '**Your mother** has promised you.' Promises depend not on what they are, but on who makes them.

▶ Now read **Genesis 15.1–11, 17–18**.

God's words about himself beginning with **'I am'** occur over and over again through the Bible. In verse 1, God promised Abram, '**I am** your shield.' However, what reward could there be for Abram, unless he was provided with an heir? Looking at the stars in the night sky, the word that his offspring would outnumber them must have made the promise seem even more incredible. Nevertheless, 'Abram believed the Lord, and he credited it to him as righteousness' (verse 6). This well-known verse is quoted by Paul in support of his claim that justification is by faith (see Romans 4.1–3 and Galatians 3.6–9).

✳ *All my hope on God is founded;*
He doth still my trust renew.   *Joachim Neander*

Wednesday May 24

When we travel in other countries we often judge the people there by the hospitality they show to us as strangers. Friends of mine have recently returned, speaking enthusiastically of the way they were received in countries as different as Zaire, Hong Kong, New Zealand and the Philippines. Everywhere it seems hospitality is regarded as a virtue. Nowhere is this more true than among the nomadic peoples of the Middle East.

▶ Now read **Genesis 18.1–15**.

Abraham was a tent-dweller. When he looked up from his siesta and saw three men standing there, his response was immediate, even if the time was inconvenient. Everybody was sent scurrying around from the moment Abraham hurried to meet them – Sarah to bake bread quickly and the servant to prepare the selected calf.

The men were not casual passers-by. Their spokesman turned out to be the Lord telling Abraham the next stage in fulfilment of his promise – a son for Abraham and Sarah by the same time next year. We can imagine Sarah's astonishment as she overheard this from the door of the tent. Think about and contrast the way in which Sarah learned that she would have a son with the way in which God revealed his will to Mary before the birth of Jesus (Luke 1.26 – 38).

✴ *Father, when we find that our human judgement is opposed to your word, may we have the faith to believe you.*

Thursday May 25

The wickedness of Sodom and Gomorrah was well-known. Abraham may have often wondered why God did not do something about it. He probably also worried about his nephew Lot and his family living in such a place. When the Lord's two companions went on towards Sodom, God shared his purpose with Abraham. There followed a great adventure in prayer as Abraham pleaded for the righteous in those cities.

▶ Read **Genesis 18.16 – 33**.

● God took the initiative by disclosing his thoughts to Abraham (verses 17 – 21), thus inviting Abraham to speak.
● Abraham explored his new relationship with God in the questions and answers of verses 23 – 32.
● God terminated the conversation (verse 33).

From this we may learn that prayer is a two-way exchange with God. Listening to God's answers is just as important as plying him with questions. Also, we learn that the time to end a prayer is when God has said what he wants to say to us.

✴ *Lord, when we pray, give us the grace not only to speak, but also to listen when you answer.*

Friday May 26

Many people make choices early on in their lives – their career, place of living or with whom they live – which later on have unexpected repercussions. Some of these choices may lead them into situations which bring unbearable pressure. This is what happened to Lot.

▶ Now read **Genesis 19.15 – 29**.

Although Lot never accepted for himself the attitudes and behaviour of the citizens of Sodom and Gomorrah, by choosing to live among them he exposed himself to such pressure that he could see no way out other than by sacrificing his daughters.

In this sort of situation, it is scarcely possible to resist on one's own, and outside help is needed. The indecisiveness that Lot showed, so that he had to be dragged away into safety, is characteristic of a person who is compromised. It is what happens when we try to serve two masters.

Lot was saved by God's messengers, but verse 29 indicates that Abraham's prayer was also instrumental. Can we recognise the times when our prayers are needed for others if God is to rescue them from desperate situations?

✳ *Lord, instead of condemning those who have got themselves into difficulty by past mistakes, may we, with the help of your Holy Spirit, plead for their salvation.*

Saturday May 27

▶ First read **Genesis 21.1–7**.

Sarah, despite the doubts which led her to laugh in derision when she had first heard she was to bear a son to Abraham, did give birth to Isaac. Now she laughed for joy, welcoming all who would share her joy with her. The fulfilment of God's promises always brings with it a joy that flows over.

▶ Now read **Genesis 21.8–14**.

There was joy for Sarah, but the birth of Isaac must have dashed Hagar's hopes for Ishmael, whose birth is recorded in Genesis 16. Abraham found himself caught between Sarah's jealousy and his own love for the boy, Ishmael.

It is easy for situations like this to arise – for example, in families where there are step-parents. There may be jealousy between children and half-brothers or half-sisters. Children often find it hard to get on with a step-parent. It may seem that some past mistake has got us into the situation where, whatever we do, will be wrong for one of those involved. If, like Abraham, we take our dilemma to God, we may discover that he can resolve the situation and, despite our mistakes, he can still use us.

✳ *Thank you, Lord, that when we turn to you in repentance, you relieve us of the burden of our past mistakes.*

For group discussion and personal thought

How do this week's readings show that Abraham lived by faith in God and in God's promises to him? In what ways was Abraham's faith a way of life rather than a set of beliefs? What do you mean by 'faith'? What are the promises by which you, as a follower of Christ, can live?

Sunday May 28

The account of Abraham offering Isaac is probably well-known to us and so we need from time to time to take a fresh look at it. The Bible presents it as a test of Abraham's faith. The peoples among whom Abraham lived would sometimes go as far as human sacrifice to their gods. Perhaps Abraham wanted assurance that his religion was as good as theirs. He may also have sought assurance that his God was better than theirs. He found both!

▶ Now read **Genesis 22.1–14**.

Abraham had confidence that, in some way, God's promise would be fulfilled despite the sacrifice of Isaac. He told his servants, '**We** will come back to you' (verse 5).

Moriah, if it is the place referred to in 2 Chronicles 3.1, may be in the region which was later known as Calvary. This has led to the suggestion that Isaac carrying the wood is symbolic of Jesus carrying the cross. Furthermore, Abraham saying that 'God himself will provide a lamb for the sacrifice', has been interpreted as a prophetic message pointing us to Jesus as the Lamb of God who was sacrificed for our sins.

✳ *'God so loved the world that he gave his one and only Son, that whoever believes in him shall not perish but have eternal life.' (John 3.16)*

Monday May 29

Abraham feared that Isaac would choose a woman from a local tribe as his wife and so endanger his faith. As Isaac was heir to the promises of God this was a risk that could not be taken. Abraham was anxious to settle the matter before he died. The obvious place to look for a wife was among his own

107

relatives. Too old to make the journey himself he entrusted it all to his faithful servant. This servant must surely be one of the finest characters anywhere in the Old Testament. His faith shone through everything that he did.

▶ Read **Genesis 24.1–4, 10–27**.

The test that was used at the well by Abraham's servant would identify a woman with certain qualities desirable in a wife – kindness to strangers, and a willingness to go further than strictly necessary. He could also observe her appearance. However, he did not depend on his own judgement, but trusted God to do the choosing.

This method may well be a pattern for us when we have to make important decisions. While making the best judgement that we can on the basis of our own knowledge, we should also proceed in such a way that God has the final word.

✳ *Thank you, Lord, that because you have a plan for our lives we can trust you to guide us in the important decisions we must take.*

Tuesday May 30   Genesis 24.28 – 34, 50 – 67

In verses 28 – 34 we get a picture of the priorities of Abraham's servant. He had already worshipped God (verse 27); now we see that he put his mission before his personal comfort (verse 33). We might all learn a lesson from this.

The account that the servant gave to Laban and his wife, Bethuel, convinced them that the whole matter should be entrusted to God. They offered no views themselves because what they thought was irrelevant in a matter that God had already decided. Again we note the servant's priorities: first, he honoured God; then he presented gifts to Rebekah and her family; finally, he ate and slept (verses 52 – 54).

Next morning the servant continued to carry out God's business. In one sense his journey had been successful but the task would not be completed until Rebekah was married to Isaac. We, too, when working for God, should consider our priorities – God first, others second, ourselves last – and then go on to complete the task.

✳ *Behold the servant of the Lord!*
   I wait thy guiding eye to feel,
  To fear and keep thy every word,
    To prove and do thy perfect will.   Charles Wesley

Isaac prayed for Rebekah because she had no children and eventually she gave birth to twins. Clearly they were not identical twins for it would be difficult to find two boys who differed more in appearance and character.

None of the characters in this family seem very admirable to us. Isaac does not seem to have had the drive of his father Abraham. Perhaps he was overfond of good food. Esau was keen on hunting and may have fulfilled some of his father's unrealised ambitions, thus becoming his favourite. He was shallow, however, placing little value on God's promise. Rebekah favoured Jacob, and conspired with him, encouraging him to take any advantage he could of the weakness of others.

Here was a family situation in which the seeds of deception had been sown. Let us remember that many families today are similarly fraught with tension. Indeed we ourselves may belong to such a family – we may not be very promising material for God to use. However, God is never thwarted, and so we can take heart – for, if he can succeed with people like Isaac and Jacob, he can also succeed with people like us.

✳ *We thank you, Almighty God, that you choose the most unlikely people for your kingdom. As you have chosen us, now change us that we may become the people that you want.*

When Indian people fled from Uganda in the time of Idi Amin, many came to England. Some of them worked hard, set up businesses and prospered. One day I was walking along a street with a man who complained to me that all these Indians seemed to be driving cars when he could not afford one. Natives are always likely to be jealous when an immigrant is successful. Isaac, as a successful immigrant, was faced with the hostility from the local people to such an extent that, when at last he dug a well which was not disputed, he named it 'Room' (*Rehoboth*), and gave thanks to God.

All his difficulties may have caused Isaac to doubt God's promises until, at Beersheba, God met his doubts with the words, 'I am the God of your father Abraham. Do not be afraid, for I am with you' (verse 24a). God assured Isaac that he would care for him and bless him.

Likewise, when we suffer from fears and doubts, we can be assured that God is with us – providing for all our needs. Our deepest needs are met by Jesus Christ, who said: '**I am** the bread of life . . . the good shepherd . . . the way, the truth and the life' (see John 6.35; 10.11; 14.6).

✳ *O Lord, we thank you for the assurances you give of who you are and of your presence with us. May we remember them to strengthen our faith in time of trouble.*

Friday June 2   Genesis 27.1–20

It seems that the only thing which made Jacob hesitate about following his mother's plan, to secure for himself the blessing intended for his older brother, was the fear of being found out. Once Rebekah, who had a dominating personality, took the responsibility for any untoward consequences on herself she had little difficulty in persuading him to proceed. So Jacob lived down to his name, which figuratively means 'Deceiver' or 'Supplanter'.

We might wonder whether God would ever be able to use Jacob while he was still so much under his mother's influence. However, as we shall see, within a short time she had to organise his departure to escape Esau's wrath. This meant that Jacob would have to stand on his own feet.

Learning to stand on our own feet is often an uncomfortable process. It is surprising how often God can use unexpected ways to accomplish this – even events that we have brought on ourselves by wrongdoing. In being separated from unhelpful influences we are brought to the point where we have to rely on God alone.

✳ *Thank you, Lord, that you discipline us through events, making us face the truth about ourselves and so opening up the way to repentance and forgiveness.*

Saturday June 3   Genesis 27.21–40

We would regard deceiving a person by taking advantage of their blindness as being particularly despicable. Jacob, however, continued to deceive his elderly father, lying again to maintain the deception. Many people find themselves locked into a situation of repeated lying from which there can be no escape until they decide to 'come clean'.

Deceit is not only a matter of words – actions can be just as deceitful. So we read how Isaac was finally convinced when Jacob, hands covered in goatskin to simulate Esau's hairiness, kissed his father. We are reminded of another kiss of deceit – Judas' kiss in the garden of Gethsemane (Mark 14.44–45). How long had Judas been pretending to be a faithful follower before he betrayed Jesus?

Jacob had already been promised seniority and Rebekah knew this (Genesis 25.23). God's purpose was to be fulfilled despite, and not because of, the actions of Isaac, Rebekah, Esau and Jacob. Failing to trust God, we often try to get the results we want through methods of our own. God will still achieve his end, but how much better it is when we do things in his way.

✳ *Lord God, give us the grace to resist the temptation to take your plans into our own hands.*

For group discussion and personal thought
Read again **Genesis 26.24**. Isaac knew God as the God of his father, Abraham. How can faith be passed on through families? In what ways can the family of your church ensure that its faith is passed on to each new generation?

Sunday June 4   **Genesis 27.41 to 28.5**

Esau was so angry with Jacob that he wanted to kill him. When Rebekah realised this she decided that Jacob would have to go away for a time, to enable Esau to cool of. As it happened there was a good reason for sending Jacob to her relatives so that he, like Isaac, could take a wife from his own people. So Isaac sent Jacob to Paddan Aram, reminding him that God's promise still had to be fulfilled through him – therefore, in due time, Jacob would have to return.

Sometimes we may need a reason to get away from a difficult situation – for example, when a parent remarries, or when someone is promoted over our heads. Yet we know that, in due time, when things have cooled down and attitudes have changed, we shall have to return and face the situation. However, God can use our experiences in the meantime to prepare us for reconciliation. When we come to face things again, we shall find just how much he has done for us.

✳ *Lord Jesus, you remind us of our need to be reconciled with others. When we are too angry to do this at once, may your love help to bring us to the point where we are able to be reconciled later on.*

Monday June 5

Tribal gods, such as those of the people among whom Isaac and his family had been living, were usually considered to be local gods. Jacob, sent away from his home, must have been feeling particularly lonely. He must also have realised that his deceitful behaviour was the cause of his problems. Feeling guilty, he would hardly expect to have a sense that God was with him as he journeyed.

▶ Now read **Genesis 28.10 – 22**.

What a surprise for Jacob – the Lord was in this place too! Note again that God says, '**I am**', and makes it clear that he, the God of Jacob's father and grandfather, will be his God as well.

Let us not be too scornful of Jacob's bargaining with God. If we look more carefully at our own relationship with God we shall probably discover that sometimes we offer him a conditional allegiance, expecting in turn that we shall prosper. Some people seem to think that they will only receive from God, what they have already paid for. If this is the stage we have reached in our relationship with God then, like Jacob, we still have a long way to go.

✳ *Hold thou my hand, and lead me by thy side;*
  I dare not go alone: be thou my guide.   Jane E. Saxby

Tuesday June 6   Genesis 29.16 – 30

This reading might be entitled *'The Biter Bit'* or *'Jacob Meets His Match'*. Laban proved to be as astute at fixing things to his advantage as was his sister Rebekah. Probation Officers, who are experienced in dealing with confidence tricksters, report that these people are themselves particularly easy to deceive.

Was it love that made Jacob blind to the nature of the bargain that he had struck with Laban? Laban took his opportunity. The parallels between these events and Jacob's deception of Isaac are intriguing. Did Laban coach Leah for her part in the deception just as Rebekah had coached Jacob?

And did the feasting that Laban arranged aid the deception of Jacob, just as the tasty meal Jacob took to Isaac blunted his perception? Like his brother Esau, Jacob realised too late what had happened.

We might well be warned by Jacob's experience. If we set out on a course of deceit, we are only too likely to finish up as victims of our own dishonesty. We can easily forget that God in his righteousness requires justice as well as mercy and has many ways of achieving it. How often are we really honest with others or even with ourselves?

✳ *Think about Jesus' words: 'With the measure you use, it will be measured to you – and even more.' (Mark 4.24b).*

Wednesday June 7

At Arlington Court in North Devon, it is possible to see a flock of Jacob's sheep, so named because they have brown and white blotches. Jacob and Laban struck a strange bargain whereby Jacob's wage was to be the streaked, spotted and dark-coloured animals. Laban, having removed all the potential parents of such animals, must have thought he had the best of the bargain. However, as we shall see God intervened to make Jacob prosper.

▶ Now read **Genesis 31.1–21**.

The time for Jacob's return had come (see verse 13). God's words would have reminded him of his experience at Bethel (Genesis 28.10 – 22).

Dishonesty and trickery exact their price. One lie leads to another. Family relationships break down. Others get involved in our lies. There seems no end to the damage that is done. We can see all this in today's reading. Also it is the pattern of many lives today. Rivalries never make for happy families.

✳ *Lord, bless us with honest and loving relationships within our families.*

Thursday June 8

Having reached an agreement with Laban, Jacob now had to face a more difficult situation with his brother Esau. It has been pointed out that Jacob could have gone back to Bethel without going anywhere near to Seir where Esau was living.

God's way, however, is a way of reconciliation and that is the way that Jacob had to go.

▶ Now read **Genesis 32.3–18**.

The news that Esau was coming with four hundred men did not sound good for Jacob. Perhaps for the first time, as he made plans for the meeting, he began to think of others as well as himself. Dividing the party into two meant that if the worst happened at least half of them would survive. Besides planning, Jacob prayed. In this prayer we find a new honesty, as he recognised his unworthiness. Only God had brought him to his present prosperity – so to God he made his plea, 'Save me I pray . . . for I am afraid' (vere 11). After praying for himself and his family, he selected gifts to pacify Esau.

In our lives, prayer and action are closely linked, and so are salvation and reconciliation. We cannot expect God to help us if we are not prepared to do our part.

✴ *Jesus said, 'First go and be reconciled to your brother; then come and offer your gift.' (Matthew 5.24b)*

Friday June 9

It is when we have divested ourselves of everything and everyone on whom we depend and who depend on us that we can most truly come to grips with God.

▶ Read **Genesis 32.22 – 32**.

Some see this story as Jacob wrestling with his conscience, others as him wrestling with the temptation to run away. Perhaps both these are aspects of his struggle to come to terms with the true nature of God. But Jacob was convinced that he had wrestled with God and there are some clues which indicate this:

● He had to go at daybreak. To see God's face fully was thought to be a fatal experience. The darkness of night would have prevented Jacob from really seeing his face.
● He gave Jacob a new name meaning, 'He struggles with God.'
● He refused to reveal his name, but gave Jacob a blessing.

Jacob's experience left a permanent mark on him (verses 25, 31). Do we have any experiences of the living God which have left their marks on us?

✴ *'Finally, let no one cause me trouble, for I bear on my body the marks of Jesus.' (Galatians 6.17)*

Saturday June 10

After reconciliation with Esau, Jacob did not go at once to Bethel. Before he could go, there had to be a spiritual clean-up in his household. There were idols – including the ones Rachel had taken from Laban – to be got rid of. Also they had to purify themselves, removing the ear-rings which may have been like lucky charms, and change their clothes for ceremonial cleanliness.

▶ Read **Genesis 35.1–14**.

From the time Jacob left Bethel (28.19) until he returned there, must have taken well over twenty years. God is always ready to give time to changing a person. For Jacob the change was affirmed by God using his new name again and repeating his promise.

We, too, may need a spiritual clean-up. There may be unsuspected 'idols' that we are carrying with us. Nevertheless, however long our journey through life and however roundabout the way, we may be sure that God intends us to end up in right relationship with him.

✳ *Lord, we often hold back when we are getting close to you because we realise how much we still fall short of what you want us to be. Give us grace to get rid of all that impedes our return to you.*

For group discussion and personal thought

What obstacles did Jacob have to overcome during his life? What are the main obstacles you have had to face? Which of these have most threatened your faith? What gifts do we receive from God which encourage our faith?

Brand NEW

series for

young people

Bible Breakthrough

Write for details

2 PETER

Notes by the Revd Michael J. Cleaves, BA, BD

Michael Cleaves is a Baptist minister, a member of the team ministry in an ecumenical parish in Milton Keynes, England. He is also Chair of the International Relations Committee of the Baptist Union of Great Britain.

The notes in this section are based on the Revised Standard Version.

2 Peter, although ascribed to the apostle Peter, is generally considered not to have been written by him. It is a passionate and closely-argued sermon, containing a wealth of teaching and detail. The author appears to have been familiar with other parts of the New Testament, particularly the letter of **Jude** which is similar to 2 Peter 2.1–18, and he also includes several Old Testament references.

This book was probably written as late as AD 140, by which time the Christian Church was well-established and the main elements of its faith had been worked out. However, false teachers of heresy had infiltrated the Church and this writer warns of their dangerous influence. He encourages his readers to hold fast to the true faith, and exhorts them to be prepared for the Day of the Lord while at the same time striving to grow to a more mature faith.

Suggestion for further reading

James and Peter by William Barclay, Daily Study Bible (Saint Andrew Press).

Sunday June 11

A cynic, who was criticising the process of early specialisation in schools and universities in Britain, said: 'The problem is that you go from knowing nothing about everything to knowing everything about nothing.'

▶ Read 2 Peter 1.1–11.

The writer of these verses sees knowledge in a very different way from the cynic quoted above. Far from being a narrowing experience, knowledge of the Lord will enable grace and peace

116

to 'be multiplied' in our lives. The possession of this knowledge is a necessary part of the process of our salvation. Growth in faith and knowledge enables us to be effective against the corruptive influences in the world. However, this requires the integration of other qualities into our lives, and these are listed in verses 5 – 7.

This list is similar to Paul's in Galatians 5.22–23a, and can also be compared with 'the whole armour of God' (see Ephesians 6.11–17). As a soldier clothed himself with armour, so we must endeavour to add to our faith these qualities – qualities that do not weigh us down, but free our lives from the world's corruption.

✷ *Lord, help us to grow spiritually throughout our lives.*

Monday June 12

It was a wet winter's night when the careless motorist behind me did not stop in time. His car struck mine from behind with a sickening thud and damaged it so badly that the insurance company declared it a 'write-off'. How thankful I was that there were witnesses who were able to testify on my behalf!

▶ Read **2 Peter 1.12 to 2.3**.

The New Testament writers often make use of eye-witness accounts. These verses contain an 'eye-witness' account of the mysterious and spectacular transfiguration of Jesus (see Matthew 17.1– 8). This event is used as confirmation of:

● the historic reality of Jesus;
● his relationship with God the Father;
● the faith which Christians have received and accepted.

Television technology enables us to see news events from many parts of the world, and we happily believe their interpretation by newscasters and reporters. Faith, however, requires more than 'seeing' and 'believing'. It is important that we think carefully about what we see and hear, only responding to and passing on that which is true.

✷ *Lord, give us the quiet assurance of faith which stands firm when untruth seeks to lead us astray.*

Tuesday June 13   2 Peter 2.4–16

'People and governments never have learned anything from history,' said Hegel in the early nineteenth century.

However, his contemporary, Samuel Taylor Coleridge, claimed that if men could learn from history, what lessons it would teach us. In today's verses we read more about false prophets and teachers who were both foolish and dangerous because they did not learn from the lessons of history.

We may be fairly familiar with the famous stories of God's judgement which are recorded here, but they were imprinted on the minds of the Jews. The writer of **2 Peter** used these stories of **faith** to impress upon his readers that God is consistently faithful to those who live righteously, but will bring judgement against the unrighteous.

Today we sometimes want to avoid these judgement stories, because we prefer to keep in mind the idea of a loving and forgiving God. However, it remains true that a righteous God cannot tolerate the injustices of **our** day any more than he did in the days of Noah and Lot.

We must therefore learn the lessons of history and be aware of our role in society today – to speak out against all forms of injustice and bring Christ's love to the whole of humankind.

✳ *O God, we thank you for the true prophet and teacher, our only Master and Lord, Jesus Christ.*

Wednesday June 14

In 1987, some friends and I visited the Dead Sea. It was very hot and the heat intensified as we got nearer to this lowest point on the earth's surface. We crossed bridges which spanned waterless riverbeds. These waterless springs reminded us of the harsh barrenness of desert areas. Our spirits rose as we got closer to the Dead Sea and saw the inviting waters. But we knew that this was a deceptive sight for the water in that famous sea could never quench our thirst. It would only leave a terrible taste in our mouths.

▶ Read **2 Peter 2.17 – 22**.

Here the writer accuses false teachers of being 'waterless springs' and deceptive – failing to fulfil the promise which they had held out to Christian believers. The faith they professed was not according to Christ's teaching but merely justified their own passions and philosophies. It could never satisfy the spiritual thirst of people seeking to know God. The only one who can truly satisfy our spiritual thirst is Christ himself. The 'water' he gives will become in us a spring 'welling up to eternal life' (John 4.14b).

118

Thursday June 15

Ever since the early days of the Church, people have differed and argued over the meaning, timing and implications of the 'second (or final) coming' of Christ. From time to time religious groups inform the world that this event is about to happen. They may even go to some appointed place in confident expectation of the return of our Lord. When nothing happens they soon disperse or find an alternative explanation of their 'revelation'. In contrast to this there are some people today who scoff at any mention of Christ's return, just as they did at the time when **2 Peter** was written.

▶ Read **2 Peter 3.1—7**.

In the Holy Communion service, Christians often affirm their faith in the words: 'Christ has died. Christ is risen. Christ will come again.' By doing this they are following Jesus' command to be vigilant **and** prepared (see Mark 13.32—33 and Luke 12.35—40).

It is said that when Ignatius Loyola was asked what he would do if the Lord were to return suddenly, he replied, 'I will continue to sweep the floor.' Very few of us will become great Christian leaders, but we are all called to remain faithful in the ordinary things of life.

❋ *Lord, help me always to be ready for your return.*

Friday June 16

We do not need to understand a complex scientific theory in order to know that we experience time in different ways on different occasions. A busy parent says that 'time flies' and that there are not enough hours in a day, while a patient waiting in a doctor's surgery feels that time is dragging and minutes can seem like hours. However, these differing human experiences of time are minor compared with the difference between **our** concept of time and **God's** sense of timing.

▶ Read **2 Peter 3.8—13**.

We cannot fully understand God's timing but we can always be sure of his dependability. **2 Peter** contains a deep hope in people's repentance and the promise of 'new heavens and a new earth' (verse 13). This seems far removed from the idea that God will destroy creation in a fit of vengeful wrath against humankind.

While we must always be prepared for 'the day of the Lord', we must not fall into the fearful trap of presuming that the very graphic words in today's reading refer to a nuclear holocaust. Rather, we should focus our attention on growing 'in the knowledge of God and of Jesus our Lord' (2 Peter 1.2).

✶ *We thank you, Lord, that the earth is yours; and that you are a God of righteousness and love, a creator and not a wanton destroyer.*

Saturday June 17   2 Peter 3.14 – 18

Like a number of the other New Testament letters, **2 Peter** ends with a list of instructions and exhortations to its readers. In verse 14, the writer encourages us to be:

- **'Zealous'.** We must be constantly aware of the need to live a life that will be acceptable to God, a life 'without spot or blemish'.
- **'At peace'.** Having written a vivid account of Christ's coming and the destruction and restoration of creation, the writer does not want fear to take hold of our imagination. Rather, he declares that we should be at peace with God.

The writer's concern that Christians remain vigilant in their faith then comes to the fore once more. There will always be false teachers, false prophets and scoffers, so he reminds his readers that none of us can know all the mysteries of the Christian faith (see verse 16). Humble admission of this helps us to avoid the pitfalls of false belief.

Finally, in verses 17 – 18, we are reminded that, even though we are aware of the dangers of false teaching, we must be constantly on guard in order to maintain a deep, stable and growing faith.

✶ *'May grace and peace be multiplied to you in the knowledge of God and of Jesus our Lord.' (2 Peter 1.2)*

For group discussion and personal thought

The writer of **2 Peter** warned his readers to be on their guard against false teachers (see **2.1** and **3.17**). How are we able to recognise false teachers and false teaching? What are the dangers and pitfalls of false belief, and how can we avoid them?

HOSEA

Notes by the Revd Howard Rady, BA

Howard Rady is minister of St Margaret's United Reformed Church, Finchley, North London. He is a retired teacher and headmaster.

The notes in this section are based on the Revised Standard Version.

Hosea's origins are unknown, although the book's language suggests that he was from the northern kingdom of Israel. Certainly his message was primarily directed to the people living there, whom he calls 'Israel' or 'Ephraim', the name of the nation's principal tribe.

Central to any real understanding of **Hosea** is the place of 'Baal' worship in the religion of Israel. For the earlier settlers in Canaan, Baal was the 'lord', 'owner' or 'husband' of the land, who controlled all its fertility. So Baal worship was the deeply-rooted religion of Canaan when the Hebrews arrived there. Soon, they began to incorporate elements of it into their worship.

However, according to their covenant with God, Israel was to 'have no other gods before Yahweh' (Exodus 20.3). So the stage was set for a titanic struggle, the latter scenes of which Hosea was to observe during his ministry. How he sought to recall the nation to her first love, Yahweh, is the theme of the book.

Suggestions for further reading

The Twelve Prophets Volume 1 (Hosea, Joel, Amos, Obadiah and Jonah) by Peter C. Craigie, Daily Study Bible (Saint Andrew Press);

The Message of Hosea: Love to the Loveless by Derek Kidner (Inter-Varsity Press).

Sunday June 18   **Hosea 1.1–11**

Communication is essential for a prophet. However to be truly effective a prophet must both discern God's message and sense how God **feels** towards his people. Hosea was preeminently able to do this owing to the circumstances of his domestic life. He had married the shallow, good-time girl Gomer, because he believed that God had commanded it. When he came to suffer rejection at her hands he realised something of God's pain at the unfaithfulness of Israel.

How was Hosea to communicate God's message to a people who gave little heed to prophets? His method was to give Gomer's children such outlandish names that they were bound to arouse public interest. Thus, by calling their son **Jezreel**, Hosea was reminding the people of the bloody massacre at Jezreel (see 2 Kings 10.1–11) and of God's impending judgement. To emphasise this, he subsequently gave Gomer's second child the name **Lo-ruhamah** – 'Not pitied' or 'Not loved'. But it was to the off-spring of one of his wife's extra-marital liaisons that he gave the bleakest name of all: **Lo-ammi** – 'Not my people'. It seemed to Hosea that, like the prophet himself, God was entitled to disclaim paternity for a 'bastard child'; and Israel had certainly been behaving like one!

✳ *Lord, may we always be ready to listen to your message – even when it is difficult.*

Monday June 19

The opening scene of **Hosea** is a tragic one – Hosea and the three children have been deserted by Gomer and they are required by Hebrew law to lay the facts before a judge. Typical of Hosea, however, the actual facts soon become absorbed into an allegory of God's relationship with Israel.

▶ Read **Hosea 2.1–13**.

As the scene shifts from the human to the divine court, Israel is charged on three counts:

● Israel has deluded herself into believing that 'flirting' with Baal will ensure a rich provision for her material needs.
● She has wilfully ignored the truth that it is God, her lawful husband, who has showered material gifts upon her.
● She has actually forgotten all about her covenant relationship with God in her infatuation with the excitement and passion of Baal worship.

Guilty though Israel is, the hope is that she will return to her true 'husband' (verse 7). When people have known something of the love of God, it is not possible for them to be satisfied for very long with the blandishments of lesser gods.

✻ *Ponder on verses 11—12. The very materialism in which*
many put their trust will let them down in the end.

Tuesday June 20   **Hosea 2.14—23**

It was never the purpose of the prophets to deliver a message
of unremitting condemnation. True to this ministry, Hosea
looked beyond the period of tribulation expected to fall upon
his nation to a restored relationship between God and his
people. Three analogies describe that new era.

● There will be a **new marriage** between God and Israel.
  Gone will be the former fascination with 'folk' religion —
  the outlook that confuses one god with another and mixes
  faith with superstition.

● There will be a **new covenant** between God and his
  people. Gone will be the instability of the former
  relationship. Instead, it will be one of acceptance, love and
  fulfilment.

● There will be an entirely **new status** given to Israel. The
  land, long ruined and deserted — presumably through the
  removal of the population — will be sown once more with
  inhabitants. The negatives of judgement will give way to
  the positives of divine acceptance.

✻ *Name before God those you know to be walking through the*
valley of trouble (Achor, verse 15) at this present time and
pray that it may become for them a door of hope.

Wednesday June 21   **Hosea 3.1—5**

This reading brings to a climax the biographical events
touched upon in the first two chapters of **Hosea**. Gomer might
have thrown off the marriage bond in search of freedom but
she had not found it. The money scraped together by Hosea
represented the going price for a slave, although it is possible
that it was compensation demanded by Gomer's current 'boy
friend' or by a 'pimp' for whom she was working.

The whole incident demonstrates the supremacy of love and
grace over law. After all, no law required Hosea to have
anything more to do with the woman who had betrayed him.
Indeed, what appears to have prompted him to search her out
and redeem her was not just his love for her, but also an
awareness that this was how God treated Israel — with
undeserved grace.

The need for Gomer and Hosea to live together in seclusion for a period (see verse 3) may have been a practical necessity following years of estrangement. During this time Hosea would seek to restore the close and loving relationship he once had with Gomer. Similarly, God would go on seeking to renew his relationship with his people – loving them and longing to forgive them.

✳ *O God, your love for us goes on and on,*
  never throwing us aside as worthless.

(From 'Everyday Prayers')

Thursday June 22

As soon as society shows signs of moral decline, then there are plenty of voices calling on the Church to 'give a lead' and demanding that schools should teach 'right from wrong'. Today, Hosea would probably say that society's problems are caused by people's ignorance of the 'knowledge of God'.

▶ Now read **Hosea 4.1–10**.

When speaking of the 'knowledge of God' Hosea was probably not referring to any intimate relationship with God, but to a working understanding of the ethical laws given to Israel, particularly the ten commandments (verse 2). Also, Hosea firmly believed that such knowledge could, and ought to, be taught. The fact that the priests had failed to do this was a dreadful indictment against them.

However, was Hosea right? Is a knowledge of what God requires the same as knowing him? It was a later prophet, Jeremiah, who proclaimed that a true knowledge of God involves an altogether different kind of covenant (see Jeremiah 31.31– 34). Under this, God's people would be so at one with him that they would be able to comprehend his will without the need for external laws.

✳ *It is the Holy Spirit who makes the new covenant effective.*

Friday June 23

'Why is it,' asked a young minister, 'that whenever I begin to talk to people about a spiritual dimension to life, I either meet with blank indifference or a load of superstition?' His problem was not a new one.

▶ Read **Hosea 4.11–19**.

Hosea found various causes for people's indifference to his message. They are worth pondering:

- Too much drinking and sexual licence.
- Paying court to idols while feigning respect for the nation's religious traditions.
- Dabbling with the occult and a fascination with magic. The 'staff' (or 'fetish' – verse 12, NEB) may well have been a special stick used by practitioners when seeking to 'divine' a future course of action.

We do not have to look far to see similar forms of escapism and superstition in modern society. It must always be a cause of deep concern to us, as Christians, when otherwise intelligent people resort to devices like fortune-telling, astrology or witchcraft.

✴ *Pray for people who think they have dispensed with the idea of God, and have filled their lives with false religion and illusion.*

Saturday June 24   **Hosea 5.1–7**

Christians can all too easily slip into playing the 'numbers game', but in doing so they may make some false equations. For example, they may assume that, as long as a church is getting large congregations, it must therefore be offering true worship. However, this may not always be the case.

No doubt the numbers flocking to the sanctuaries such as those at Mizpah and Tabor gave the impression that all was well with the religious life of Israel; but Hosea was not deceived. To him the crowds were like the victims of the hunt being lured into a trap (verse 1). Moreover, it was the very guardians of the national life – the priests, the elders and the royal house – who were abetting the adulteration of the faith.

Ostensibly, the traditional worship of Israel might be continuing as before, but what drew the crowds was the additional excitements of pagan worship. Perhaps the priests saw these as harmless pursuits, justified by the needs of a changing society. Nevertheless, to Hosea, they were evidence of a fatal double standard that was bound to bring its own retribution. Because the worshippers no longer desired to find God, he would not be found.

✴ *Hosea implied that it is a terrible thing to seek God and not be able to find him (verse 6). Compare this with Jesus' words in Luke 19.10.*

For group discussion and personal thought

In this week's readings what does Hosea say about the society in which he lived? What similarities and what differences do you see between the society of Hosea's time and our modern society? What can the Church do to help raise moral standards today?

Sunday June 25

The historian, Arnold Toynbee, spent much of his life producing a detailed study of the world's twenty-one major civilisations. The reasons for each one's decline and collapse fascinated him. Eventually he concluded that none had broken down solely as the result of external attack; all had first been subjected to internal corruption and discord. Successful external attack was only the final stage in a long process of collapse.

▶ Now read **Hosea 5.8–15**.

The opening words of this prophecy sound like trumpet-calls raising an alarm. Hosea was alerting the nation to the approach of an external foe who would destroy Israel like a flood of water, and tear apart the nation like a lion – something that ultimately happened in 722 BC. However, the prophet's essential concern was not this external threat, but the nation's internal decay. A poison was affecting the life-blood of the nation. Recourse to foreign powers could not solve the problem.

The human tragedy is that people and nations fail to recognise the extent of their malaise. Furthermore, they think they can cure themselves; this delusion blinds them to the reality of God's judgement.

✴ *And they who fain would serve thee best*
   Are conscious most of wrong within.   Henry Twells

Monday June 26   **Hosea 6.1–11a**

A recurring and tragic element in the history of Israel was the superficiality of its repentance. Time after time the anguished language of penitence was on the lips of the religious leaders but their deeds seldom matched their words.

126

Verses 1–3 give us an idea of the sentiments expressed on occasions of national repentance, but all the talk of 'pressing on to know the Lord' led nowhere. The trouble was that such knowledge was seen in terms of placating God with sacrificial offerings (verse 6). Real renunciation of evil practices was entirely absent; indeed, the leaders of the nation were known to condone a host of appalling crimes. Hosea only alluded to the nature of these atrocities, but it is quite possible they involved child sacrifice at Gilead and the murder of men seeking sanctuary at the refuge city of Shechem.

During the early days of the Second World War, C.S. Lewis wrote an article about the 'Dangers of National Repentance'. He argued that specially appointed 'national days of prayer' tended to encourage people to repent of others' sins rather than their own. Although he may have overstated the case, it remains true that superficial repentance is always a danger facing God's people.

✳ *Repentance is a costly business. Always it costs our pride; often our prestige; sometimes our pockets.*

Tuesday June 27　　　　　　　　　　Hosea 6.11b to 7.7

Six men ruled in turn over Israel during its last three decades as an independent kingdom. Four of these obtained the throne by assassinating his predecessor and only one died naturally.

With everyone in the court manoeuvring for position, it was hardly surprising that law and order were breaking down in Israel, and that fraud, house-breaking and robbery were rampant. 'Any excuse for an orgy' seemed to be the motto of the court, well typified by the drunkenness at the king's celebrations (verse 5). Even so, something far more sinister was going on. For, while many at court were engaged in banking up the fires of lust, others kept their envy and rivalry smouldering until it was ready to burst out in yet more political intrigue or another assassination plot (verse 7).

If Israel's rulers were obsessed with lust and ambition, Hosea knew why: they had ceased turning to God. Obedience to God, seeking him through prayer and honouring him in worship, are the only means by which we may bring sanity and order into social chaos and our personal relationships.

✳ *Pray for your national leaders, that they may seek God's help to govern with integrity and justice.*

Wednesday June 28

According to some informed observers, the problem for Christianity in the West is that, for the last century and a half, it has become progressively more influenced by the surrounding culture. This problem, however, is limited neither to the West, nor to Christian communities. This is why Hosea's words are often strikingly relevant.

▶ Now read **Hosea 7.8–16**.

In these verses Hosea vividly illustrates four abiding spiritual principles:

● Lack of conviction by God's people produces half-baked religion. To assimilate the values of materialistic society is to be like a cake cooked on one side only (verse 8).

● Loss of spiritual vitality often goes undetected for a long time. Constantly trying to rely on alien ideas is weakening, and can only be remedied by turning to God (verses 9–10).

● Panic measures and silly opportunism inevitably lead to unforeseen consequences. Only loyalty and truth can keep God's people out of the net (verse 11–15).

● Insincerity leads to ineffectiveness. No warrior can make use of a flawed weapon; neither can God use a people warped by deception and lies (verse 16).

✳ *Lord, renew our spiritual youth and love of truth.*

Thursday June 29   Hosea 8.1–14

There is much repetition in **Hosea**. This is inevitable, for it is an anthology of sayings from different periods of the prophet's ministry, rather than a carefully planned book. Today's reading, for example, reiterates some familiar themes; although, it also reflects Hosea's realisation that Israel's day of reckoning was fast approaching.

Hosea understood God's judgement of Israel in concrete terms. Punitive armies were going to strip the land and destroy the nation's identity. Further, the very diplomatic schemes Israel devised to keep the nation safe, would in fact have the effect of hastening the end. By continually changing sides Israel had forfeited international respect and become 'like a crock' that no one wanted (verse 8, JB). Thus friendless, she was easy prey, indeed.

The idea that judgement is never arbitrary but the logical outcome of human folly is perfectly contained in the words 'sow the wind . . . reap the whirlwind' (verse 7). This principle can be applied to many aspects of living (see Galatians 6.7 – 8).

✻ *For frantic boast and foolish word –*
Thy mercy on thy people, Lord!   *Rudyard Kipling*

Friday June 30   Hosea 9.1 – 9

Prophets are seldom popular figures. Because they are for ever wanting to strip away religious embellishments and recall God's people to their fundamental loyalty, they are seldom welcome in religious circles. Often treated as mad fools, they are the victims of clever traps and the objects of persecution (verses 7 – 9). However, such treatment does not in the least invalidate their message.

It was precisely because Israel would not take seriously the warnings of her 'watchmen', the prophets, that the nation's whole fabric of religious observance was to suffer a devastating blow. As Hosea saw it, the day would soon come when food laws would be pointless, sacrifices would cease, festivals would be unobserved, and homes and treasures would be ruined (verses 3 – 6). Why? Because the land would have been dismembered by war and the population displaced.

To make religion an end in itself, and to allow it to cut one off from the reality of God, is always a danger facing devout people. This was the tragedy of the Pharisees and it has blunted the cutting edge of many a Christian. Significantly, when a Samaritan woman began to discuss the merits of different places of worship with Jesus, he give her this word:

✻ *'God is spirit, and those who worship him must worship in spirit and truth.' (John 4.24)*

Saturday July 1   Hosea 9.10 – 17

✻ *Where is the blessedness I knew*
When first I saw the Lord?
Where is the soul-refreshing view
Of Jesus and his word?   *William Cowper*

Why do so many Christians lose the freshness and fruitfulness of the early days of their discipleship? How is it that once vigorous congregations are left with no young people growing up in the church? Certainly there are psychological and sociological factors to be taken into consideration, but it is equally important to study the possible causes of spiritual regression. In this context, Hosea's analysis of Israel's decline is highly instructive.

Hosea identifies the story of Baal-peor (see Numbers 25.1–5) as the turning-point in Israel's history. Both physical and spiritual adultery took place there; and from then on Israel began to treat Baal as a deity almost equal to God. Consequently, in order to safeguard life's deepest values, God withdrew the reality of his presence (verses 11–12, 17). Does this mean that one remedy for spiritual regression is to make sure that we have no secondary gods in our lives?

*   *The dearest idol I have known,*
    Whate'er that idol be,
  Help me to tear it from thy throne
   And worship only thee.   William Cowper

For group discussion and personal thought
Study **Hosea 6.1–6**. In the light of this discuss what true repentance involves. What do we need to repent of today (a) as individuals, (b) as a church, (c) as a nation?

Sunday July 2

▶ First read **Hosea 10.1–2**.

The way people react to prosperity often tells us a great deal about them. Israel gladly received the divine bounty, but soon chose to lavish her affection on Baal. Perhaps we do the same when we extol modern technology and forget God, the great source of all creative power.

▶ Now read **Hosea 10.3–4**.

How people co-operate socially helps us to understand their attitude towards God. What struck Hosea was his fellow-citizens' great reluctance to be bound by their promises, unless reinforced legally. Signs of similar suspicion are becoming visible in different parts of the world today.

▶ Read **Hosea 10.5–8**.

What moves people to tears is usually an indication of what they hold most dear. Mourning for the loss of the calf-idol at Beth-aven was ironic – it had failed to deliver Israel from Assyrian blackmail and was about to be used to pay off the blackmailers! Even so, people still clung to their failed superstitions and ignored the rising tide of judgement. Hosea's pictures of retribution are comprehensive, not least that of people begging for either protection or extinction (verse 8b).

✳ *Where superstition reigns, suspicion flourishes.*

Monday July 3   **Hosea 10.9–15**

Not everyone will be able to accept Hosea's argument in these verses. War seems such an obscene way of chastening a recalcitrant people. Also, how can a righteous God use such unrighteous instruments as the Assyrians to carry through his purposes? However, before we attempt to form our own opinion we must follow the steps in the prophet's argument:
● Israel has always been a wayward people.
● Therefore God will use foreign nations to chastise her.
● Because Israel has refused God's easy yoke, the people will have to wear the collar of slavery.
● The hope is that Israel will then cease to be impervious to God's calls to lead a new life.
● The chastisement will be both appropriate to Israel's own belligerence and the people's lack of humility.

To take this line of argument seriously may mean our having to ask questions about international history. For example, should we see wars and other national calamities as a 'form of collective chastisement'?

✳   *Take not thy thunder from us,*
    But take away our pride.   *Gilbert K. Chesterton*

Tuesday July 4   **Hosea 11.1 to 12.1**

In the early 1960s, Bishop John Robinson was associated with the view that man had now 'come of age' and was free to make his own moral decisions based on the principle of love. It was a daring thesis and it is still being debated whether or not Robinson's book, *Honest to God*, contributed to Britain's subsequent 'permissive society'.

Today's reading tells how Israel 'came of age'. After an idyllic childhood (hardly in accord with the account in **Exodus**), the developing nation came of age when it entered· the land of Canaan. There it soon came under the spell of pagan worship and, like some carefree young man-about-town, it scorned or forgot what it owed to God. Chastisement was bound to follow, yet only as a means to an end. God's holy compassion yearned to restore the broken relationship and bring the prodigal home.

The New Testament knows nothing of any 'coming of age' within discipleship. What is spoken of is 'spiritual maturity'; and this does not imply any independence from God, but rather the very opposite. In fact, Christian maturity comes about through a growing union with Christ (see Colossians 1.28).

✱ *O Jesus Christ, grow thou in me,*
And all things else recede.   *Johann C. Lavater*

Wednesday July 5   Hosea 12.2 − 14

These verses read almost like notes for an evangelistic sermon. Like many sermons there are three main points!

- **An illustration from history** (verses 3 − 6). This is drawn from the story of Jacob − later known as Israel. Deceitful and arrogant though he was in the earlier part of his life, the patriarch then had a series of experiences that made him highly aware of God's claim upon his life. Consequently he changed from being a grasping opportunist to a man who wanted to take a firm hold on God.
- **Jacob's descendants must learn the same lesson** (verses 7 − 9). They are just as he was − deceitful and arrogant. Also they have forgotten how their forefathers were rescued from slavery in Egypt by the intervention of God. To forget him is to go back into bondage.
- **The ones appointed by God** to bring his word to the people **are the prophets** (verses 10 − 14). They are not a new breed but can trace their lineage back to Moses, the greatest prophet of all. This is why it is such a provocation to God not to attend to the prophets he has sent.

✱ *No one can have the burning heart of a prophet who does not possess the burdened heart of an evangelist.*

Thursday July 6   Hosea 13.1 − 11

It is the sign of a bankrupt intellect when people continue to apply discredited solutions to their problems. Both internally and internationally Israel was staggering from crisis to crisis, yet the only solution in the minds of the majority of people was increased veneration for the 'old religion' of Canaan (verse 2). They were seeking salvation in their own, not God's, way.

The problems facing Israel were ostensibly political, but in reality they were moral and spiritual. The vital question to be answered was whether God was of limited power or absolutely sovereign. That is still the question needing to be answered by today's people of God; and it is a question which has many ramifications. For example, to what extent can the inequalities and injustices of society be put right without a willing acceptance of the reign of God on the part of the population?

- Should AIDS be treated like any other disease, or does it also demand a total reappraisal of sexual attitudes in the light of Christian teaching?
- Is it possible that many of the world's disasters are brought about by self-opinion, indifference and greed on the part of national leaders and people?
- Is the Western world's obsession with pleasure and money as debilitating as the worship of any Baal?

✱ *'Alleluia! For the Lord God omnipotent reigneth' (Revelation 19.6, AV). What does this mean for us?*

Friday July 7 **Hosea 13.12–16**

'You do not want a great faith, but faith in a great God,' wrote the pioneer missionary, Hudson Taylor. Hosea's confidence that God held the destiny of Israel in his hands was based on his idea of divine sovereignty. This was far in advance of the limited vision of his contemporaries. For Hosea, God was no mere territorial deity but One who used nations to execute his purposes. Nor was his power limited to this life only; for he also had authority over the world of departed souls (verse 14).

The fate in store for God's rebellious people is a constant theme in **Hosea**; and is portrayed very graphically in the closing parts of the book. Even so, there is still a remote chance of deliverance – Ephraim must be born again! But alas, all the signs seem to indicate that this will not happen (verse 13).

To see men and women turning their backs on the chance of new life in God through Christ is always a bitter experience. Yet, it is this very anguish of heart that can enable the Christian to enter into a deeper sense of fellowship and suffering with Christ (see Luke 13.34; 19.41–44).

＊ *Think and pray about Jesus' words to Nicodemus: 'No one*
can see the kingdom of God unless he is born again.' (John
3.3b, GNB).

Saturday July 8

▶ First read **Hosea 14.1−3**.

Are these words yet another call to repentance in the hope
of averting catastrophe? Or should we read them as a call to
the remnant of the nation that would survive the bitter years
following the impending fall of Samaria in 722 BC? The latter
seems preferable in view of the stress on Israel's orphan state.

▶ Now read **Hosea 14.4−7**.

What promise there is in these verses! A new **freshness** is
indicated by words like dew, blossom and fragrance; a new
stability is pictured with trees striking root; and a new
vigour is anticipated by the presence of fresh shoots and
flourishing vines.

▶ Read **Hosea 14.8−9**.

Grace had triumphed for the remnant of Ephraim, whose
name means 'God has made me fruitful in the land of my
affliction' (Genesis 41.52). Yet they could not afford to be
presumptuous or complacent. As for us who read this book, we
always need to apply it to our own life and times.

＊ *God has spoken − by his prophets,*
  Spoken his unchanging word,
  Each from age to age proclaiming . . .
  God, the first, and God the last.   *George W. Briggs*

For group discussion and personal thought

The steadfast love of God for his people is an important theme
running through the book of **Hosea**. Look especially at
Hosea 2.14−20; 11.1−9 and **14.1−9**, and discuss the essence
of God's love. How can we avoid taking his love for granted? In
what ways have **you** experienced the love of God?

EPHESIANS

Based on notes by the Revd Lesley M. Charlton, BA

Lesley Charlton is a minister of the United Reformed Church serving in Wallington, Surrey.

The notes in this section are based on the Good News Bible.

Ephesians was probably written in about AD 80 – 90 by a disciple of Paul, rather than by Paul himself. As there are no personal greetings, it is thought to be a general, circular letter directed to Gentile Christians in Asia Minor.

It has been said that of all the books in the New Testament **Ephesians** is the most relevant to our time, because it brings before us a vision of the Church as Christ's body, working to unite all people in a fellowship of worship and love.

Suggestion for further reading

Ephesians by C. Leslie Mitton, New Century Bible Commentaries (Marshall, Morgan & Scott).

Sunday July 9   **Ephesians 1.1–14**

Obviously no one had instructed the writer of **Ephesians** how to use dramatic effect. His opening verses give away much of what he has to say. In today's reading we are told of the wonderful spiritual blessings to be found in Christ. God's free grace has been lavished upon us, and we have been forgiven and chosen by God. God has called us and has cleared a path for us to be with him. We are welcomed in spite of our blotches and blemishes.

The path-clearing has been done by Jesus Christ, who was willing to pay the price and die so that we might be forgiven. Most of us find forgiveness easy to speak of, but hard to practise. Many wrestle with the hurt another has caused them, and then wrestle with trying to forgive them. Even though we ourselves have done wrong, we still find it hard to forgive those who hurt us. God has never hurt anyone, needs no one's forgiveness, yet is hurt by the things we do to one another.

✳ *Praise God for all his goodness to you. Ask for forgiveness for your blotches and blemishes.*

Monday July 10

Have you ever been given a present for which the words 'thank you' seemed too small? When I was newly ordained, I received a gift of a series of Bible commentaries from the church secretary. I could never have afforded to buy these books myself. To say 'thank you' seemed far too small an appreciation. Sadly, when it comes to our faith – the greatest gift we have received – we often forget to say 'thank you'.

▶ Read **Ephesians 1.15–23**.

The writer of **Ephesians** never ceases to give thanks for the people who are to receive his letter, and never stops being grateful to God because of the faith of others. This example of constant thanksgiving is one we would do well to follow. We are surrounded by good things and we should learn the importance of saying 'thank you'.

Thanksgiving helps us to recognise that God has given us all we have – nothing is to be taken for granted. What we have we owe to God, so let us give thanks.

✳ *Lord, help me to concentrate on saying 'thank you' for all your gifts.*

Tuesday July 11   Ephesians 2.1–10

By grace God has brought us into a new relationship with himself. What is grace? It is God's goodness, God's love that saves people in spite of their wrongdoing, and establishes a new relationship between them and God.

The ancient debate of good works versus grace as the means of achieving salvation may seem academic but it has a great bearing upon the way we live our life. Many of us keep up such a pace in life that the way we behave could indicate that our salvation depends upon good works. We take on more and more jobs – yes, we will organise the Christmas fair; of course, we will collect for Oxfam; yes, we will be on this or that committee.

What is this pressure that makes moderately busy people into workaholics? God does not want us to flog ourselves to death. Do we think that God will not love us if we take life easier and enjoy it? Do we not trust God to work through a church unless we personally do everything?

✷ *Do you trust God to love you and want you as his follower even when you relax and enjoy life? Think and pray about this.*

Wednesday July 12 **Ephesians 2.11–22**

Today's reading speaks of the debate between those who welcomed Gentiles into the Church and those who wished to keep Christianity as a purely Jewish religion. Because we are separated by many years from the beginnings of Christianity, this could appear to us to be nothing more than a history lesson. However, had the debate gone the other way, Christianity would certainly be very different today.

The message of **Ephesians** is that the Gentiles are no longer alienated from God but, rather, they have the same status as Jews. The early Christians who followed this teaching could see the importance of being united with people across a racial divide. This would have been a radical change in beliefs for Jewish nationals who had become Christians.

Today we can look back and see that there was a time when Christians were able to debate something very difficult and come to a consensus without splitting the Church.

✷ *Pray for those situations in the Church where people are not able to debate and reach a consensus. Pray also for those who feel excluded because of their race.*

Thursday July 13 **Ephesians 3.1–13**

The writer of **Ephesians** proclaims the good news 'about the infinite riches of Christ' (verse 8). We are called to do the same today. People outside the Church often think they know about Christianity. They believe that it has no surprises for them, no mystery, no secrets. But what they actually know about is a childish religion remembered from their schooldays. Their vision is very limited and they do not know of the depths within Christianity from which their spiritual needs could be met. Therefore, in their search for spiritual food, many ignore Christianity, and instead turn to other teachings, including the more way-out sects and cults.

Certainly, in **Ephesians**, the writer is able to speak about the newness of the gospel, and invites his readers to explore the secret of the faith – the secret which had never before been revealed to the human race (verse 9).

However, we must remember that all this newness would have presented problems for some, just as the supposed familiarity of Christianity handicaps certain people today.

✴ *Lord, may we be inspired by the great ideas of our faith, even if we have known them for a long time; and help us to cope with new ideas.*

Friday July 14   Ephesians 3.14 – 21

Do you know how much God loves you? Some people can easily understand that God loves the 'good' people of this world, but find it difficult to accept that God loves them.

God's love for us is so great – have another look at verses 18 – 19. His love is not a grudging acceptance or a mere nodding of approval, but a massive love. It extends beyond anything we can ever imagine. We can only begin to glimpse the immensity of God's love as we grow in faith. The more we get to know God, the more we realise just how much we mean to him.

Perhaps, through the experiences of human love and growing relationships, we can catch a glimpse of the potential of love. As we love someone more, as we learn more about them, we grow closer to one another. However, no matter how long we have loved someone, we can never know everything about them – they still surprise us. If that is true of our human relationships, how much more true it is of our relationship with God!

✴   *It passeth knowledge, that dear love of thine,*
     My Saviour, Jesus! Yet this soul of mine
     Would of thy love, in all its breadth and length,
     Its height and depth, and everlasting strength,
       Know more and more.   Mary Shekleton

Saturday July 15   Ephesians 4.1 – 6

What difference does it make to me if I am a Christian? Does it matter to others if I believe or not? What effect does it have on the world? It would certainly make a great difference to the peace of the world if we all took today's verses, and the challenge they contain, seriously.

How wonderful it would be if all the world were united and

served the 'one God and Father of all mankind' (verse 6)! As Christians we should long for this and do all we can to work for peace, justice and harmony in our world.

Perhaps it will only be in very small ways – in our own spheres of influence – that we can contribute to world peace. That is how the writer of **Ephesians** sees it (verse 2). The Christian life is about being gentle with one another, giving people space, being patient with them, forgiving and loving them. It is about that kind of tolerance and respect that can transform both the recipient and the giver. These are very important matters, things that occur in our everyday life.

✳ *Lord, help me to be humble, gentle, patient, forgiving and loving for the sake of Jesus Christ, our one Lord.*

For group discussion and personal thought

Read **Ephesians 2.4–10**. What do we mean when we claim that we are saved by God's grace? Having responded to God's grace and love we must build our personal faith 'with deep roots and firm foundations' (**Ephesians 3.17b**,NEB). How can we do this?

Sunday July 16   Ephesians 4.7–16

Every one of us has a gift – gift in the sense of an ability we have received through no merit of our own. In the world's eyes some gifts are more valuable than others, but this should not be so within the Church. If each gift is given by God, then there is no room for pride or jealousy.

The gifts of God are indeed varied. One of the problems in a church is learning to live with the great diversity of interests and abilities, while maintaining unity in mission and service. Unity does not mean that we should all behave in the same way. Rather, it is accepting and recognising that each person's gift is valuable – and to be used – even though it is completely different from our own.

We **all** have different contributions to make, and each is necessary to complete the whole. So, the next time we feel irritated by someone in our church who spends hours in silent meditation, or who is always singing choruses and playing the guitar, let us remember the gifts of God and the importance of valuing the gifts of others.

✴ *Lord, when our gifts seem to bring us into conflict, help us to be patient and to speak 'the truth in a spirit of love' (verse 15).*

Monday July 17   Ephesians 4.17 – 32

What does it mean to be a Christian when it comes to spiritual morality? The writer of **Ephesians** is trying to get us to recognise that we have become **new** people. This transformation must affect the way we live. We must reject our 'old self', and learn to put on the 'new self' of God's creating. This means putting aside all our sins, and putting on a completely 'new personality, which was divinely created, and which shows itself in that justice and holiness, which are the product of truth' (verse 24, WB).

However, Christians must remember that we are not the only people with an understanding of morality, nor do we have a monopoly on good works. In the past, social reform and help for those in need, both in Britain and overseas, mainly came from those within the Church. We can be glad that secular agencies now continue these good works. Nevertheless, we should continue to lead the way to a more just and ethical society. We still need to show the world that it is possible to live without bitterness and hate – that it is possible to be kind, tender-hearted and forgiving (verse 32).

✴ *Lord, now that you are transforming me by the power of your Holy Spirit, help me to know how to live in the way of truth.*

Tuesday July 18   Ephesians 5.1 – 7

Today we continue to think along similar lines to yesterday – morality arising out of our faith. The key to the whole ethical question is set out here in the word, **love**. But note that the word 'love' is almost immediately followed by 'sacrifice' (verse 2). This indicates the type of love that God expects us to show. It is not something easily offered and which brings instant happiness. Rather, it involves pain and suffering for the person who loves.

Although the issues mentioned in verses 3 – 5 include sexual morality, they do not concentrate on that issue alone. For instance, greed is to be condemned as much as fornication; also the danger of vulgar language is exposed. Some

Christians act as if sin was only to do with sex. They seem unable to recognise the dangers of the sins of gossiping, acting unjustly and worshipping material success.

We need to look again at the life of Christ and compare his priorities with ours.

✳ *Lord, forgive my wrongdoing. Help me to live life doing your will in all things.*

Wednesday July 19   Ephesians 5.8 – 20

What are the dark corners in your life? Are there things that you would rather keep hidden – parts of your life where you hope God's light will never shine?

Today, scientists have discovered the healing properties of light, and use it in modern medicine. We have probably heard of psychiatrists and psychologists saying how important it is to bring problems out 'into the light'. This is part of ancient wisdom. In many places the Bible speaks of living in the light – but what does this really mean?

There is a picture, painted by Holman Hunt, showing Jesus standing outside a door and holding a lantern. That door is meant to represent our hearts (see Revelation 3.20), and maybe we can imagine that inside there are rooms with many dark corners. Jesus, through his Holy Spirit, wants to shine his light into **every** part of our lives. When we allow him to do this, we gradually become aware of all that is wrong in our lives – all that we are ashamed of. Then we shall be ready to confess it to people whom we trust and to God. In this way we are healed – made whole.

When the Holy Spirit works like this in our lives, we shall indeed want to praise God and thank him for everything.

✳ *Lord, you know my problems and my joys; help me not to keep them to myself, but to share them.*

Thursday July 20   Ephesians 5.21 – 33

Often in the past, verses 22 – 23 have been used to support the subjection of women to men. Such an interpretation misunderstands what the writer intended.

At the time when **Ephesians** was written, a woman was looked upon as a piece of property, owned by her father and then by her husband. Women had no rights; they could be divorced for very trivial reasons and be left with no maintenance or support. Against this background, it can be seen that some of the ideas in today's reading are in fact quite revolutionary.

A husband is to love his wife, taking for his model the way Christ loved the Church; and he is to respect his wife as though she were a part of his own body. A wife who experiences this kind of love will no doubt respect and willingly submit to her husband – husband and wife will be united in bonds of love.

This is the essence of Christian social relations – that we treat each other with respect. The ideas contained in today's reading do not challenge, but transcend, the established order of life. They show us that Christian love is not confined to religious matters; rather it is to be a part of all our relationships.

✳ *Lord, help me to follow your example of love and respect for all people.*

Friday July 21   Ephesians 6.1 – 9

Yesterday we read how **mutual respect** should be the basis of Christian marriage. Today's reading tells us that respect should be the foundation of **all** relationships – including those between parents and children (verses 1 – 4), and even between slaves and masters (verses 5 – 9). While today we regard slavery as deplorable, it was accepted when **Ephesians** was written. The main point of these verses is that, in whatever situation we find ourselves, we are responsible before God to show respect and care for one another.

Many family and work relationships break down because of selfishness, mistrust and harsh treatment. Often, individuals in families and in work situations fight for their own rights without considering the needs of others. This contradicts the Christian teaching of mutual respect. Love and respect must be worked at and developed.

When we find ourselves in a situation where relationships seem to be breaking down, we can be encouraged because change is possible. We can always learn afresh, and apply, the principles of Christian discipline and instruction (verse 4b).

✳ *'Don't do anything from selfish ambition, but be humble towards one another, always considering others better than yourselves. And look for one another's interests, not just for your own.' (part of Philippians 2.3 – 4)*

Saturday July 22

When you get up in the morning do you take time to put on your 'armour'? Do you take time to prepare yourself for the 'battles' of the day?

▶ Read **Ephesians 6.10 – 24.**

The language of armour and war is unhelpful to many Christians today. Nevertheless, the picture that the writer is trying to paint in these verses is of God's all-surrounding love and protection, which is available to us every day. 'Putting on God's armour' means finding our strength in the Lord. Too often we expect to do things in our own strength, to provide the power necessary from our own resources.

It is not easy to be a Christian in today's society, so we need God's power and protection to enable us to 'fight' against the evils and injustices around us, as well as the conflicts within us (see Romans 7.19). If we, as Christians, and members of the Church, are to fulfil our mission to the world – to bring all people together in a fellowship of worship and love – we each need to put on God's armour of truth, righteousness, peace, faith and salvation. Also we must learn to pray for one another and for ourselves in the power of the Spirit, always keeping alert and never giving up (verse 18).

✳ *Use verses 23 – 24 as your prayer today.*

For group discussion and personal thought

Look at **Ephesians 4.11 – 12.** What special gifts and talents are you using in the service of your church and community? What other gifts do you have? In what ways could you use these? What gifts does your local church have which could be used to enrich and strengthen the wider Church community?

JEREMIAH

Notes by the Revd David Cornick, MA, BD, PhD

David Cornick is Director of Training in the South Western Province of the United Reformed Church. Previously he was chaplain of Robinson College, Cambridge. He has also ministered as a University Chaplain in Central London and in two churches in Hertfordshire.

The notes in this section are based on the Revised Standard Version.

Jeremiah's ministry as a prophet lasted from about 627–580 BC. These were difficult and dangerous years in Judah's history, coinciding with the rise of the Babylonian empire, principally under Nebuchadrezzar (605–562 BC). Jerusalem was captured in 597 BC. Many leading citizens were deported: Zedekiah was placed on the throne as a puppet-king and he reigned for a decade until he rebelled in 589 BC. His revolt was eventually crushed, and Jerusalem and the temple were destroyed. In 587 BC everyone, except a few peasants, was taken into exile.

Jeremiah's message was controversial but simple:
- God was involved in the ebb and flow of political events.
- He was using the Babylonians as instruments of his will.
- Only by the 'death' of exile could God create a new covenant with his people.
- Therefore, the people of Judah should accept God's judgement and let the Babylonians have their way.

Suggestions for further reading

Jeremiah Volume I and *Jeremiah Volume II and Lamentations* by Robert Davidson, Daily Study Bible (Saint Andrew Press);

Book of the Prophet Jeremiah (Chapters 1–25 and *Chapters 26–52)* by Ernest W. Nicholson, Cambridge Bible Commentaries on the NEB (Cambridge University Press).

Sunday July 23

God's presence in the depths of our personalities can be

frightening and disturbing, for he can sweep away our carefully balanced life-plans with a word or a feeling. Yet, paradoxically, that can also be a comfort, for when a vocation overwhelms us our lives are given a purpose and we discover who we really are. Jeremiah was a deeply sensitive young man when that experience gripped him.

▶ Read **Jeremiah 1.4−10**.

Called by God, what could have been Jeremiah's weakness was made perfect in God's strength. He was sensitive to the signs of the times and interpreted them as the judging activity of God, to a people who considered themselves to be saved and safe.

▶ Read **Jeremiah 1.11−19**.

Prophets see the same things as everyone else, but they see them differently. Jeremiah saw an almond branch in early bloom (in Hebrew, *shaqed*, and by a simple pun realised that God was 'watching' (in Hebrew *shoqed*)−'watching to see that my word is fulfilled' (verse 12, NIV). Similarly, the sight of a cooking-pot tilted away from the north led him to see that an invasion by the kingdoms of the north would be God's way of judging his people.

✳ *Lord, give us ears to hear the prophet's word.*

Monday July 24   Jeremiah 2.1−13

Sometimes relationships turn sour, and marriages which begin with ecstatic honeymoons end in the divorce court. Israel, God's precious and chosen people, had deserted him for the Canaanite fertility god, Baal. Jeremiah imagined God as a plaintiff in court asking if there was any evidence of a similar breach of faith from the farthest east to the farthest west (verse 10); and then summoning the heavens, where his will is done perfectly, to be appalled at such unfaithfulness.

In a land where rainfall was uncertain, a fresh water spring would have been an incalculable blessing. Israel's great spiritual folly was to forsake God, the fountain of living water in favour of man-made cisterns. These cisterns were carved out of the porous limestone rock and lined with plaster to save the rainwater during the long hot summer. Once the plaster cracked, the water seeped away. Irresponsible civil and religious leaders had led the people away from God (verse 8), preferring the gaudy ritual and cheap advantage of the fertility cult of Baal to the holiness and demands of God.

Tuesday July 25   **Jeremiah 4.19 – 28**

It hurts to be a prophet – all who speak God's word are torn
between the way things are and the way God wants them to
be. Jeremiah was a man of two worlds, and the tension
between them nearly destroyed him. Although he was the
messenger of God's judgement, he remained one of the people,
part of the nation, in solidarity with them as they faced
political disaster.

Salvation, the triumph of God, seemed a long way off (verses
21 – 22). Creation itself seemed to have gone into reverse gear,
for Jeremiah saw a vision in which creation, as described in
Genesis 1, had returned to waste and void. The entire God-
given environment was in chaos because Israel had turned
away from God.

Creation is an inseparable whole which cannot be divided
into spiritual, social and physical elements. If the purpose of
creation is that God be glorified through the praises of his
people, then the Church has much to learn from Jeremiah
about the anguish of living in two orders – identifying with
the world in its brokenness and pain, while announcing God's
word of consolation. We must never forget that it was this
kind of tension which cost our Lord a cross.

✻ *Lord, help us bear the tensions of Christian living.*

Wednesday July 26   **Jeremiah 5.1 – 11**

Abraham once bargained with God to save Sodom if he could
find ten righteous men there (Genesis 18.22 – 33). Here God
promised Jeremiah that if he could find **just one man**, 'who
does justice and seeks truth', then he may pardon Jerusalem
(verse 1).

Jeremiah began his search among 'the poor' (verse 4). This
probably means simple, ordinary people who respond to the
climate and style of an age but do not create it. Because the
search proved fruitless in the back streets and markets, he
turned to the 'great' – the leaders and intellectuals of the
nation – but there, too, he was doomed to futility because they

were like oxen that had broken free of their yokes and become an easy prey for predators (verses 5 – 6). The rejection of God in favour of fertility gods and goddesses and attendant cultic prostitution had brought disastrous social consequences (verses 7 – 8).

Worship can often seem irrelevant to the life of the world around us, but a society is subtly influenced by what it worships and honours. Many false gods of wealth, pleasure, power and security abound in our world. Like Jeremiah we must proclaim God's alternative way, and search out and support those who 'do justice and seek truth'.

✳ *O worship the Lord in the beauty of holiness.*

John S. B. Monsell

Thursday July 27   Jeremiah 7.1–15

Some sermons are uplifting; others are meant to be disturbing by the truth they reveal. Jeremiah delivered this sermon in the winter of 609 – 608 BC after King Josiah, the great reformer, had been killed by the Egyptians at Megiddo (2 Kings 23.28 – 30; Jeremiah 26.1) and his son Jehoiakim installed as a puppet-king. In spite of this disaster, the Judeans continued to believe that Jerusalem was inviolable because it was the city of the temple, and the temple was the house called by God's 'name' (verse 10) or personality. However, trust in empty formulae like 'This is the temple of the Lord' (verse 4) was misplaced, because the words had been robbed of their potency by the immorality of the people.

Faith without works is dead; religious language without changed lives is hollow. The Judeans had so separated behaviour from belief that even their most cherished assumptions about God and religion had to be smashed before they could be rebuilt on a sound ethical foundation. Jerusalem would therefore suffer the same fate as Shiloh, an ancient Israelite holy place which had been razed by the Philistines several hundred years before.

✳ *Lord, may our lives always be a fitting garment for your living word.*

Friday July 28   Jeremiah 7.29 to 8.3

Religion is the finest and noblest human activity, but it is still human and cannot bring life – only God can do that. In this sombre and frightening reading Jeremiah highlights three aspects of Judean religion:

- They defiled the temple with **false symbols and images**.
- They even **sacrificed their children** in the misguided belief that the greater their sacrifice the more likely was God's protection.
- They **worshipped the heavenly bodies** because they believed the movements of sun, moon and stars influenced their fate.

All this was an occasion of mourning and lament, so Jeremiah commanded Jerusalem to cut off her hair — a traditional sign of mourning (verse 29, compare with Job 1.20) — because of God's anger. The valley of the son of Hinnom, the 'shrine' of child sacrifice would be renamed the valley of Slaughter as God changed the thriving land of Judah into a wasteland.

No human activity must be allowed to obscure God's truth. All delusions, illusion and false securities have to be destroyed because only the truth can set people free.

✶ *Jesus said, 'When the Spirit of truth comes, he will guide you into all the truth'* . . . *'and the truth will make you free'.*
(John 16.13a; 8.32b)

Saturday July 29

Love cannot be abstracted. It has to do with real people. We are called to love those whose lives touch ours, however difficult or irritating they may be. Those who endeavour to live at the interface of God's kingdom and humanly-ordered society will find such loving a bitter-sweet affair, for their visions may well be rejected and their dreams trampled underfoot by the people they love.

▶ Read **Jeremiah 8.18 to 9.11**.

To be a channel of God's grace means being open, and openness means being unprotected and vulnerable. Jeremiah was vulnerable. He felt the pain of openness throbbing throughout his life. He loved his people just as he loved God, but God was judging and purifying his people. No medicine in Gilead, no physician could ease that hurt, and no words of his could make the people repent.

When we are caught in similar tensions, and paradox threatens to undermine our service, we must remember that our vocation is simply to love, not judge. Judgement is God's and his alone, and is but the reverse side of his saving love.

148

＊ Belovèd, let us love: for only thus
  Shall we behold that God who loveth us.

Horatius Bonar

For group discussion and personal thought

Read **Jeremiah 7.29 to 8.3**. If Jeremiah were a prophet today, what do you think he would say about our religious life? What are our 'idols'? With what false securities do we surround ourselves? How does our faith help us (a) to recognise these and (b) resist them?

Sunday July 30   **Jeremiah 11.6–17**

In 621 BC King Josiah had called his nation to renew their covenant with God (2 Kings 23.1–3) and accept the serious obligations laid upon them to live according to God's will. However, just as they had failed to keep the original covenant, so too they only paid lip-service to Josiah's reform and transferred their worship to the petty deities which were 'two a penny' in Judah and Jerusalem (verses 12–13).

With sad irony Jeremiah heard God contrasting what might have been, with what had actually happened. God's 'beloved' had forfeited the right to share his 'house'. The 'green olive tree', which had promised to bear exquisite fruit, faced destruction.

Israel had been the recipient of an inestimable privilege, for she had been chosen to be God's people, the channel of his communication with his world. Privilege always entails responsibility, but Israel preferred to ignore her obligations. As Christians we are privileged citizens of God's kingdom and we must not ignore the responsibilities which this involves.

＊ *Lord, may we be responsible citizens of your kingdom.*

Monday July 31

Even the most honest autobiographies can hide the deepest secrets of a person's life. Total honesty is a rare attribute, especially in matters of faith and spirituality. There are several sections in **Jeremiah**, called his **'confessions'**, where the masks are ripped away and we see a soul in turmoil, wrestling with himself, with God and with the misery of his life.

▶ Read **Jeremiah 11.18 – 23**.

It may have been Jeremiah's sympathy with Josiah's reforms, including the centralisation of worship at Jerusalem and the closure of local shrines, which made the men of Anathoth plot against him. Jeremiah felt as vulnerable as a sacrificial lamb in the face of their anger and opposition and he yearned for vengeance.

▶ Now read **Jeremiah 12.1 – 4**.

We, too, may be angered by the prosperity of the faithless (compare Psalm 73.12) and the seeming impotence of good in the face of evil. However, faith in God means living in trust, and not expecting an answer to all our questions.

✳ *Have faith in God, my heart,*
  Trust and be unafraid.   *Bryn A. Rees*

Tuesday August 1

Those who have faith in God know what it is to live with unanswered questions. They also know what it is to receive answers they do not expect. It must have been cold comfort to Jeremiah to hear that the worst was yet to come!

▶ Read **Jeremiah 12.5 – 6**.

It was to be through shared suffering that Jeremiah would grow closer to God, and find that even in the depths of darkness light could shine. Jeremiah's sorrow at his alienation from his fellows was echoed and magnified by God's lament at the devastation wrought upon Judah by the Babylonians and their allies following Jehoiakim's rebellion against Nebuchadrezzar in about 602 BC.

▶ Read **Jeremiah 12.7 – 13**.

There were deep tensions in God's heart. Judah was still his 'beloved' (verse 7), his 'vineyard' and 'pleasant portion' (verse 10), yet he hated her (verse 8) and was using her enemies to destroy her (verse 12). As his people suffered, so God suffered. There is no detachment, no remoteness about our God. Although he is judge, he is in solidarity with those he judges. Is there already a cross in his mind's eye?

✳ *Never was love, dear King,*
  Never was grief like thine.   *Samuel Crossman*

Jeremiah understood that medium and message are closely related. This symbolic act or 'acted parable' was intended to be far more than a visual aid. Such acts were believed to have the power to bring about that which they symbolised.

Before Jeremiah had even washed his brand new waistcloth, which was probably a short skirt worn next to the skin under a long robe, he went and hid it in the cleft of a rock. The NEB and NIV are probably correct when they say that he hid it at Perath, a few miles north-east of Anathoth, rather than by the Euphrates, for that would have involved two round trips of 700 miles!

Although such details are debatable the meaning of Jeremiah's action was clear. Even though God's relationship to his people had been as close as Jeremiah's to his waistcloth, they too would be ruined (verses 8 – 9). Their overweening pride had led them into the arms of other gods and made ruin inevitable.

There was a profound relationship between the political events which were overwhelming Judah and her spiritual state. Similarly, what we believe and what we do are closely related and have far-reaching consequences.

✳ *Lord, help me to keep you in the centre of my life.*

Jeremiah must have frequently passed the potter's shop, and it was out of this ordinary situation that God spoke to him of something extraordinary – God's relationship with Judah.

The potter was at once a destroyer and a creator. When a pot was not coming out right, the potter flattened the clay and began the work of re-creation, producing something beautiful and useful. That was what God was doing with the nation – and what he does with every nation. He was using historical events to destroy his imperfect people, but only so that they may be made perfect.

This compelling picture takes us to the heart of God's anger and judgement. It is not vindictive and vicious in intent, but loving and creative. Judgement is but the obverse side of salvation. God can save and perfect us only by judging us – bringing to light those faults, fears and sins which are hidden in our inner darkness. If we allow God to judge us, he can then remould and re-create us.

Friday August 4

▶ Read **Jeremiah 19.1−2, 10−13**.

God told Jeremiah to buy a narrow-necked water decanter from the local potter. The word translated 'earthen flask' is derived from a verb meaning 'to make a gurgling sound' because that was the noise the water made, when pouring out of it. Jeremiah was to smash it at the Potsherd Gate, which was probably the potters' rubbish dump for broken and imperfect pots. God's judgement began at that moment because such acts were believed to have power to bring about what they symbolised as we saw on August 2.

▶ Now read **Jeremiah 19.3−9**, which is written in a different style. Some scholars suggest that a later editor took the incident of the broken flask and used it to explore the reasons for God's judgement.

Judah's attraction to the fertility cult had so alienated her from God and annihilated her moral sense that child sacrifice had become a normal part of her life (verse 5). This abomination would meet with God's judgement.

God's people should have a strong moral sense, be whole and integrated − their words and actions should be at one. Jeremiah had the courage to act according to his convictions, but the cost would be high.

❋ *Lord, make us whole, and give us the strength to bear the cost of integrity.*

Saturday August 5

▶ Read **Jeremiah 19.14 to 20.6**.

Pashhur the priest was only doing his job, and a very important job it was! As 'chief officer' in the temple he was responsible for decorum and good order there. It was all very well for Jeremiah to smash pots at the city gate, but preaching seditious nonsense within the temple precincts was altogether different. Jeremiah's reaction to Pashhur's disciplinary measures was not motivated simply by animosity. Rather, he was saying that Pashhur would be **personally** involved in God's judgement – he and his friends would be taken into exile. The guardian of law and procedure would be overtaken by a divinely inspired breakdown of law and order.

God's word was unwelcome, for his searing light threatened the comfortable darkness of both religious and civil establishments. Jeremiah stood alone against those dark forces which were clothed in the robes of decency and righteousness, just as, years later, one greater than all the prophets – Jesus – stood alone before the high priest and the Roman governor. This was Jeremiah's 'Gethsemane'.

▶ Now read in **Jeremiah 20.14–18**, another of the prophet's 'confessions'.

Jeremiah's courage masked spiritual turmoil, but in the loneliness of failure he held on.

✱ *Pray for those whose ministries today seem to be failures.*

For group discussion and personal thought
Read **Jeremiah 18.1–12**, and discuss the meaning of the acted parable of the potter. Jeremiah consistently claimed that God was working out his will through political events. To what extent can **we** speak usefully of God's activity (a) in the history of our age and (b) in our lives?

Sunday August 6   **Jeremiah 21.1–14**

Zedekiah was a puppet-king appointed by Nebuchadrezzar (see introduction on page 144) in 597 BC. He was a weak man, torn between serving his Babylonian master and placating the anti-Babylonian power groups which still held sway in Jerusalem. He consulted Jeremiah several times during the two-year Babylonian siege of Jerusalem (see Jeremiah 37.17; 38.14), which followed his hapless rebellion in 589 BC. The city's fate was politically and militarily inevitable. Only an incorrigible optimist could have expected otherwise.

Zedekiah seemed to have realised that the political writing was on the wall, but he completely misunderstood the spiritual dimension of the nation's crisis (verse 2). Miracles – wonderful deeds – were not on the agenda. Before God could save his people there had to be wholesale destruction. Death had to precede resurrection. In this the Babylonians were the agents of God. The power exercised through them was the same as that which freed his people from slavery in Egypt (compare verse 5 with Deuteronomy 5.15). Dark and oppressive powers were — and still are — the unwitting servants of the Lord of heaven and earth.

✳ *God moves in a mysterious way*
   His wonders to perform.   *William Cowper*

Monday August 7

▶ Read **Jeremiah 23.1–4**.

From the darkness, light is born; out of judgement, salvation arises. The God who scattered his people into exile would gather them together. Bad shepherds (rulers) would be replaced by caring, good shepherds who lived the life-style of the shepherd God. 'Shepherd' was an ancient title for the king. This oracle, therefore, gives a vision of an ideal political future in a divinely ordered society.

▶ Now read **Jeremiah 23.5–6**.

The hope that sprang from exilic despair was centred not just on a society but on a person, a 'righteous Branch' of the Davidic kingly line. This hope for a Messianic king was meant to contrast sharply with the disastrous reign of Zedekiah. Although his name meant 'The Lord is my righteousness', his rule expressed everything but faith in God. 'One day', said Jeremiah, 'in God's good time, there will be a true "Zedekiah".'

▶ Finally, read **Jeremiah 23.7–8**.

This is a marvellous vision of a new exodus. Even the people of the northern kingdom of Israel, which had been scattered over a century before, would also return to their homeland. God's ultimate purpose is always to create and restore, not to destroy.

✳ *Gather us to yourself, loving Lord.*

Tuesday August 8   Jeremiah 24.1–10

After the first deportation of leading Jews to Babylon and the establishment of Zedekiah as a puppet-king by Nebuch-adrezzar, false hopes arose among those who remained in Jerusalem (see 28.1–4). They appear to have regarded those who had been deported with a mixture of pity and contempt. They thought that the worst was past; they were still in the city of God and close to his presence in the temple.

As at the beginning of his ministry, Jeremiah was confronted with an ordinary experience which was given an extraordinary meaning. The good figs were not the self-satisfied citizens of Jerusalem, but the exiles who wept by the waters of Babylon (see Psalm 137). The future lay with them in their isolation, loneliness, bitterness and confusion. Much as it seemed otherwise, God was with them. They were the seeds of reconstruction, the community of the faithful from which God would raise up his 'righteous Branch'. It is often when we seem to have lost most and have failed completely, that God is closest to us and most active.

✴ *There's a wideness in God's mercy*
  Like the wideness of the sea;
  There's a kindness in his justice
  Which is more than liberty.   *Frederick W. Faber*

Wednesday August 9   Jeremiah 27.1–11

Prophets in Old Testament times were political beings, concerned with discerning the will of God in the flux of human affairs. Jeremiah could not help but be in conflict with Zedekiah's regime, for its facile patriotism directly contradicted God's purposes.

At the beginning of Zedekiah's reign, Jerusalem became the centre of a conspiracy of some of the small vassal states at the western end of the Babylonian empire. The time seemed ripe for revolt because Nebuchadrezzar was dealing not only with external pressure, but also with civil war at home.

Jeremiah's response to such intrigue was dramatic and desperately unpopular, for it seemed cowardly and an affront to national pride. He proclaimed that the way of salvation lay not in armed rebellion but in submissive acquiescence to the arrogant power of Babylon.

It is never easy to contradict the ways of the society in which we live. However, like Jeremiah, Christians have a prophetic ministry to perform whenever rulers choose the easy way of popularity rather than the difficult path that leads to life.

✴ *Pray for those who are called to a prophetic ministry in their country today.*

When there is a Babel of conflicting voices within the Church, how can we know who is correctly interpreting the will of God? God does not fully reveal his plans to any one individual – he refuses to write them across the night sky.

Although Jeremiah would have liked Hananiah's prophecy to be true (verse 6), he responded with common sense – the proof of the pudding was in the eating. Only forthcoming events would reveal the truth.

The people of Judah were left to choose between Hananiah's sincere optimism and Jeremiah's sincere pessimism. How should they choose? These two prophets were part of a community which, throughout its history, had been guided by prophets. The prophets of the past (verse 8) were critics of the establishment. It was not their business to speak peace when there was no peace, because God does not ignore sin, but rather he deals with it.

Often the past can help us to discern what is happening in the present. When voices contradict each other, a sense of what God's activity has revealed of his nature can be a spiritual 'litmus' test. If we are truly open to God, he will always make his will known to us.

✴ *'God is always at work in you to make you willing and able to obey his own purpose.' (Philippians 2.13, GNB).*

This letter which Jeremiah wrote to the exiles in Babylon was sent through Zedekiah's diplomatic channels (see verses 1–3), probably because Zedekiah thought that Nebuch-adrezzar would be relieved to hear that the Judeans were not sowing seeds of sedition. However, this letter is in fact one of the most revolutionary documents in the Old Testament.

● The exiles were told to settle in Babylon; but more than that, they were to work for its welfare, its *shalom*. They had been used to praying for the welfare and peace of Jerusalem and Judah and for the annihilation of their enemies. However, the way of God lay in seeking the good of those who persecuted them. A new spirituality was struggling into being, which eventually emerged in the teachings of Jesus (see Matthew 5.43–44).

● This new spirituality was the direct result of an astonishing new understanding of God. The God who used the arm of Nebuchadrezzar, and who would bring forth resurrection from the death of exile, was no narrow nationalistic god – he was the Lord who summoned forth all that had been, is and shall be. He is not bound to a temple or a nation, but will be present to all who seek him in sincerity and truth.

✳ *Lord, may we seek to worship you in spirit and in truth.*

Saturday August 12   Jeremiah 29.15 – 23

Not only did Jeremiah have to contend with a weak king, a corrupt establishment and false prophets at home, he also had to deal with false prophets in Babylon (verse 21). Jeremiah boldly predicted their execution at the hands of the Babylonians, presumably for sedition. This punishment may have been politically based, but according to Jeremiah the 'real' reason for their deaths was a religious one. These prophets had disregarded God's laws and had failed to discern God's will – they spoke lies in the name of God.

Central to Jeremiah's spirituality was the belief that God is deeply involved in, and has something to say about, the movement of human affairs. Therefore, there could be no distinction between political and religious responsibilities.

It is dangerous to misunderstand the signs of the times as Ahab and Zedekiah were to find out. However, to interpret them correctly and proclaim the will of God, can invite hostility, even to the point of violence, as Jeremiah knew.

A spirituality for today must be a 'Jeremiah spirituality' – we must take time to understand the signs of the times, be courageous enough to speak and live out God's truth, and recognise that prayer and action are inseparable.

✳ *'Be of good courage, the Lord your God will not fail or forsake you.' (part of Deuteronomy 31.6)*

For group discussion and personal thought

Read **Jeremiah 28.1–17**, and compare the messages of Jeremiah and Hananiah. What kind of prophetic ministry are we called to today? Is it right for the Church to have a political voice? Why? In what instances in our modern complex society do we need to compromise either as individuals or as a Church?

Sunday August 13   **Jeremiah 31.23–34**

Today's reading takes us to the heart of Jeremiah's message of hope and renewal. Jeremiah dreams of a time when everything will again be as it once was in Judah and Jerusalem. The blessing of God will rest upon it and the decimated, strife-torn land will return to normal living.

God's people were the children of history – they reaped the consequences of the actions of their ancestors (verse 29). But always God cared for them and acted for their good. God spoke to Jeremiah of a new age that would dawn when God's relationship to his community would change. There would be a **new covenant** – a new relationship with God – which would depend on an **inner experience** rather than on an external demand.

The concept of covenant is central to the Old Testament, and Christians believe that this new covenant was established by the life, death and resurrection of Jesus. However, before we sit back in smug satisfaction, let us ask ourselves whether we have let this **living** relationship wither, as once the old covenant was laid to waste.

✱ *Lord Jesus, remind me always that you are the living Lord.*

Monday August 14   **Jeremiah 32.1–15**

Jeremiah was not afraid to back his talk with actions. At a time when Jerusalem was under siege and the city was likely to fall to the Babylonians, property prices must have been at rock-bottom. It was hardly a propitious time to invest in a piece of land. However, in order to fulfil his family obligations (see Leviticus 25.25–28), Jeremiah agreed to purchase a family field in Anathoth.

This is the most detailed description of a business transaction in the Old Testament. Everything was done in perfect order and regularity at a time when the social and economic life of the nation was disintegrating. It was because of this context that such an ordinary transaction became symbolically potent as a sign of confidence in God's future for Judah (verse 15).

It was God who first told Jeremiah to buy the land, but Jeremiah did not act until God's message was confirmed by a normal family visit. God works through the ordinariness of life and confirms his plans for our lives through our everyday experiences.

Tuesday August 15   **Jeremiah 36.1–19**

Fast days (verse 6) were held at times of national crisis. We know that this incident occurred in December 604 BC (verse 9), when the political situation was worsening. Judah's Egyptian allies had been defeated by the Babylonians at Carchemish in the previous year, and they had then advanced as far as the coastal plain. The people gathered in the temple to seek help and reassurance from God. Jeremiah had been banned from the temple, possibly because of his seditious teaching, and so he relayed his message through Baruch his secretary.

The politically powerful leaders, who advised the king and helped formulate policy, heard the message of the scroll (verses 11–14). We do not know exactly what it said, but we may surmise that, among other prophecies of Jeremiah, it contained his teaching about the necessity of capitulation to the Babylonians. It is the way of the world that friends in high places can be extremely useful. Jeremiah and Baruch had good reason to be grateful for sound advice and solid help from sympathisers in the court (verse 19), for these were dangerous times for people who spoke God's word.

* *Pray for those for whom it is dangerous to speak God's truth today, that they may have courage and, like Jeremiah, find government officials who are sympathetic to them.*

Wednesday August 16   **Jeremiah 36.20–32**

The only way King Jehoiakim could find comfort in Jeremiah's words was to turn them into fuel for his winter fire! In spite of opposition from members of his 'cabinet' (verse 25), Jehoiakim treated the word of the Lord with contempt. We can almost hear a cynical laugh with each slash of the knife. Censorship is always the first resort of the frightened, but it rarely works. God's word never returns to him void. The process of judgement is inexorable.

From the security of his secret hiding-place Jeremiah simply redictated his 'sermon' to Baruch, adding a few words about the fate awaiting Jehoiakim. The stupidity of Jehoiakim compared badly with the wisdom of his father, Josiah. When Josiah heard a reading from a scroll, he heeded it and began a movement for national renewal and reform (2 Kings 22); whereas his son, Jehoiakim reacted to a similar scroll with derision and contempt.

The decisions that we make have inevitable repercussions – we reap what we sow. Let us not live like the foolish son who preferred to follow his own reckless judgement, but rather live like the wise father who let God be part of his decision-making.

✱ *Lord, be part of my decision-making.*

Thursday August 17   **Jeremiah 38.1–13**

The surprise was not that the anti-Jeremiah faction should have tried to get rid of him, but that it took them so long. To all appearances he was subverting the war effort, and traitors have been shot for much less. Zedekiah showed his weakness by handing Jeremiah over to the princes (verse 5) which enabled them to leave the prophet to die of hunger and exhaustion in a muddy cistern. Was this intended to be Jeremiah's 'Calvary'?

Ebed-melech was an Ethiopian eunuch, an outsider to the Jewish faith. Sometimes eunuchs attained high positions in court circles (see Daniel 1.3), but it must have taken much courage, and involved considerable risk, for Ebed-melech to speak so bluntly to the king (verse 9). God can always weave such humanity and decency into the fabric of his will.

Little acts of kindness reveal a greatness of spirit. Ebed-melech was the sort of person who would have instinctively thought that the rescue ropes would cut and burn, and so he sought out rags and old clothes to provide padding. Stupidity and disobedience may have ruled long in the court and demanded the judgement of God, but the light of humanity and compassion still burned in the concern of this foreigner.

✱ *Help us to help each other, Lord,*
   Each other's cross to bear.   *Charles Wesley*

Friday August 18

Christians sometimes think it is easy to be as innocent as doves, but agonise over what it might mean to be as cunning

160

as serpents (see Matthew 10.16). Compromise and doing deals in world affairs have always gone against the ethical grain. Sometimes the choices that we have to make are not simple ones between good and evil, but complex ones between bad and worse. Jeremiah was working in times of political crises and had just survived an assassination attempt. The 'cabinet' was divided in factions, the king was deeply insecure, and the Babylonian army was advancing every day.

▶ Read **Jeremiah 38.14 – 28**.

After his secret consultation with the king, Jeremiah was sworn to secrecy and when the princes confronted him he told a downright lie about what had passed between them (verse 27). He did this in order to protect the king, possibly because keeping the king in power would prevent a political purge and bloodshed in the city.

From the comfort of our armchairs, we can debate forever about the rightness of such a decision, but for those who live in corridors of power such decisions are a daily reality, and the way they are taken may result in life or death for others.

✳ *Pray for Christians who have difficult political decisions to make.*

Saturday August 19   **Jeremiah 39.1–18**

Jerusalem was finally captured by the Babylonians in July 587 BC. Zedekiah tried to escape, but was caught, dealt with brutally, and taken in chains to Babylon. Jeremiah's prophecies proved all too true. All the people of note in Jerusalem were taken into exile – only a few poor people were left in Judah. However, Jeremiah, a collaborator in Babylonian eyes, was treated well and his ministry was vindicated.

It was a sad tale, but at the end of it Ebed-melech, the Ethiopian eunuch who had saved Jeremiah's life, remained a sign of hope. His deep humanitarianism was recognised and interpreted as trust in God (verse 18). Ebed-melech put his own life in jeopardy to save another, and by risking his life he found it. Zedekiah, however, by only seeking his own security, lost his life (see Luke 9.23 – 24).

The Babylonian exile marked the end of an era of the history of God's people. They had not heeded the advice of their prophets, but God would continue to teach them and care for them during this absence from their homeland.

✱ *As we finish reading this section of **Jeremiah**, let us be mindful of the need to listen to God. His words are not always comfortable but they are always meant for our well-being.*

For group discussion and personal thought
Read **Jeremiah 31.23 – 34**. Dreams and visions of the future have always been important in the life of God's people. Share some of your visions for the future. How can we test whether they coincide with the will of God? Is the new covenant a vision for the future or part of the pattern of living now?

FURTHER
EVERYDAY PRAYERS

A third collection of original prayers for everyday use. Also prayers for special occasions including the Christian year. This book makes a very acceptable gift.

The first two books in this series – **Everyday Prayers** and **More Everyday Prayers** – are still available.

● *UK price:* **£2.40** each

Order through your IBRA group secretary or from the appropriate address on the back cover.

ACTS 21–28

Notes by the Revd J. David Bridge, BA, BD

David Bridge is a Methodist minister who has served on the staff of the British Methodist Home Mission Division, and has now returned to circuit ministry. He has written on such diverse topics as the ministry, preaching and the cinema.

The notes in this section are based on the Revised Standard Version.

After completing his three great missionary tours Paul returned to Jerusalem. In this third and last section of **Acts** we shall read how Paul was finally able to further the work of the gospel in Rome, even though he was taken there as a prisoner to be tried before the emperor. Rome was the centre of communications of the then-known world. If the gospel was to be preached to the whole world, there was no better place than this for the Church to be firmly established.

Although there is plenty of adventure and danger in these chapters – more than most of us experience in a lifetime – the pace is much slower than in the previous sections of **Acts**. This allows us to take a close look at Paul as a person. How was he able to achieve so much, driven by the vision of Christ whom he had met on the Damascus road and whom he believed was the Lord of all nations?

In a sense the story of **Acts** is incomplete – as the story of God's mission is still incomplete. It continues today as God invites us to share in it, and it will go on until all things are made new.

Suggestion for further reading

The Acts of the Apostles by William Barclay, Daily Study Bible (Saint Andrew Press).

Sunday August 20   **Acts 21.17 – 26**

Paul returned to Jerusalem at the end of his third missionary journey to a warm welcome from the leaders of the church there, but also to disturbing news about malicious lies being spread by his enemies. How easy it is to distort what a person

163

has said, or to misrepresent their actions, if you want to believe the worst!

Paul had consistently taught that Gentiles need not follow Jewish customs where these were not essential to the Christian faith. Nevertheless, he himself valued many aspects of his Jewish heritage and saw no reason to abandon them, nor had he encouraged his fellow-Jews to abandon them. In order to make this crystal clear, he joined four men in making a solemn vow according to Jewish traditions.

God does not begin to work in our lives at a particular time – he has always been at work. In our personal history, and in the history of our nation, there are signs of God at work. As Christians we are not called to cut ourselves off from our roots. There will be much in the past of which we need to repent, but there will also be much to thank God for. When we invite people to become Christians we do not ask them to leave their culture behind, but to offer the best of that culture to God.

✱ *Thank you, God, for my heritage and for all your past gifts.*

Monday August 21   Acts 21.27 – 36

One of the saddest aspects of the history of the Church has been the number of times religion appears to have been the cause of war and suffering, prejudice and oppression. In our own day there are conflicts in many parts of the world in which religion plays a major part. It seems as if religion, like any other important aspect of our lives, can enrich or destroy life. Because it is something about which people feel deeply, their passions may overrule their judgement.

Paul was accused of violating the temple by taking a Gentile into the area reserved for Jews. Those who stirred up the trouble, which rapidly led to violence, were acting in the name of religion. They were Jews from the province of Asia. Sadly it seems as if the experience of living with Gentile neighbours had done nothing to lower the barriers between them. On the contrary, their religion had been used to support their prejudices.

There are many warnings in the Bible about false religion – that is, religion directed towards our own ends rather than towards God. 'Not everyone who says to me, "Lord, Lord,"' warned Jesus, 'shall enter the kingdom of heaven' (Matthew 7.21a). Let us take care that the aim of our devotion is to seek God's will and to do it.

Tuesday August 22   **Acts 21.37 to 22.5**

This reading illustrates three stages in the process by which faith is shared:

- At the start there is a **barrier**. In this case the barrier was formed by a pre-conceived idea. The Roman tribune assumed that Paul was an Egyptian revolutionary. He did not expect Paul to be able to tell him anything. There is a similar barrier in the minds of people who do not know what Christianity is, and who do not expect it to have a message for them.
- Then comes a **breakthrough**. In this case it was the discovery that Paul and the Roman tribune had a language in common. Our search for a breakthrough may take longer but it will also involve looking for common ground with those with whom we seek to share our faith.
- Finally, there is **testimony**. This is the most important way in which faith is shared. Even the hostile crowd found itself listening to Paul's words as he recounted his experience of God's power.

The order of the stages is important. We cannot give a testimony to those who will not hear us. First, we must discover what the barrier is and then find some common ground. The time to speak is when people are open to our words.

✱ *Father, teach me not only how, but when, to speak about your love.*

Wednesday August 23   **Acts 22.6 – 16**

In Paul's account of his conversion here we see the same pattern of events that we noticed yesterday.

There was a **barrier** between Paul and God, largely due to Paul's pre-conceived ideas about God. He believed himself to be a zealous and God-fearing man. Yet, when God spoke to him on the Damascus road, he did not know who it was.

The **breakthrough** came in two stages. We are familiar with the account of the bright light and the heavenly voice. Less spectacular, but equally important, was the trust shown by Ananias. He welcomed Paul as a friend, although Paul had left Jerusalem with the intention of finding Christians in order to punish them. Had Ananias withheld his friendship, the barrier in Paul's mind would soon have moved back into place.

Instead, Paul had the opportunity for **testimony**, and in response he took his first faltering steps as a Christian.

✴ *'Who are you, Lord?' (verse 8). You know us better than we know ourselves. Thank you for those who trust us and whose testimony has enabled us to see you and know you.*

Thursday August 24   Acts 22.17 – 29

The attitude of Christians to the State must be determined in the light of local circumstances. In some countries the State gives every encouragement to the Church; in others it is neutral, or even hostile. Paul frequently had reason to be grateful for the State's protection. Further, we can all agree that being a Christian does not release us from the obligation to be a good citizen.

The crowd listened to Paul's testimony until he mentioned his commission from God to minister to Gentiles. Then their prejudices came to the surface again and Paul's life was threatened. He was saved, and spared an agonising beating, because he could claim his rights as a Roman citizen. He did this, not for his own sake, but because his mission was not yet accomplished.

Good laws provide a framework in which people can live at peace. They uphold justice and they create the conditions in which people may be free to hear and respond to the gospel. Therefore, as far as our circumstances allow, we should be glad to claim the privileges and obligations of our citizenship.

✴ *Give thanks for the ways in which the law in your country helps the church to do its work.*

Friday August 25

One could not blame the Roman tribune if he took a rather dim view of religion. One day he had to quell a riot which had broken out over whether foreigners should be allowed in the temple, the next he had to intervene to stop people fighting over the resurrection.

▶ Read **Acts 22.30 to 23.11**.

This episode shows us three ways of dealing with differences of opinion.

● The Sadducees and Pharisees resorted to violence to try and prove their point (23.10).

● The tribune was a curious onlooker, willing to hear all points of view but personally uninvolved (22.30).

● Paul had respect even for those with whom he disagreed strongly and who may have done him wrong (23.5).

Sadly, religion has often been the cause of conflict and even of war. It happens when religious people forget that God is both truth and love. It is important to contend for the truth, but the way we do so is part of the truth we are defending. Jesus said, 'Love your enemies and pray for those who persecute you' (Matthew 5.44).

✳ *Think about the people with whom you disagree most strongly. Ask God to help you respect them as persons even though you dislike their ideas.*

Saturday August 26   Acts 23.12 – 22

Throughout this week we have seen how religion can be a source of division, prejudice and violence. Now we see the most appalling thing of all – men plotting to commit murder as a religious act. Jesus had warned his followers this would happen (see John 16.2). Now this prophecy was coming true. Forty men made a sacred vow to take Paul's life.

Thanks to the alertness of Paul's nephew, news of the plot was passed to the tribune, and Paul was spirited away by night with a large bodyguard for protection. What happened to the forty men, who made the vow, we are not told. At the very least they must have been very hungry and thirsty!

History is full of the most dreadful acts committed in the name of religion. These warn us that enthusiasm can turn into fanaticism, and commitment can become intolerance, unless linked to genuine prayer. There is much in the Church's past for which we should thank God, but there is also much that dishonours Christ and about which we can only feel shame.

✳ *Father, forgive all in the life of the Church, past and present, that makes it hard for people to see you.*

For group discussion and personal thought

Read the account of Paul's arrest in the temple at Jerusalem
(Acts 21.27 – 36). These Jews had strong and exclusive
nationalistic feelings about their faith. Why is it that religion
often appears to cause so many problems? Consider some such
problems in the world today, and how we, as Christians, can
help to resolve them.

Sunday August 27   Acts 23.23 – 35

Since becoming a Christian, Paul had been a traveller. Here
he began his last, and in some ways his most significant,
journey of all. In a vision, God had called him to be a witness
in Rome, the capital of the empire (see 23.11). The journey to
Rome was to be a more perilous and uncertain journey than
any he had previously undertaken. But the call of God cannot
be ignored, and to this Paul devoted himself.

We see how this journey began in a most unpropitious way.
It began with a muddle, as Paul ought not to have been
arrested in the first place. It began with weakness, the local
tribune lacking the courage to do what he knew to be right. It
began almost with farce, the tribune having to mobilise a
small army of 470 soldiers to protect his prisoner. It began
with helplessness as Paul, no longer a free man, was kept
under close guard.

It is from such unlikely beginnings that God is able to work
his mighty acts.

✷ *Father, when I feel that life is against me, may I remember
that you are still for me. When I am in despair, help me to
know that you can bring life even out of death.*

Monday August 28   Acts 24.1 – 9

Paul was tried before the governor, Felix, and his accusers
had their say. Their spokesman, Tertullus, revealed a most
unpleasant set of human failings:

● There was **hypocrisy**. The Jewish people were most
   unwilling subjects of Roman rule. Yet Tertullus, to
   ingratiate himself with the governor, claimed the opposite.
● There was **wilful ignorance**. Far from stirring up Jews
   throughout the world, Paul had devoted the greater part of

his ministry to the Gentiles. This was what had provoked the crowd to wrath in the first place (see Acts 22.21–22).
● There was **deceit**. Tertullus did not mention the real reason why the crowd had tried to kill Paul – his special concern for the Gentiles. Such an argument would not have gone down well with a Roman governor.

Those who oppose the way of Christ usually have to resort to tactics such as Tertullus used. Christians must take care that they do not descend to such a level but use only the weapons of truth, faithfulness and love.

✻ *Father, when I am accused wrongly, or insulted, or abused, grant me the spirit of Christ that I may seek to overcome evil with good.*

Tuesday August 29   Acts 24.10–21

Because most of those responsible for the death of Jesus were Jews, and because most of Paul's enemies seem to have been Jews, it is possible to form the impression that Jews and Christians can only be deeply hostile towards one another. Such an impression is false as a careful reading of the New Testament will quickly show. Jesus was himself a Jew, as were all his earliest disciples. Also, Paul was a Jew and proud to be so. In his speech to the governor he made it clear that although he had become a 'follower of the Way' – as the first Christians were called – he had not turned his back on all his past.

Paul's accusers had told only lies about him, but he did not respond in the same manner. Instead, he reminded them that he had come to Jerusalem to bring help to those Jews who were suffering on account of the famine, and his reason for being in the temple was to fulfil a Jewish religious observance. Despite the behaviour of some Jews he had not lost sight of what was precious to him about Judaism.

As Christians, we should reach out to Jews and people of other faiths, not in hostility, but in friendship and in appreciation for what their traditions may be able to teach us of God.

✻ *Father, forgive the bitterness that has so often soured relationships between Christians and Jews. Heal the wounds caused by ignorance and prejudice. Help me to be ready to learn of you from people whose culture and traditions may be very different from my own.*

Felix seems to have been an odd mixture. He was not a callous
man, for he refused to hand Paul over to his enemies and he
kept him in conditions which were not too harsh. Yet,
although he did not do the wrong thing, he had a number of
weaknesses which prevented him from doing what was right.
He was curious about Christianity without seeing the need for
commitment. Although he refrained from pleasing Paul's
enemies, he would not anger them by releasing his prisoner.
He put off making a decision as long as he could. In a word, he
was a weak man open to the highest bidder. Of course Paul did
not offer a bribe – he was a very strong man, with a clear idea
of where he was going.

The gospel themes on which Paul lay special emphasis
(verse 25) were just those the governor needed to hear. He had
lost sight of **justice** in his concern for a quiet life. His lack of
self-control meant that he was at the mercy of whoever could
exert the greatest pressure against him. In his eagerness to
postpone awkward decisions, he had forgotten that there
would be a **future judgement** when it would be impossible to
put things off – when he must either be for or against Christ.

✴ *Are there difficult decisions which you are reluctant to face*
up to? Pray for wisdom to perceive what is the right course
of action and for courage to take it.

When a new governor, Festus, took over from Felix, the
Jewish authorities soon pestered him to bring Paul to
Jerusalem for trial. However, this did not suit Paul at all – he
had been called by God to witness in Rome, and to Rome he
would go. He, therefore, appealed to his right as a Roman
citizen to be tried before the emperor himself. Festus had no
alternative but to grant this appeal.

There is an important lesson to be learned here about
timing. Jesus chose his moment carefully to go to Jerusalem
for the final conflict. There were previous occasions when
death had threatened, but he had withdrawn from
confrontation (for example, see Luke 4.29 – 30; 13.31 – 33).
The right thing has also to be done at the right time.

It is wrong to think that Christians should be in a
permanent state of conflict and that anything else is
inexcusable compromise. The examples of both Paul and

Jesus teach us that, while we may be called to witness through confrontation, the time and place of that confrontation should be carefully chosen for the witness to be effective.

✴ *God, may your Holy Spirit guide me to know when it is the time for reconciliation and when for conflict. In times of trial, give me courage and a sure trust in your power.*

Friday September 1   Acts 25.13—27

At this point in the story let us pause and reflect on why Paul was at the centre of so much fuss, requiring the attention of chief priests, governors and royalty. To his contemporaries Paul would have been just another travelling preacher. Why should so much effort and expense be devoted to his trial?

● To Festus, Paul was a **disturber of the peace**. The province of Judea was a turbulent place. Within a few years there would be a major revolt leading to the destruction of Jerusalem and the heroic last stand of the Jewish people at Masada. The most important task of a Roman governor was to keep the peace, even if that peace was built on oppression and injustice.

● To some Jews, Paul was a **disturber of their prejudices**. Jews saw themselves as a superior race, specially favoured by God. They did not like to think that God also looked with favour on the Gentiles.

● To others, Paul was a **disturber of their pre-conceived ideas**. They believed that death was the end, and that life after death was out of the question. The claim that Jesus was alive challenged all this.

As Christians we are not people who have chosen a quiet life. We are constantly being disturbed by God as we seek to live in his way and not our own.

✴ *Father, may I always be open to your word, even when it makes me feel uncomfortable.*

Saturday September 2   Acts 26.1—11

We saw previously how Paul was proud of his heritage (see August 20). In his testimony to King Agrippa Paul developed this theme, admitting to his own persecution of Christians. He echoed Jesus' teaching (see Matthew 5.17) and implied that God's promises to the Jewish people had been fulfilled in the life, death and resurrection of Jesus. By this time Paul, himself, had realised that the many Jews who had become Christians had not turned their backs on the law and the prophets. Rather, they had recognised that Jesus was the Messiah, God's chosen One, about whom their sacred Scriptures spoke.

All this may seem rather obvious to us today, and indeed it is only necessary to repeat it because, in some quarters, Paul had acquired the reputation of being anti-Jewish. It is true that, if parts of Paul's writings are read in isolation from the rest, they may seem to have an anti-Jewish flavour. Throughout history, some people have read the Bible selectively to justify their own prejudices. It is important, therefore, to consider Paul's teaching as a whole. His words to Agrippa make it clear that Paul saw Jesus as One who came in fulfilment of the Jewish faith.

✵ *Pray for your Jewish friends. If you do not have any, offer a prayer of thankfulness for the faith of the Jewish people.*

For group discussion and personal thought

What do Paul's speeches of defence (**Acts 22.1–21; 23.1–7; 24.10–21; 26.2–23**) teach us (a) about Paul himself and (b) about presenting the gospel to others?

Sunday September 3   Acts 26.12–23

Paul's experience of conversion was sudden and spectacular. Many people could tell a similar story of a dramatic change in their lives, although it is probable that for most of us the change is more gradual. However, whether our conversion is sudden or gradual, there are certain things we shall have in common with Paul.

● **God takes the initiative**. Becoming a Christian is not something we achieve for ourselves; it is a response to God who has loved us and called us from the beginning.
● **God calls us for a purpose**. He needs our response because he has a place for us in his mission. When we open our lives to his Spirit, he is able to work through us.
● **It is costly to respond to God's call**. Paul's life was threatened many times and it is probable that he eventually died a martyr's death. Our lives may not be

required of us in the same way, but we should not forget that Christ called his followers to carry a cross. It is Christ's sacrifice that gives meaning and purpose to ours.

✸ *Not disobedient to the heavenly vision,*
  Faithful in all things, seeking not reward;
  Then, following thee, may we fulfil our mission,
  True to ourselves, our brethren, and our Lord.
                                        William Jenkins

Monday September 4   Acts 20.24 – 32

Compare these two statements of fact: 'Your train has six coaches,' and, 'Your train leaves in six minutes.' The first may or may not interest you and can be ignored, but the second requires a response. The mark of an effective testimony is that it cannot be ignored. It challenges and evokes a response.

Paul gave his testimony effectively and it put Festus and Agrippa on the defensive. They knew they had to make a response, although in both cases it was a negative one.

Festus tried to avoid the challenge of Paul's words by claiming that they were not to be taken seriously – they were the ravings of a lunatic. Agrippa tried to avoid the challenge by playing for time. 'You surely don't want an answer straight away,' was what he implied.

Do we feel challenged by the gospel message? If it has become just an interesting story which we can take or leave, let us try to read it afresh. We ignore the challenge of the gospel at our peril.

✸ *Father, may I hear your call – even if I have heard it many times before – in such a way as to require my response.*

Tuesday September 5   Acts 27.1 – 20

Today's reading contains a vivid account of the difficulties faced by sailors at this time. However, what may interest us most is the role of four people who are mentioned.

First there was **Julius**, the Roman centurion. He seems to have been willing to treat Paul generously, allowing him a great deal of personal freedom and being willing to discuss the progress of the voyage with him.

Then there were **Aristarchus** and the **author of *Acts*** who were with Paul in the boat (note the use of the pronoun 'we').

173

They were Paul's faithful companions on many of his journeys, and their loyalty to him was shown in their willingness to share his imprisonment.

Finally, there was **Paul** himself in a role which came naturally – Paul the master seafarer who would have known a great deal about ships and navigation. He was a very experienced traveller. Paul's combination of skill and experience enabled him to predict a disastrous voyage, but his warning went unheeded. The ship was soon caught in a terrible storm!

✳ *Pray for those who travel by sea, whether for business or for pleasure, and for those who serve seafarers – lighthouse keepers, lifeboat crews and others.*

Wednesday September 6   Acts 27.21 – 38

Here was an extraordinary thing – the prisoner had taken charge of the boat. Almost too late, Paul's authority on matters of seamanship was recognised and his words were heeded. He had a twofold message about **trust in God** and **practical action**. These belong together; they are not alternatives.

- **Trust in God.** Although their situation was precarious and their physical world was in turmoil, God had not changed. He could be trusted and they were all in his care.
- **Take the necessary practical measures.** Trusting in God did not mean neglecting what they themselves could do. The ship's crew needed all their strength to cope with the storm, and so Paul ordered them to eat.

On the deck of the ship, in the heart of the storm, Paul invited people to remember Jesus who was once with his followers in a storm, and through whose power the storm was mastered (see Mark 4.35 – 41). Paul demonstrated his trust in God with action. He took the bread and gave thanks – as Jesus had done – before he distributed it to them all.

✳ *O hear us when we cry to thee*
  For those in peril on the sea.   *William Whiting*

Thursday September 7   Acts 27.39 to 28.6

The Roman centurion again revealed his outstanding qualities. His men planned to kill the prisoners lest any should take advantage of the storm to try to escape. This

174

seems cruel to us but, according to Roman law, if a prisoner escaped the soldier guarding him suffered the penalty which that prisoner would have paid. However, the centurion would not allow any of the prisoners to be killed and eventually the whole party reached shore safely.

The restless spirit which had driven Paul on his great missionary journeys gave him no rest even now. He had to be constantly active and so, instead of resting to recover from his ordeal, he went off looking for firewood. The fact that this was a rather menial task did not deter him.

The natives of Malta, setting aside any resentment they might have felt towards the Romans, or any hostility towards members of other races, gave a warm welcome to the distressed strangers. It is often the case that a crisis will bring the best out in people, drawing them together and helping them to forget their differences. But it is sad that when a crisis passes people often revert to their former pattern of life.

✴ *Thank you, God, for the good qualities which are in everyone. Help me, so that the better side of my nature may more and more gain the upper hand.*

Friday September 8 Acts 28.7 – 22

The Maltese people received healing and were generous in return. Verse 10 reads, 'They presented many gifts to us.' Many believe that the author of Acts, and Paul's frequent companion, was Luke the physician, and so it would have been natural for him to share in the healing ministry. If that was the case, we have here the earliest account of a medical missionary at work.

We can only guess at Paul's feelings when he came ashore at Puteoli, Italy's main seaport. Everywhere he would have seen signs that indicated he was near the heart of the great Roman empire. What sort of impact could he, a Jewish tentmaker (Acts 18.3), hope to make in such a place? Then he was overjoyed to be welcomed by local Christians who had heard of his arrival. He was not alone; he was among friends.

There is an important lesson to be learned here about the missionary strategy of the Church. We know the names of great missionaries like Paul and Barnabas, and it would be hard to exaggerate the importance of their work. Yet, when Paul came to Rome, the Church was already there. Who brought the gospel message so far from its origins in Palestine? We do not know their names but we can guess the kind of people they were – slaves, businessmen, soldiers, civil servants, ordinary people whose lives had been transformed by Jesus and who were sharing their faith wherever they went. This is how the gospel spreads today.

✳ *Whenever I go into new situations, O God, help me to remember that you have gone ahead of me and that I am never alone.*

Saturday September 9   Acts 28.23 – 30

Here we see Paul being true to the same principles which had guided him throughout his life as a missionary.

- He wanted to be **financially independent**. This was not something he expected of other apostles but it was important to him to support himself and so retain his dignity.
- He **ministered to Jews and Gentiles**. Despite the problems which certain Jews had caused him, and despite his call to be an evangelist to Gentiles, Paul never gave up his longing for his own people to accept Jesus as Messiah and Lord.
- His **preaching** was about the **kingdom of God** and the **Lordship of Jesus Christ**. Faith is both social and personal.

The account of Paul's life in Rome is tantalisingly brief. Perhaps the author planned to write another volume. Paul wrote several letters from Rome, and these give us glimpses of his life at this time. However, the purpose for which **Acts** was written had been fulfilled – to show how the Church grew from its beginnings in a small group of people in Jerusalem on the day of Pentecost to a movement numbering tens of thousands, poised to sweep across the whole world.

✳   *Jesus shall reign where'er the sun*
     Doth his successive journeys run;
       His kingdom stretch from shore to shore,
       Till moons shall wax and wane no more.   *Isaac Watts*

For group discussion and personal thought

In the story of the shipwreck (**Acts 27**) Paul stands out as a commanding figure, a leader full of confidence and courage, and a calming influence. What reasons can you give for this, and what help are they to us today?

INTERNATIONAL APPEAL

'The enthusiasm with which our friends in India promote the IBRA puts us to shame,' remarked our General Secretary after his visit there early in 1988. 'Promoters do not just sell books; they also visit people's homes to talk about the value of Bible reading.'

The same enthusiasm shines through IBRA reports from other parts of the world. But **their** enthusiasm is not enough – **we** have a part to play, too. Translating into local languages, producing and distributing books, costs the kind of money that many Christian groups throughout the world do not have.

Through grants, and gifts of books in English, the IBRA International Fund makes it possible for many thousands of Christians to have regular help with reading the Bible.

Are you enthusiastic enough to share in the work of the IBRA? Please give generously. Place your gift in the envelope provided and hand it to your local secretary, or send it direct to the *IBRA International Appeal, Robert Denholm House, Nutfield, Redhill, Surrey RH1 4HW, England.*

Thank you for your prayers and your gifts.

A TIME FOR EVERYTHING

Notes by the Revd Christopher Ellis, MA, MPhil

Christopher Ellis is a Baptist minister serving in the ecumenical Central Church, Swindon. He has also ministered in Brighton and Cardiff.

The notes in this section are based on the New International Version.

In this section we shall be reflecting on some of the themes which occur in **Ecclesiastes 3.1–8**. **Ecclesiastes** is part of what is usually called the 'wisdom literature' of the Old Testament, along with **Job** and **Proverbs**. Although traditionally **Ecclesiastes** has been attributed to Solomon, it is unlikely that he was the author.

The writer of this book reflects on the variety of human experience and sees God in it all. However, the ways of God are a mystery and we are warned to remember that we are only creatures. We can encounter God, but we cannot control the Lord of the universe. Like much of the 'wisdom literature', **Ecclesiastes** is a book born of realism and a concern to tackle life as it is, not as we would wish it to be.

Sunday September 10   **Ecclesiastes 3.1–8**

GOD IS IN THE WHOLE OF LIFE

Ecclesiastes, with its pessimism and resignation, might seem a strange book to be included in the Bible. Here is no great statement of faith amidst the uncertainties of life, as we might find in some of the **Psalms**; nor do we find in it the dramatic questioning of the book of **Job**. However, it is part of the total witness of the Bible, for its very realism makes us face the realities of life. Here is no gospel, but it does prepare us for the kind of self-examination which enables us to embrace the good news in Jesus.

In the next two weeks we shall look closely at some of the individual themes from today's reading, but first let us note that they are written in pairs, reminding us that there is a tension and rhythm to life's experiences: for example, birth and death; weeping and laughter. God is not only to be found in the good events, with their opportunities for praise; nor is

178

he only to be found in moments of desperation, when we pray in time of trouble. He is God in the whole of life and calls us to find and praise him in everything.

✷ *Fill Thou my life, O Lord my God,*
In every part with praise,
That my whole being may proclaim
Thy being and thy ways.   *Horatius Bonar*

Monday September 11
A TIME TO BE BORN

Today we read the story of the birth of Samuel. Hannah desperately wanted a son and when she and her husband went to the shrine at Shiloh she offered prayer to God.

▶ Now read **1 Samuel 1.9 – 20**.

Hannah's prayer shows us that she recognised that life is a gift of God. God is indeed the source of all life and this awareness requires of us a response in the way we view life. Hannah made a very particular commitment in dedicating Samuel for the service of God. Similarly, if we believe that life is a gift, then there are implications for the way we see our own lives, what we do with them and how we treat other people.

This story also reminds us that, while birth is a beginning, it is not the beginning. The birth of Samuel was preceded by a deep yearning on the part of Hannah and a relationship of love between her and Elkanah which brought Samuel to life. We are made for relationship – with each other and with God. Husband and wife, the baby in the womb of the mother, parent and child – each of these reflects our relationship with God, the giver of life.

✷ *Give thanks for the people whose love brought you into this world, and for the love of God which worked through them and which surrounds you now as the womb of your mother once surrounded you.*

Tuesday September 12   Ecclesiastes 7.1 – 4; 8.6 – 8
A TIME TO DIE

The writer of **Ecclesiastes** brings us face to face with a pre-Christian view of life and death. However, there is still much that we can learn from this writer's attitude.

Verse 2 reminds us that death is the destiny of everyone. We may try to delay the ageing process, we may try to eliminate all risk from our lives, we may try to ignore the fact that the day of our death approaches, but we shall be deluding ourselves. We would be living our lives in a dream without substance, a shadowy world of fantasy rather than the acceptance of years that are the gift of a gracious God.

Verse 8 reminds us that no one has power over the day of their death. Life and death are both mysteries, and death makes us face the meaning of our life on earth. Death is a natural event and a necessary one if others are to live. Christian hope is based not on immortality here in an increasingly crowded world, but life in God through the power of the resurrection of Jesus.

＊ *I'll praise my Maker while I've breath,*
And when my voice is lost in death,
  Praise shall employ my nobler powers. *Isaac Watts*

Wednesday September 13 Isaiah 5.1−7
A TIME TO TEAR DOWN

In this, one of the great parables of the Old Testament, the prophet uses rhetoric to invite the opinion of his audience. Only when they had passed judgement on the 'bad' (wild) grapes were they told that Israel was the vineyard in question.

God had made all the preparations through leaders, prophets, teachers and commandments, but to no avail. God's plan was that his justice and compassion should be reflected in the community life of his people, so that Israel might be a light to the nation. However, instead of finding justice, there was injustice and bloodshed.

Here was a time for breaking down the structures of violence, the systems of injustice that made the rich richer and the poor poorer. Prompted by such verses as these, the Church is called to a prophetic ministry − identifying the sins and seeking to break down the power of evil in the world. What evils are there today which you believe Christians are called to resist and fight?

＊ *Lord, break down those evils within my heart that oppress me and cause me to oppress others. Have mercy on the wilderness of my living that I may know the harvest of your Spirit− 'love, joy, peace, patience, kindness, goodness, faithfulness, gentleness and self-control' (Galatians 5.22−23a).*

Thursday September 14

A TIME TO BUILD

The prophet Amos offered a message of judgement and a call
to repentance. He saw injustice and exploitation in a
community that had been called by God to live a different
kind of life. Yet at the end of the book of **Amos** there is a
looking forward, beyond the judgement, to a time of
prosperity, rebuilding and fullness of living.

▶ Now read **Amos 9.11–15**.

However much we may talk about the judgement of God, the
resisting of evil and the denouncing of injustice, we must
never lose sight of God – the giver of life, the Creator. His will
is that life should be lived to the full, that we should enjoy the
fruits of his earth. God's judgement is not an end in itself – it
has a place in pointing us towards God's hope for creation.
Real hope enables us to see the world as it really is, as well as
giving us a direction for the future. Christian hope is based on
the promises of God, because he has shown us our future in the
resurrection of Jesus Christ.

✳ *What is the place of hope in my life and in the witness of the
Church? Think and pray about this.*

Friday September 15

A TIME TO WEEP

David was told of the death in battle of Saul and Jonathan.
Despite Saul's jealous attempts to kill him, David offered a
most moving lament at the death of this father and son.

▶ Read **2 Samuel 1.17–27**.

David's lament expressed grief; likewise we should never be
afraid of giving expression to our feelings of loss. Indeed,
when we lose someone close to us, it can be dangerous to try
and bottle up our feelings. There is no shame in tears that are
shed over the loss of someone dear, for it is human and it is
right to grieve.

Notice that David's lament distinguished between Saul and
Jonathan. Saul was mentioned for his greatness and the
prosperity that he brought to Israel (verse 24–25a), while
Jonathan was mourned as a friend (verse 26). Sometimes we
mourn the loss of greatness, or of someone who has given us
much. At other times we simply mourn the loss of a friend.

However, let us remember that in all our grieving there is the promise of new life in Jesus Christ.

✴ *Pray for those who have recently lost a loved one, or who are still grieving over the loss of someone close, that they may know the love of God and the peace of Christ.*

Saturday September 16
A TIME TO LAUGH

Many people think that happiness is the most important thing in life, but so often they find themselves chasing an 'elusive butterfly'. As they reach the goals they have set for themselves, they do not find the contentment and joy for which they had hoped.

Metropolitan Anthony Bloom, a great man of prayer, said that happiness, if it has no meaning, can lead to despair. For him the meaning which underpinned deep and true happiness could only be found in God.

▶ Read **Joel 2.21 – 29**.

The prophet Joel prepared the people for a time of rejoicing, but it was all centred around God and his promises (verses 26 – 27). It is in God that we gain the meaning of our rejoicing, as well as receiving hope amidst our despair.

Thanksgiving is a basic attitude for the Christian. We give thanks for creation and the blessings of this life, but above all we give thanks for Jesus Christ. He is *Immanuel* – 'God with us' – and in him we discover the God who comes close to us in our laughter and weeping.

✴ *Thou Christ of hope, thou Door of joy,*
  Golden Sun of hill and mountain,
    All hail! Let there be joy!   *Gaelic, 6th century*

For group discussion and personal thought

Read **Ecclesiastes 3.1 – 8** and the notes for **September 10**. These verses remind us 'that there is a tension and rhythm to life's experiences' (Christopher Ellis). Discuss what this means, using specific examples. Why do we need both positive and negative experiences in life?

Sunday September 17

A TIME TO BE SILENT

In the middle of great, unexplained suffering, Job maintained his innocence and complained to God.

▷ Read in **Job 33.31−33**, what God said.

The meaning of suffering is never explained in the book of **Job**. There is no philosphical or theoretical answer to suffering, but through it there is a meeting with God, the Lord of all. In the presence of the creator God, there is nothing that can be said. Complaints dry up before his greatness and questions cease to have meaning.

We sometimes spend so much time talking that we are unable to listen. Prayer becomes a monologue, with God as the audience. However, if prayer is to be an encounter, then we need to be silent as well, to listen and be still.

▷ Now read **Habakkuk 2.18−20**.

There is no image which does justice to the greatness of God. The prophet was talking about idols, but we could include language, ideas and theological definitions in the same way. There is a need and a right desire to praise God, but when the noise has ceased there must be the silent adoration of the heart.

✳ *Be still in the presence of God. Reflect on his greatness which made the world, and on his love which is closer to you than the air you breathe.*

Monday September 18

A TIME TO SPEAK

▷ First read **Amos 7.7−9**.

This vision of the plumb-line highlights the message of Amos. With a vision of God's truth and the path of justice God wanted his people to walk, the prophet challenged Israel on their performance. They could not plead ignorance, for they had the commandments to lead them in God's way and to help them build a community of justice and peace. Yet they were like a crooked wall, exposed by the simple test of a plumb-line. Here was judgement, but those who were guilty did not want to hear such things. The call to speak out can be a dangerous business.

▷ Now read **Amos 7.10−17**.

Amos had travelled from the southern kingdom of Judah to the north in order to speak out at the royal shrine of Bethel. Then the priest, Amaziah, told him to get back to Judah, calling him a 'seer' – a professional prophet. But Amos replied that he was a shepherd who had heard the call of God and responded. God calls all kinds of people to speak out on his behalf and many suffer imprisonment and death as a result. The word of judgement is never welcomed and the voice of the prophet is one that the unjust always try to silence.

✻ *Pray for those who are imprisoned or threatened because they speak out against injustice.*

Tuesday September 19
A TIME TO LOVE

▶ First read **Song of Songs 8.6 – 7.**

The **Song of Songs** is a marvellous series of love poems and its place within the Bible reminds us that sexual love is a part of being human. These verses tell us of the intensity of love and the bitter-sweet experience of passion. However, human love also points us to that love in which we all may find meaning and new life.

▶ Now read **Ephesians 3.14 – 19.**

Paul prayed that his readers might receive the power of God to strengthen and enrich them in the faith. But this power is no earthly strength – it is the power which comes from Christ dwelling in their hearts. Thus may we be able to grasp the sheer intensity of God's love. We are not simply called to follow the example of a good man, but to participate in the love of God which floods the whole universe, and which is focused in Jesus. Here is the fullness of God and the measure of our true humanity.

✻ *May the mind of Christ my Saviour*
  Live in me from day to day,
By his love and power controlling
  All I do or say.   *Kate B. Wilkinson*

Wednesday September 20   Amos 5.10 – 15
A TIME TO HATE?

The reason for the question mark should be obvious. Of all the aspects of human experience in Ecclesiastes 3.1 – 8, hatred is the one which most sharply challenges us to face the differences between the Old and New Testaments. Or does it? Amos certainly believed that hatred was a valid emotion. The problem with the Israelites was that their hatred was directed at the wrong things – at truth and justice, rather than at evil. Here was a society where the powerful manipulated the courts and exploited the weak. How often do our actions display a hatred of justice and truth, even when our words claim otherwise?

In verse 15, Amos tried to direct the people's hatred to evil, while encouraging them to love goodness and justice. However, we must be careful not to over-simplify these two alternatives – life is more complex than that. We talk about loving the sinner and hating the sin, but sins are manifest in people and hatred is a dangerous word. Much wrong has been done in the name of hating evil – self-righteousness can easily breed violence and then where is love?

✳ *Think about this: 'Justice should always serve love and its helpmate must be forgiveness.'*

Thursday September 21
A TIME FOR WAR?

There can be few issues that divide Christians more sharply than the question of war. In the Old Testament it was not an issue and it is only with the coming of Jesus that a radical challenge is made to our common sense assumptions. As we read the words of Jesus it is important that we apply them to ourselves and not just to others.

▶ Read **Matthew 5.38 – 48**.

The Old Testament law (see Exodus 21.23 – 25) limited the reprisals which had until then often resulted in widespread tribal warfare and family feuding. That limitation led to the idea of punishment as a part of a system of justice rather than as revenge. Jesus took this a stage further and has transformed our relationships by his own example and his invitation for us to follow him. Love, not hatred; service, not domination, are the parents of peace. Yet we must heed the warning that he who invites us to follow also promises us a cross.

✳ *Drop thy still dews of quietness,*
   Till all our strivings cease;
Take from our souls the strain and stress,

> And let our ordered lives confess
>   The beauty of thy peace.   *John Greenleaf Whittier*

Friday September 22
A TIME FOR PEACE

The prophet Isaiah had a vision of Mount Zion, on which the Jerusalem temple was built, becoming a centre for the nations.

▶ Read **Isaiah 2.1 – 4**.

Here is no imperialistic dream which said there will be peace when **our** nation is in control. Rather, we have a vision in which God is at the centre of life, settling disputes. Peace will only come when God is in control – when we walk in his paths; when we stop building weapons of destruction and concentrate our energies on the production of food and other necessary resources; when we stop training for conflict and concern ourselves with justice and peace. What are we able to do for the cause of peace? What relationships can be healed, what priorities need to be changed?

✳ *Ponder upon, and pray slowly, these words of St Francis:*
  Lord, make me an instrument of your peace.
  Where there is hatred, let me sow love;
  Where there is injury, pardon;
  Where there is doubt, faith;
  Where there is despair, hope;
  Where there is darkness, light;
  Where there is sadness, joy.

Saturday September 23
ETERNITY SET IN THE HEARTS OF ALL

After the breadth of human experience held in the tensions of Ecclesiastes 3.2 – 8, the writer makes some general remarks about God and the world, about life and work.

▶ Read **Ecclesiastes 3.9 – 15**.

Reflection on the ways of the world led the writer to comment that, although people chase after attainment, they would do well to make the most of each moment. Ambition can be a healthy drive in the search for fulfilment, but it can also be a runaway beast that drags us headlong. It is foolish to ignore the present in order only to think of the future –

whether that future be the top of the promotion ladder, or retirement.

Ecclesiastes reminds us that although God 'has set eternity in the hearts of men . . . they cannot fathom what God has done from beginning to end' (verse 11). In the middle of our living we can encounter the God who, by his grace, comes close to us. However, we can never contain God by our thinking, or control him by our praying. He is the eternal God, yet we can meet him in Christ – who 'is the same yesterday and today and for ever' (Hebrews 13.8).

✳ *'Thou awakest us to delight in thy praises; for thou madest us for thyself, and our heart is restless, until it repose in thee.' (St Augustine)*

For group discussion and personal thought
There is 'a time to be silent and a time to speak' (**Ecclesiastes 3.7b**, NIV). Consider when it is most helpful to be silent in the presence of others and when it is necessary to speak.

PHILIPPIANS

Notes by Mrs Eileen Jacob

Eileen Jacob has lived in India for over thirty years where she has served as a missionary, taught in a city grammar school and been superintendent of a village hostel for girls. She is now retired and living in Hyderabad, South India.

The notes in this section are based on the New International Version.

During Paul's first visit to Philippi, in the course of his second missionary journey, he and Silas were put in prison. At midnight they praised and sang hymns to God (Acts 16.25). Some years later when Paul was in another prison – probably in Rome, awaiting trial and possible execution – he wrote a letter to the Philippians which breathes the same spirit of praise, joy and thanksgiving.

Philippians reveals a very warm bond of affection between Paul and the Christians in Philippi. They had not only sent a gift to help him but they had also sent one of their number, Epaphroditus, to be with him during his time of detention. Paul wished to thank them for their gift and to send back Epaphroditus who had been seriously ill. He used the opportunity to encourage and strengthen them in their faith.

Suggestion for further reading

The Letters to the Philippians, Colossians and Thessalonians by William Barclay, Daily Study Bible (Saint Andrew Press).

Sunday September 24   **Philippians 1.1–11**

There are times when we can actively and vigorously engage in the service of others who are in need. There are other times when we may be frustrated to find ourselves totally unable to help on account of infirmity or sickness, lack of resources or the pressure of other commitments.

Paul's missionary service involved long and hazardous journeys, action-packed programmes of preaching and teaching, and physical work as a tentmaker. For such a person to be confined to prison could have been a most frustrating and depressing experience. However, instead we find him brimming over with hope and joy. Why was this?

- During his years of active work, Paul had developed the ministry of writing letters to his Christian friends and praying for them. He was able to continue this ministry even in detention.

- Paul knew from his own experiences that nothing could confine the mighty power of God's love. The Lord would continue to work in the lives of Christian converts even when his servant, Paul, could no longer be physically present. What amazing prayers resulted from this confidence (see verses 9–11)!

✳ *Lord, when circumstances seem to cramp and confine me, set my spirit free to rejoice in you and to trust you; and teach me how to serve others through my letters and my prayers.*

Monday September 25   Philippians 1.12–18a

Paul could rejoice that the work of God had not suffered, but rather advanced, because of his imprisonment. Through him a new work had begun in the heart of the Roman empire, among the most prestigious soldiers in the Roman army. Although Paul was living in a private house in Rome, he was chained to one of a succession of detachments of these soldiers. He had used the opportunity to introduce them to Christ.

From the time Paul had encountered Christ on the Damascus road (Acts 9.3–6), it had been his consuming passion to preach Christ crucified. He could therefore rejoice over every proclamation of the gospel, even when he knew it to be motivated by envy or rivalry (verse 15a) in an attempt to undermine his influence while he was in prison. Thus Paul showed true greatness.

We must try to follow Paul's example, for so much of our Christian service is marred by narrowness and petty jealousy. When we turn our eyes away from ourselves and fix them on Jesus and his kingdom, we shall be able to see God at work in and through the most unlikely people and circumstances.

✳ *'The important thing is . . . Christ is preached.' (verse 18)*

Tuesday September 26   Philippians 1.18b–26

Psychologists tell us that one of the ways in which we can

combat our fears is to ask ourselves the question, 'What is the worst thing that could happen?', and then face up to the situation. Paul seems to have been doing something like this in today's reading.

Living as he was in daily expectation of a call to trial, which could result either in his execution or his release, Paul calmly and objectively examined the two possibilities and their respective advantages and disadvantages to himself and to others. Then, from his knowledge of God and his purposes, he concluded that he would be freed. However, what in fact did happen to Paul remains a mystery.

Paul's greatest fear was not that he might be killed, but that he might fail to witness for his Lord, whether by his life or by his death. This letter from prison, like letters written today by prisoners of conscience, may arouse such a fear in us, too. However, in verse 19, when Paul writes of his 'deliverance' (salvation), he assures his readers that whatever happens, it will be for the best. Paul's confidence did not lie in himself, but in the help of the Holy Spirit and the prayers of his Christian friends.

✳ *Again and again Jesus says to us, 'Fear not!'*
  Lord, give me courage to face my fears and, by your perfect love, to cast them out.

Wednesday September 27   Philippians 1.27 – 30

When we recall the circumstances of Paul's first and final visit to Philippi (Acts 16 and 20.6), we realise that the new converts there must have been well aware that in deciding to follow Jesus they were embarking on a road that was likely to lead to opposition and suffering. Paul's teaching to them about the way to meet such experiences echoes that of Jesus in Matthew 5.11–12.

Suffering for the sake of Christ is not to be viewed as a grim duty or as a burden to be borne stoically. Rather, it is to be regarded as a high privilege and joy. Countless Christians, throughout the history of the Church, have proved that this is possible. Their eyes were open to see beyond the temporary suffering to the incomparably greater and eternal glory (2 Corinthians 4.17). Also, however injustly they were treated, they trusted their Lord to vindicate them and uphold their cause (Romans 8.33 – 34). In their trials they experienced a close fellowship with the Lord and all the faithful witnesses of Christ. Let us take courage from their example.

Thursday September 28   **Philippians 2.1–11**

Like many other local congregations, the Philippians faced a
problem of discord and disunity among their members. Paul
prescribed the 'attitude . . . of Christ Jesus', and then quoted
from a magnificent, early Christian hymn on Christ's
humility. The sheer beauty of these words should not blind us
to the stark reality of what it cost Jesus to be our Saviour.

Can we, who find any small reduction in our standard of
living or adaptation to a different culture so difficult, begin to
imagine what it meant for Jesus to leave the glory of heaven's
perfection to become one with us in our sin and suffering? Can
we, like him, identify not only with the victims of violence,
prejudice, ignorance and injustice, but also with their
perpetrators? Can we continue to show compassion and
concern for people in all their desperate needs of body, mind
and spirit, even when they press upon us to the extent that we
are jostled, have no time for meals, must sacrifice family life,
or are interrupted when we plan a time of quiet with our
friends?

Through it all, will we never become bitter or disillusioned,
never resort to self-assertion or relax into self-satisfaction,
but quietly and faithfully accept and do the Father's will?

* *Lord, help me to empty myself so that you can fill me with
yourself.*

Friday September 29   **Philippians 2.12–18**

During the sweltering heat of summer in India one of the
great joys is to sleep outside or on the flat roof of one's house,
with the cloudless canopy of the night sky above lit by
millions of stars shining as bright as diamonds. All the day's
weariness falls away as one's spirit soars into that mystery of
serenity and peace.

For thousands of years the stars have guided travellers by
land and ships at sea, bringing them safely to the end of their
journey. A star led the wise men of the east to the infant
Christ. As Christians, we are to shine in the darkness of the

world so that the weary are refreshed, the wanderer guided home and the learned brought in humility to worship God.

All this sounds very grand. However, in practice, it means that in the nitty-gritty of daily life we are to obey the Lord, not slavishly but joyfully, making his will and purposes ours. That which God works into us of himself, we are to work out in the circumstances of our lives each day.

✻ *I am like unpolished brass, Lord — dull and lifeless. Use the frictions of my daily life to remove the tarnish and stain until I reflect fully the brightness of your glory.*

Saturday September 30   Philippians 2.19 – 24

Paul invited Timothy to join him, during his second missionary journey (Acts 16.1 – 3). Being the child of a mixed marriage, Timothy benefited both from the religious upbringing of his Jewish mother and grandmother and from the education and culture of his Greek father. This enabled him to move with ease among both Jews and Gentiles as he travelled with Paul to evangelise and establish churches in the strategic centres of the Roman world. Paul often spoke of Timothy as his son and there was obviously a very close bond of understanding and affection between them.

For his part, Timothy proved a model disciple and messenger. Sharing Paul's arduous journeys, his persecutions and imprisonments, Timothy also came to share his mind and spirit. He was as concerned for the welfare of the churches as Paul was, and as ready to suffer in order to serve them. He was so trustworthy and reliable that Paul could entrust him even with the most delicate missions. Further, he was happy to work under Paul's leadership without jealousy or self-assertion.

✻ *Lord Jesus Christ, help me, like Timothy, to truly share your interests so that I may be your loyal co-worker and messenger.*

For group discussion and personal thought

Read **Philippians 2.12 – 16**. What did Paul mean when he wrote that 'it is God who works in you' (verse 13)? How is God at work in **our** lives? How do we, and how could we further, co-operate with God?

Sunday October 1 **Philippians 2.25 – 30**

It was brave of Epaphroditus to go, on behalf of the Philippian church, to do what he could to help Paul while he was under detention, and to give him the comfort and encouragement of Christian companionship. To identify himself with a prisoner, who was facing a capital charge, would certainly involve a personal risk.

While Epaphroditus was with Paul he had fallen seriously ill and nearly died. After he had recovered, Paul wanted to send him back home to relieve the fears of those who would be anxiously awaiting news of him. But since the church, which had sent Epaphroditus, had not recalled him, Paul was anxious that he should be well received and not accused of quitting. So he wrote this glowing reference for him, appreciating all he had done to help him in his trouble, and especially his courage in risking his life in order to fulfil the commission which the Philippian church had entrusted to him.

Appreciation of the services of others – especially of those who are in a subordinate position – is a sign of true greatness. It is all too rare.

✳ *Recall incidents in the life of Jesus when he expressed appreciation and approval of others. When did we last voice that kind of praise to a friend or fellow-worker?*

Monday October 2

From writings of Paul, such as Romans 9.1–5, we realise what an intense longing he had that all his fellow-Jews should accept the gospel of Christ. He had once shared their misconceptions – relying on their status as the covenant people, on their righteousness as upholders of God's law, and on circumcision which distinguished them from the Gentile 'dogs'. However, after his conversion, he prayerfully yearned that, like him, they might come into the light of Christ and salvation through him alone.

However, in spite of his deep love for the Jews, he saw that their teaching posed a grave threat to the young churches. So he had to oppose them fiercely and warn the Christians, who were still young in the faith, against their doctrines.

▶ Read **Philippians 3.1–6**.

Heretics and false teachers have appeared throughout

Church history and are with us today. At times terrible deeds
have been done by those who thought they were defending the
truth and serving God by opposing erroneous teachers. At
other times, or in other places, the Church has been careless
of the dangers such false teachers represented and has
allowed the faith of many to be destroyed and the witness of
the Church to be weakened by failing to oppose them.

✳ *In upholding truth may we never abandon love;*
In showing love may we never forsake truth.

Tuesday October 3   Philippians 3.7–11

No one can possess the pearl of great value (Matthew
13.45–46) unless they are willing first to let go of everything
they previously regarded as precious. God cannot pour out his
blessings upon us unless we come to him with empty hands.
However, our hands are forever clutching at things which will
boost our egos – we pride ourselves on our race, nationality,
education or professional accomplishments; our looks or our
temperament; our property or possessions; even our religion
or our social service. All of these are temporary gifts of God to
be used by us as good stewards, for his glory. As we pass
through the gateway of death we have to surrender them all
again to God. What will then remain?

Have we really understood the words of Jesus: 'Apart from
me you can do nothing' (John 15.5b)? Harriet Auber wrote:

And every virtue we possess,
  And every victory won,
And every thought of holiness,
  Are his alone.

Anything we offer to God, we have first received from him;
and we always gain far more than we give.

✳ *Open our eyes, Lord, to see what is worth possessing.*

Wednesday October 4

Once when I was travelling by train in India there was a
jockey in the compartment. I was amazed that, in order to
keep down his weight, throughout that long journey he ate
only a bag of ground-nuts (peanuts). The willingness of
athletes and sportsmen to accept the rigours of training, and
their complete commitment to what they set out to achieve,

are an example to us. For us the Christian life, as Paul reminds us, is like a race to be run.

▶ Read **Philippians 3.12 – 16**.

For those who accept the glorious gospel that salvation is by faith alone, received into our empty hands as the gracious, undeserved and free gift of God, there is a great danger. If Christ has done everything needed, can we not relax? Sure of our acceptance with God can we not do as we please, and take it easy? On the contrary! The paradox is that to become disciples, to enter into our inheritance, we have to go flat out for the finishing tape. No past successes should cause us to rest on our laurels – no previous failures or fear of future ones need discourage us. All the strenuous effort of pressing on towards the goal is abundantly worthwhile.

✳ *Remember that the Christian life is like riding a bicycle – either you keep moving forward or you fall off!*

Thursday October 5

The picture of the Christian life as a race, which we looked at yesterday, is not a perfect analogy. There is no element of competition since all who complete the race receive the same prize, and every person is as concerned for the progress of others as for their own. Everyone has a large influence, for good or ill, on those about them, and one of the important lessons we have to learn is to choose as our models those who are doing well in the race.

▶ Read **Philippians 3.17 to 4.1**.

Philippi was a Roman colony. Such colonies were places of strategic importance where veteran soldiers had been settled with their families to help keep the peace in the far-flung empire. Each colony was linked by excellent roads to its neighbours and, in time of crisis, military reinforcements could quickly be summoned. The people in such colonies were more 'Roman' than the Romans, most meticulously keeping the language, dress, customs, titles and ceremonies of the capital. Probably the greatest joy in life for them would be a visit from the emperor. What a marvellously evocative picture this is of 'our citizenship of heaven' (verse 20) and our Christian position in relation to the world!

✳ *Jesus said of his disciples, 'They are not of the world, even as I am not of it' (John 17.16). Ponder on these words.*

For two oxen to pull an agricultural implement or cart satisfactorily, they need not only to be fully under the control of their human master but also in accord with one another. In the Church, we may find ourselves yoked together with unlikely partners but, as we yield to our Master's direction, we can work together harmoniously. There is no place for total individualism in the body of Christ.

Perfect submission to the Lord will also bring us security. When we hand over our lives to him, his peace will stand guard like a Roman sentry over our hearts and minds. Then no anxious, untrue, ignoble, evil, impure, or ugly thoughts can gain entry. What a wonderfully comforting and encouraging picture this is! The power of evil in the world around us often seems so great, and corrupt influences that mock and undermine our faith so subtle that, left to ourselves, we feel we shall be easily destroyed. We are so weak and vulnerable – but praise God we are never left to ourselves!

✱ *The soul that on Jesus hath leaned for repose*
He will not, he cannot, desert to its foes;
That soul, though all hell should endeavour to shake,
He never will leave, he will never forsake.   Richard Keen

A person who has been in love will know what ecstasy lies in the knowledge that they are loved by the beloved one. Enormous value is placed on the most trivial token of that love. The preciousness of any gift always depends on the degree of love it conveys and not on its market value.

The Philippians had rejoiced Paul's heart by sending him gifts which showed their continuing care and concern for him. But he was dependent neither on the articles, nor even on their love, for he was already full to overflowing with the love of God in Christ.

To be filled is to be set free from the voracious hunger for love with which we are all born – set free to love ourselves and others. We can now be perfectly content for we have everything we need in Christ Jesus.

Is it not true that all the troubles in the world spring from the unsatisfied hunger of human hearts for God's love?

✱ *Jesus said, 'I am the bread of life. He who comes to me will never go hungry.' (John 6.35)*

For group discussion and personal thought

Paul's letter to the Philippians has been called 'The Epistle of Joy'. Look again at Paul's many references to 'joy' and 'rejoicing' in **Philippians**. What are the characteristics of true joy? To what extent is 'joy' an essential part of the Christian life? List the reasons you have for rejoicing in your church today.

JONAH

Notes by the Revd Michael J. Cleaves, BA, BD

The notes in this section are based on the Revised Standard Version.

After the Jews returned from exile in Babylon, they became increasingly exclusive, believing that God cared only for them. The book of **Jonah** was probably a protest against this exclusive attitude. Written in the form of a parable, it shows that the God of the Jews was also the God of the Gentiles. More importantly, it shows that God is a loving, merciful God who is ready to forgive and save all those who truly repent.

Suggestion for further reading

The Twelve Prophets Volume 1 (Hosea, Joel, Amos, Obadiah and Jonah) by Peter C. Craigie, Daily Study Bible (Saint Andrew Press).

Sunday October 8 — Jonah 1.1–6

Jonah was hardly a heroic figure, but from this very human character we have much to learn. Faced with the terrifying responsibility of being God's prophet, Jonah turned and fled. He had no intention of risking his life by going to the city of Nineveh. Instead, he aimed at putting as much distance as he could between himself and God.

However, Jonah was soon to realise that he could not get away from God. Even far-off Tarshish, which was probably in the west Mediterranean and represented the farthest distance from his country by sea, would not be far enough.

There are times in our lives when we, too, want to escape from our responsibilities. Even today some people literally try to run away. For example, in East Germany recently, Christian youth leaders have been worried by what they call 'the flight to the West'. Many young people there are attracted by the freedom, life-style and affluence of the West and tend not to care about the country in which they live.

Most of us, however, avoid our responsibilities in more subtle ways. Perhaps we busy ourselves with tasks which we find enjoyable and neglect the rest; or perhaps we ignore our responsibilities because of an underlying fear. But the story of

Jonah shows us very clearly that we cannot run away from our responsibilities, nor from God.

✳ *Pray for help and courage to face up to your responsibilities.*

Monday October 9

There is something fascinating, and at the same time terrifying, about the sea. If you stand on the shore and watch the endless restlessness of the waves, there is a quality of eternity in it; but its mood and nature can quickly change. The Jews had a great fear of the sea; they believed it was a powerful evil force to be resisted.

▶ Read **Jonah 1.7–17**.

In these verses the author contrasts the fear and cowardice of Jonah with the genuine response in faith of the Gentile seamen. Their response reminds us of the way many people discover faith in God for the first time – they find him quite unexpectedly. Furthermore, these seamen were concerned for Jonah's welfare even though he appeared to be the cause of their distress. For those who believe in God, faith and compassion must always go hand in hand.

Jonah soon learned that there was no place where he could hide from God. God was even with him in the sea! God is the Lord of every part of our lives, wherever we are. We believe that he is in control of our lives and we must open ourselves to his guidance and call.

✳ *O God, help me to see that you must be Lord of all my life.*

Tuesday October 10

When people experience a calamity in their lives a common reaction is to say, 'The only thing to do now is to pray.' Although this is often the desperate cry of the normally unreligious, believers can be prone to such reactions as well. Jonah was no exception when he sought deliverance from his awful predicament.

▶ Read **Jonah 2.1–10**.

This is one of the great prayer-psalms of the Old Testament, and provides us with a good example of the process of prayer:
- a sense of being a long way from God (verse 4);
- genuine remorse and a renewed faith in the God who hears (verse 7);

- joyful thanksgiving for the mercy of God and proclamation of his love (verse 9).

By all appearances Jonah's fate was sealed and there was no hope of rescue. Perhaps only those who have gone through a deep experience of hopelessness are able to understand the anguish of Jonah's cry.

While Jonah was delivered from his predicament, we must not be so simplistic as to expect immediate deliverance from all our difficult situations. Often our prayers seem to be unanswered, especially in times of prolonged suffering. And yet, those who have cried out to God from these depths of despair can bear witness to God's answering love.

✳ *Prayer is the soul's sincere desire,*
Uttered or unexpressed.   James Montgomery

Wednesday October 11

We live in a world with a vast number of huge, growing cities. London was the largest for many decades, but several have now overtaken it including developing mega-cities such as Tokyo, São Paulo and Mexico City. This is a graphic illustration of the urban expansion of the twentieth century.

For a long time the Church has realised the particular problems of sustaining religious life in the large cities. Generations of people have lived with poverty and unemployment, and have felt excluded from many aspects of society — including the Church. 'Faith in the city' — the theme of much recent theological reflection in Britain — contains a hopeful note.

▶ Read **Jonah 3.1–5**.

The city of Nineveh, to which Jonah went, was huge. It was a metropolis of its day with a great population, but in God's eyes it was full of wickedness (Jonah 1.2). Jonah arrived there and preached God's warning message. Much to Jonah's astonishment the people of Nineveh were transformed by his words. The reluctant prophet was a great success.

We can learn much from this hesitant prophet whom God used effectively. If we feel inadequate when we are confronted by a seemingly hopeless task, we can be encouraged by the response of the Ninevites to Jonah.

✳ *The word of God is able to bring about change in situations which seem hopeless. Think about this.*

Thursday October 12

Today we are surprised when we hear of national leaders actively incorporating their religious beliefs with affairs of state. However, in Jonah's time, political and religious matters were not separated.

▶ Read **Jonah 3.6–10**.

The king of Nineveh could have been expected to react with alarm and anger at the arrival of this stranger, Jonah, in his city. Jonah could have presented a dangerous threat to the king's power over his people, and no doubt the king could have removed Jonah from the scene quickly and permanently. But this did not happen. On the contrary, the king reacted in a similar way to the people, and ordered everyone to fast and wear sackcloth.

When God saw this genuine sign of repentance he revoked his judgement of the city. God's judgement is always combined with mercy, for he longs to be in relationship with all those he has created.

It often takes the threat of a calamitous event to remind us of our human frailty and vulnerability – a near-miss car accident teaches us to be more alert and careful. While God is patient and is ready to forgive us, it is far better always to live according to his way.

✳ *Lord, help me to trust you especially when I am fearful.*

Friday October 13   Jonah 4.1–5

These verses make us wonder whether Jonah would have ever been satisfied. By the end of chapter 3, God had done what he had wanted to do – change the hearts of the Ninevites. But this did not satisfy Jonah and he vented his anger on God. Why?

We now recognise that **Jonah** was written for a special purpose. In the story of the storm and of the Ninevites the author has shown that God is the God of all creation and all nations. Thus the message to the exclusive-minded Jews was clear – Yahweh is the God of Israel, but he also shows his love and mercy to the whole world. Jonah's irritation that the Ninevites actually repented, and so did not suffer destruction, clearly indicated his underlying hostility to the Gentiles. If he knew, as he claimed, that God was merciful (see verse 2), then he should no longer have been a narrow-minded Jew.

Here is a vital lesson for us. Many people now live in communities that are both multi-racial and multi-faith. As

Christians we are called to get to know our neighbours, whether they are Buddhists, Hindus, Jews, Muslims, Sikhs or of any other faith. We can only do this from the standpoint of mutual respect. Arrogant, prejudiced Christians cannot hope to show Christ to the world. The gospel is for **all** people and we must be prepared to show this in all we do and say.

✳ *Lord, help me to see you in the face of my friend, in the loving spirit of my neighbour, and in the care-full actions of all people.*

Saturday October 14

Jonah, disappointed with God's attitude to the Ninevites, waited to see what would happen in the city, no doubt expecting to be proved right about the sinful people there. Instead, he became obsessed with a plant that sprang up to give him shade.

▶ Read **Jonah 4.6–11**.

A friend of mine thought he had a prize leek. He had grown it from seed and nurtured it to prime condition for a show. Then one morning he found that a neighbour's dog had trampled on it and it was useless. Probably we all have had things that were the centre of our lives for a time. Often material possessions are important to us because they are the fruits of our labours. But what are the really important things in life?

The story of Jonah shows us that people, not things, are important. The lives of 120,000 people in Nineveh were infinitely more valuable than Jonah's 'pet' plant. Jonah's petulance and anger (see verse 9) were in stark contrast to God's pity for Nineveh.

In the end, **Jonah** is not about a great fish, a shipwreck, the plight of a reluctant prophet or a vast city. Rather, it is about the **sovereignty** of God and the power of his message – of repentance and a new life – which changes people's lives.

✳ *Lord, give us a vision for the extension of your kingdom through all the world.*

For group discussion and personal thought

Read **Jonah 4.1–4**. Why was Jonah angry when the people of Nineveh repented? Contrast his attitude with that of Jesus towards repentant sinners, and consider how we can overcome the temptation to feel as Jonah did.

THE GOSPEL OF THE KINGDOM

Luke 10–19

Notes by the Revd H. Graham Fisher, BA

Graham Fisher is a Baptist minister who has spent many years as a lecturer at colleges of further education.

The notes in this section are based on the Good News Bible.

In this third and last section of readings from **Luke's Gospel**, we shall be looking at the events and teaching of Jesus during the time between the end of his Galilean ministry and his arrival in Jerusalem on Palm Sunday. In these chapters there is a great emphasis on the **kingdom of God** – how we can enter it and what it means to belong to it.

With a clear vision of the universal outreach of the kingdom of God, the Gospel writer understood that the new world of love and peace, for which Christ died, would not come about through social reform or political change. It would be created only through the transformed lives of people who lived according to the values and priorities of the kingdom of God.

Suggestions for further reading – see page 17.

Sunday October 15   Luke 10.1–12

The keynote of today's reading is urgency. Acceptance or rejection of the announcement of God's kingdom is so important that heralds of the good news must in no way be distracted from their vital mission.

During a national election campaign, prominent political issues are debated daily. Usually the politicians who present their case with greatest effect are those who have the strongest convictions and the clearest minds.

Jesus required such people to present the case for his kingdom. His words, 'The kingdom of God has come near you' (verse 11), were to indicate that the love and power of the living God had been present in the lives of people energised by his Spirit – people who spoke with authority because of the transformation in their own lives.

Today, there is still a 'large harvest, but few workers to gather it in' (verse 2). It remains a colossal task to win the whole world for God, and the need, as ever, is urgent. As messengers of the kingdom today, like the first pioneers, we should not be turned aside from our charge by enticements of any kind.

✱ *Lord, help me to speak your word with love and power.*

Monday October 16 **Luke 10.13 – 24**

The men engaged in this first evangelistic campaign were greatly privileged – chosen, commissioned and counselled by Jesus himself. They did not let him down, but returned in jubilant mood to tell their success stories.

Many of us will remember special events when it seemed that the power of God was clearly at work – a rally, a campaign or an exceptional conference. It is easy to recall the sense of expectation, the stirring addresses and the stimulating comradeship. Perhaps some of our friends, or we ourselves, entered into a new experience of Jesus Christ. At such times the kingdom of God comes near.

For all such highlights of experience we may be truly grateful, but Jesus points to a yet more stable and lasting source of joy and gratitude. Meetings and rallies, however colourful and impressive, come and go. All evangelistic achievement is but the means to the glorious end – God's reign over all the world. The most refreshing and satisfying spring of gladness must always be the certainty that God loves us, forgives us through Christ, and reserves for us a place in his everlasting kingdom.

✱ *This glorious hope revives*
Our courage by the way,
While each in expectation lives,
And longs to see the day. *John Fawcett*

Tuesday October 17 **Luke 10.25 – 37**

In our enthusiasm to commend the caring attention of the Samaritan in the parable (verses 30 – 37), in contrast to the selfish indifference of the two religious officials, it is easy to overlook a further truth revealed by the question, 'Who is my neighbour?'

For the teacher of the law, this was an important question, partly because lawyers like to define their terms precisely, but also because he may have sensed a threat to his established ideas. Strict Jews would not acknowledge that any non-Jew was a neighbour. The answer Jesus gave in his story of the good Samaritan turned the original enquiry right round, for he really replied to the question, 'How can I be a neighbour?' The response was a rebuke and challenge both to his questioner and to ourselves.

We, too, can be very 'choosy' about our neighbours – where we sit, where we live, with whom we eat, play and worship. The result is widespread social, racial and religious separation. The story of the good Samaritan is, therefore, an answer not only to the lawyer's question, but also a challenge to the countless divisions that spoil our world.

✳ *Help me, Lord, to be a good neighbour, and so create friendship and peace in a divided world.*

Wednesday October 18   Luke 10.38 – 42

People rally to the support of either Martha or Mary according to their sympathies. William Barclay believed that, in religion, we have never allowed enough for the place of temperament. It is, indeed, true that while some are naturally active and practical, others are reflective and quiet. Mary and Martha both loved Jesus, but they expressed that love in different ways.

Nevertheless, Jesus did establish an essential priority, of which not only individuals but also the whole Church should take heed. Communion with God, close friendship with Jesus and a sensitive listening to the whispers of the Holy Spirit should always take first place. Without this central grace, practical service, however well-meaning, may become strained, fussy, and even materialistic. Jesus drove the traders – probably religious men – from the temple, proclaiming that God's house should be a place of prayer (Luke 19.45 – 46). Some activities in the Church today may well deserve a similar rebuke!

Mary chose 'the right thing' (verse 42). Perhaps her time with Jesus was followed by truly loving service.

✸ *Jesus said: 'Whoever lives in me and I in him shall produce a large crop of fruit.' (part of John 15.5, LB)*

Thursday October 19   Luke 11.5 – 13

We learn from today's reading that God gives generously to those who persistently ask. Unlike the reluctant neighbour (verse 7), he is far more open-handed than even the kindest parent. Why, we may ask, does the Gospel writer single out the Holy Spirit from all the other 'good things' that the Father bestows? Clearly he believes the Spirit to be not only the most desirable, but an essential, gift. The modern housewife desires certain gadgets for her kitchen. Yet the most desirable commodity of all is a constant supply of electricity. It is essential if these gadgets are to work.

The Holy Spirit is the 'electricity' of the Christian life, and is essential if all the good gifts of God are to be fully enjoyed. Energised by the Spirit of God, thoughts are illuminated, words are charged with meaning and actions become creative.

Jesus instructed his friends to 'wait for the gift' his Father had promised (Acts 1.4). They obeyed and waited, and the Spirit was given – in a most unexpected way (Acts 2.1 – 4). We, too, as we ask for the Spirit, should be ready for surprises!

✸ *'Those who look to the Lord will win new strength.'*
(Isaiah 40.31a, NEB)

Friday October 20   Luke 11.14 – 26

'The expulsive power of a higher affection' has been the phrase used by psychologists to mean that one emotion stronger than another can predominate in controlling a person's actions. For instance, a mother who is normally afraid of bulls, will readily go among them if her child is in danger. Love, in this case, drives out fear.

Jesus teaches the same truth, stressing that it is not enough to banish evil thoughts and wrong desires – the greater power of God must take their place. A preacher, visiting a prison, told the inmates that he would not try to reform them. There were sighs of relief – but he went on to say that the message he brought would **transform** them. He shared with them the good news that their lives could be completely changed through the love of God and the power of the Holy Spirit.

A moral clean-up is not enough, either for the criminal or for ourselves. Paul wrote to his friends in Rome: 'Let God transform you inwardly by a complete change of your mind' (Romans 12.2). Pride, selfishness, hate, greed and lust can be overcome only by the indwelling Spirit of Jesus.

✻ *Lord, help me to drive all sin out of my life by the power of your Spirit.*

Saturday October 21   Luke 11.27 – 36

In the apparently unconnected sections of today's reading, it is possible to discern the word of God as the uniting idea.

- **The word requires obedience.** Verse 28 reminds us that the Father of all humankind, in his love for his children, expects obedience from them. The need for obedience is emphasised strongly throughout the Old and New Testaments. Jesus himself made it clear that the blessings of the kingdom are only for those who do the Father's will (Matthew 7.21).
- **The Word who became a human being . . .'** (John 1.14). Jesus Christ not only spoke the word of God; he was the Word of God. Greater than all his illustrious predecessors, Jesus himself was the most powerful and appealing way in which God had revealed himself to the world.
- **The word of God is the light of life.** The psalmist declared: 'Your word is a lamp to guide me and a light for my path' (Psalm 119.105). We are indeed illuminated by the Scriptures and by the word of God conveyed in other ways. Yet, best of all, Jesus himself, 'the light of the world' (John 8.12), makes his home in our hearts through the indwelling of the Holy Spirit.

✻ *Lord, thy word abideth,*
  And our footsteps guideth.   *Henry W. Baker*

For group discussion and personal thought

Study Jesus' parable of the good Samaritan in **Luke 10.25 – 37**. How would you answer the question, 'Who is my neighbour?' In what ways can we be better neighbours (a) as individuals and (b) in our churches?

- Have you remembered to send your gift in response to the **International Appeal** (see page 177)?

- October 22 – 29 is the **Week of Prayer for World Peace** (One World Week). During this week the daily prayers reflect this theme.

Sunday October 22   **Luke 11.37 – 51**

Jesus was fiercely critical of all unreality and sham. The teachers of the law and the Pharisees were punctiliously careful about the outward observance of regulations, but lacked the spirit of love and service which their law required. By contrast – on another occasion – Jesus commended the behaviour of children. Although sometimes cheeky, disobedient and difficult, on the whole, children are honest, genuine, natural and full of life – qualities essential for entering the kingdom of heaven (see Matthew 18.3).

In today's world, evil and corruption are still masked by respectability. Sometimes we read of eminent people – politicians, judges, doctors, financial experts, and even clergy – whose serious misdemeanours have come to light. Nearer at hand, we are aware that the superficial 'niceness' of our acquaintances may conceal feelings of mistrust or dislike.

For us, as Christians, it is humbling to observe that those whom Jesus censured were religious people. We are warned that religious profession without its practice may be the most deceptive cloak of all. However, the real Christian will often attract others to the faith through friendliness, a natural warmth and a sense of fun.

✳ *Lord, help me to create peace by being warm and friendly.*

Monday October 23   **Luke 11.52 to 12.7**

John Knox, the famous Scottish preacher, said that he feared God so much that he never feared the face of man. In the concern of Christian people to emphasise the love of God, there has been a tendency to minimise the element of fear in our faith. Yet, in today's reading, Jesus strongly accentuates this aspect of belief. We may prefer the word 'reverence' to the word 'fear', but we should remember that true reverence includes a sense of profound respect, an awareness of being in the presence of One who is infinitely wonderful and holy.

Jesus contrasts people's limited capacity to inflict harm with God's unlimited power to control our eternal destiny. Only a due sense of fear or reverence in our relationship with such a God will make possible the full appreciation of his tender care. It is characteristic of Jesus that he should speak in one sentence of the awesome power of the Creator, and, then immediately follow it with words about the heavenly Father's loving care for his people (verses 5 – 7).

'The fear of the Lord is the beginning of knowledge' (Proverbs 1.7, NEB) and this beginning will lead us to 'the knowledge of God's glory shining in the face of Christ' (2 Corinthians 4.6).

✳ *Pray that fear of the Lord may lead to the knowledge of peace.*

Tuesday October 24   Luke 12.8 – 21

Both sections of today's reading speak of the value of our spiritual resources. In times of difficulty and persecution, the guidance and help of the Holy Spirit is promised (verses 11 – 12. Also, it is made clear that, throughout life, true riches lie, not in material things, but in a trusting relationship with God.

Sometimes these riches are discovered in unexpected, and certainly unchosen, ways. For example: a man, who had no faith in God, was involved in a car accident. Both his legs were badly injured and he was permanently confined to bed. Yet, through this apparent tragedy, the man found God – and peace. He became a radiant Christian. When a visitor went to see him, intending to pass on some encouragement and cheer, it was the visitor who was cheered! A happy smile, jokes galore and a well-used Bible, all proclaimed that this man was rich in faith.

People living in prosperity and affluence are warned by Jesus (verses 16 – 20) of the perils of selfishness and greed. Those in situations of poverty and need are assured that it is the 'rich in God's sight' who are truly blessed (verse 21).

✳ *Lord, may we learn, through giving and sharing, the way of real peace.*

Wednesday October 25   Luke 12.22 – 34

Food, clothes, physical appearance and satisfaction – these, said Jesus, are the things 'the pagans of this world are always concerned about' (verse 30). How easy it is to apply this statement of Jesus to the attitudes and obsessions of the present day! An item of television news revealed that, on

American Independence Day, so many millions of hamburgers were consumed that they would have stretched right around the globe!

However, Jesus addressed his words, not to 'pagans', but to his closest followers. **They** must not be absorbed in material things; **they** must 'be concerned above everything else with the kingdom of God' (Matthew 6.33). To be called a 'disciple', a 'believer' or a 'Christian' may sound virtuous; but it does not, of itself, set a person free from the lures and temptations of materialistic thinking.

In our hearts, we all know what are the things – or people – upon which we set our minds. Have we got **our** priorities right? Is the kingdom of God at the top of **our** list? If not, we should think, pray, repent and obey until it is.

✳ *Lord, help me to make the kingdom of God my primary concern and so discover the 'righteousness, peace, and joy which the Holy Spirit gives' (Romans 14.17).*

Thursday October 26

Two monks were playing chess. During a pause in the game, the conversation went something like this:

Brother James What would you do, brother Stephen, if you knew the Lord would return tonight?

Brother Stephen *(flustered)* Oh! – I expect I would hurry to my cell, confess my sins, and pray. What would you do?

Brother James *(smiling)* Well, I would go on playing chess – if I could find someone else to play with!

▶ Now read **Luke 12.35 – 48**.

The possibility of meeting our Lord suddenly might happen in one of two ways: if he should return, and no one knows when that will happen (see Matthew 24.36); or, if we should die. Jesus teaches that, however it happens, whether suddenly or not, we should be ready. Brother James felt quite ready and was not worried.

Whenever we are summoned into the presence of God, we shall be on our own. There will be no one else to blame or bear the responsibility. The white light of judgement will shine upon each person alone. As Paul wrote to his friends in Rome, 'Every one of us, then, will have to give an account of himself to God' (Romans 14.12).

✳ *Lord, help me to create peace, because I am at peace with you.*

Friday October 27

The theme of judgement, whether we like it or not, features prominently in Christian teaching. The necessity for God's judgement arises from the presence of sin in our world, sin which only Christ's sacrifice could take away.

▶ Read **Luke 12.49 – 59**.

Here Jesus indicates the cost of the way he was destined to take (verse 50). Human sin is to be judged, but that judgement would fall upon the sinless Son of God himself. Yet, Jesus does not dwell upon his own sufferings. He predicts the effect of this judgement upon succeeding generations. Some will gratefully accept the miraculous delivery from guilt which his death makes possible; others will criticise and oppose those who do. In this way, many conflicts and divisions will be caused, not least in family life.

A business man in an English city was greatly incensed when his elder son, also a promising executive, became a Christian. Deprived of his inheritance, the son found himself in a wilderness of family antagonism and distrust. Loyalty to Jesus, whatever the cost, comes first.

✳ *Drawn to the cross which thou hast blessed*
With healing gifts for souls distressed,
To find in thee my life, my rest,
Christ crucified, I come!   *Genevieve M. Irons*

Saturday October 28   Luke 13.1 – 9

Today's reading accentuates two essential requirements of the gospel message:

● Repentance for past sins, and a turning from them.
● Fruitfulness for the future, a life energised and directed by the Spirit of God.

It is all too easy for us to be concerned about other people's sins. Jesus makes the challenge personal and direct: 'If you do not turn from **your** sins . . .' (verse 5).

The pattern for the true Christian life has always been that repentance should pave the way for fruitfulness. Genuine sorrow for past sinfulness is followed by deep gratitude to God for his forgiveness through Jesus Christ, and a new life characterised by love and service. This was the way for Saint Augustine, who turned from being a dissolute unbeliever to follow Christ whole-heartedly, and greatly influenced the Church.

Similarly, when William Carey was led to Christ through a fellow shoemaker apprentice, he turned from lying, swearing and cheating to a life of conspicuous fruitfulness. He became a distinguished missionary in India and founded the Baptist Missionary Society.

What about ourselves — how fruitful are we?

✳ *Lord, help me to bear the fruits of love and joy, and so create a climate in which peace may spread and grow.*

For group discussion and personal thought

What did Jesus mean when he said, 'Seek his (God's) kingdom, and these things shall be yours as well' (**Luke 12.31**, RSV)? Look carefully at the whole of **Luke 12.22 – 31**, and then discuss what verse 31 means for us today.

Sunday October 29   **Luke 13.10 – 17**

Leslie Weatherhead said that official religion has always been the greatest enemy of the kingdom of heaven. In today's reading, we see a strong attempt by a zealous religious official to prevent one person from entering the kingdom.

Whatever the cause of the woman's affliction, the resulting condition was certainly evil. The pain, misery and restriction she was suffering cried out for the kingdom of health, happiness and freedom. Jesus knew that her pitiful state demanded immediate action; he did not put off until tomorrow — which would have pleased his critics — the good possible today.

A district nurse was reproved by her minister for frequent absences from church. He should have known better. She could not regularly attend her place of worship because she was taking health, comfort and cheer to house-bound patients. We keep the Sabbath day holy by doing the caring, creative will of God.

It is possible to be very religious, to be seen often in church, and yet to lack the humanity, understanding and love which the law of God requires.

✳ *Lord, help me to generate peace by doing your will and working for your kingdom.*

Jesus often turned a hypothetical question into a direct
challenge. Here, disregarding the statistics of salvation (verse
23), he confronted his questioner with his real need – to find
the way into the kingdom. The Greek word, translated 'do
your best' (verse 24) also means 'struggle', and is the word
from which the English word, 'agonise', is derived.

The kingdom of God, growing from small beginnings, is
destined to affect the whole world. It is open to everyone,
without exception. Yet, no one should be over-confident of
finding a place in it. The 'struggle' is not that of 'trying to be
good'. Rather, it is the pain of conviction of sin and
repentance, and the cost of continued obedience.

There will, no doubt, be surprises when the guests for the
'feast in the kingdom' become known. The poet, James Leigh
Hunt, wrote of a certain Abou Ben Adhem who, in a dream,
saw an angel compiling a roll of honour. Conscious of his lowly
state and limited achievements, he could only ask, 'Write me
as one that loves his fellow-men.' The next night, names on
the roll were revealed, 'And lo! Ben Adhem's name led all the
rest'.

✷ *'Make love your aim.' (1 Corinthians 14.1, RSV)*

Tuesday October 31   **Luke 13.31 – 35**

It is ironic that Jerusalem – the centre of Jewish faith, with its
temple, the heart of Jewish worship – should be castigated as
the place where the messengers of God were persecuted and
killed. It is unspeakably tragic that the Jews themselves,
God's chosen people, should have rejected and murdered his
Son.

Yet Jesus loved Jerusalem with a deep and warm affection.
He longed for her people to turn to God and to find in him the
peace and security for which they craved. We have in today's
reading a moving picture of the tenderness and compassion of
Jesus, met by the callous and ugly rebuttal of an ungrateful,
uncaring people. In even more poignant language, the words
of the psalmist are echoed: 'They are a people whose hearts go
astray, and they have not known my ways' (Psalm
95.10, NIV).

In the Church today, we like to regard ourselves as the
people of God. This, indeed, we are; but only if we allow the
love of Jesus to fill our hearts and change our ways. We, too,

must beware lest the dead hand of formality, the busyness of church life and, above all, the sinfulness of the human heart, cause our modern 'temples' to be abandoned – both by God and by those who are seeking him.

✽ *'O come to my heart, Lord Jesus!' (Emily E. S. Elliott)*

Wednesday November 1   Luke 14.1–14

The early messengers of the good news were said by their opponents to 'have turned the world upside down' (Acts 17.6,RSV); the implication being that Christians caused trouble wherever they went. Undeniably, the truth in this charge is that the values of God's kingdom are sometimes a complete reversal of values normally accepted and practised. The second part of today's reading (verses 7 – 14) provides two outstanding examples:

● It is normal to desire, seek – and often insist upon – the 'best place'. The meaning need not be limited to parties and other social functions. It can include the universal desire for positions of power, prestige and influence – even within the Church. How strong is the fascination of being 'number one'! Jesus taught a different way, both by word and example. Paul wrote that Christ 'made himself nothing, assuming the nature of a slave' (Philippians 2.7,NEB). We know, too, that he 'tied a towel round his waist ... and began to wash the disciples' feet' (John 13.4 – 5).

● It is normal to practise hospitality with varying degrees of self-interest. True hospitality expects no return, anticipates no reward. It is an expression of love.

✽ *'Teach us, good Lord, to serve thee as **thou** deservest.'*
(Ignatius Loyola)

Thursday November 2   Luke 14.15 – 24

Some of the Jewish leaders looked forward to the consummation of God's kingdom, certain that they would be included! Jesus countered the pious statement in verse 15 with a sobering parable. Those Jews originally invited by the prophets, and those now told by Jesus that the kingdom feast was near would find themselves left out. Their place would be filled by 'outsiders', people who were aware of their sinfulness and needs, but who, nevertheless, would respond gladly to their late invitation.

Those of us who belong to the Christian Church should take notice of this warning. Membership of a religious body, however orthodox or esteemed, is not enough. The banquet of the kingdom awaits only those who gratefully respond to Christ's loving invitation. They may be poor, unconventional, even socially undesirable, but God loves them and wants them.

Eyebrows were raised when two teen-age girls, sporting outlandish clothes and hair-styles, turned up at a church service. They received a cool welcome. Yet one old lady, with her usual sweet smile, exclaimed, 'How nice you were able to come!' She knew her Lord had said: 'I will never turn away anyone who comes to me' (John 6.37).

✳ *Lord, give me a responsive and welcoming heart.*

Friday November 3   Luke 14.25 – 34

It has been said that in the Church there are many distant followers of Jesus, but few real disciples. Large crowds of people and full churches give little indication of the level of true discipleship. It was to 'large crowds . . . going along with Jesus' (verse 25) that stern words regarding the cost of discipleship were addressed.

A disciple is a **learner** – one who seeks to follow in the steps of his teacher. Whenever a master musician gives instruction to a student, the maestro is keen that the student responds quickly and assimilates the essence of his teaching. The good student readily imitates and reflects the master's skills. However, the attainment of high standards demands tremendous and unceasing discipline.

The disciples of Christ also aspire to the high standards of their Master. It is a tough assignment. No one should embark upon this course without careful thought as to the possible cost and the ability to see it through. Loyalty to Jesus must come before every human consideration. It is one thing to say, 'Lord, Lord . . .'; but quite another to do what the Father wants (Matthew 7.21). However, with God's help everything is possible.

✳ *Lord, I want to follow you; help me to be a true disciple.*

In Luke 15 we reach the heart of the gospel, the best of the good news. We learn that God, in his love, actively searches for men and women in order to win their love. A great Jewish scholar once said that this was the only completely new thing that Jesus taught about God.

God searched for John Newton, mate and master on slave-trading ships, who became a Christian. In 1764, Newton was ordained and, later with his poet friend William Cowper, published the *'Olney Hymns'*. These included the well-loved hymn, 'How sweet the name of Jesus sounds'. God searched for C. S. Lewis, famous scholar and writer, who fought long to 'keep God at bay'. Yet he was 'surprised by joy', and became one of the greatest exponents of the faith in modern times.

Jesus came 'to seek and to save the lost' (Luke 19.10). He befriended the poor, the despised and the socially unacceptable. Only so could he fulfil the purpose of the God who searches 'until he finds'.

✴ *Lord, speak to me, that I may speak*
    In living echoes of thy tone;
    As thou hast sought, so let me seek
    Thy erring children, lost and lone.

                                        Frances R. Havergal

For group discussion and personal thought
Jesus spoke of God's kingdom in terms of a feast. Study Jesus' parable in **Luke 14.16–24**. What does this parable teach us about (a) the nature of the kingdom of God and (b) those to whom we should proclaim the gospel?

This story is really a parable about ourselves. In his letter to the church at Rome, Paul wrote: 'Everyone has sinned and is far away from God's saving presence' (Romans 3.23). None of us is a stranger to the 'country far away'; and, if we are Christians at all, we know something of the joy of God's loving-kindness and forgiveness.

Yet it is not enough to experience this joy for ourselves. We may have found – or be finding – our way back home, but countless millions are still away in the far country, impoverished, desolate and despairing. It is the work of the Church to show them the way home.

A Royal Air Force chaplain stood beside his commanding officer watching a succession of aircraft touch down on the runway. Impressed by the efficiency and accuracy of the operation, he asked the commanding officer how it was possible. 'Well, you see, padre,' was the reply, 'we're homing them in!'

Both as individuals and as a Church, we should be 'homing them in' — giving to our fellow-sinners the loving friendship and helpful counsel they need. It is a matter of great urgency. If someone does not 'home them in', they may never know the peace and happiness of the kingdom.

✷ *Lord, help me to bring others nearer to you.*

Monday November 6   Luke 15.25 – 32

It is easy to identify with the younger brother. We, too, have been in the far country; we, too, were brought home through the mercy of God. It may not be so easy, but is perhaps salutary, to compare ourselves with the elder brother.

He believed himself to be the good one; it was his younger brother, he thought, who was in the wrong and needed to change. He was jealous of the fuss made over his brother because he expected appreciation and resented not receiving it. He put the worst construction on his brother's behaviour and was not pleased when his brother did return home.

In the light of these points, we may ask:
● Am I quite free from self-righteousness?
● Do I see my own faults more clearly than those of others?
● Am I glad when others enjoy success or popularity?
● Do I like to see the best in other people?
● Am I unconcerned about how much appreciation I get?

A 'no' to any of these questions indicates some share in the elder brother's nature. However, we can be grateful that the father was kind and forgiving to the elder brother, also. There is hope for us all!

✷ *Father, 'forgive us our sins, just as we have forgiven those who have sinned against us' (Matthew 6.12, LB).*

● For a copy of the new **NCEC catalogue** write to: Robert Denholm House, Nutfield, Redhill, Surrey RH1 4HW.

Three important truths stand out in these verses:

- **Love God with all your mind.** Verse 8 suggests that Christians deal with the affairs of life less astutely than wordly people. We are reminded that the life of faith requires hard thinking as well as goodwill. We are to be 'wise as serpents' (Matthew 10.16, RSV) – not, as someone facetiously added, 'silly as chickens'!
- **The need for honesty.** Sir Walter Scott wrote:

  > O, what a tangled web we weave,
  > When **first** we practise to deceive!

  The 'small matters' referred to by Jesus in verse 10 confirm the poet's emphasis on 'first'. 'White' lies easily become black ones; 'fiddling' becomes embezzlement; petty pilfering becomes robbery. Honesty is a requirement of Christian living.
- **The need for good stewardship.** The manager in Jesus' parable was sacked for bad stewardship. Are we good stewards of the precious things God has entrusted to us – life, time, gifts, opportunities, and all the valuable resources of Bible and Church? We, too, will have to give God an account of ourselves.

✳ *Lord, may I love you more dearly, see you more clearly and follow you more nearly, day by day. (Based on a prayer of Richard of Chichester).*

The Pharisees scornfully rejected the antithesis between love of God and love of money. For the Jews, material prosperity was the sign of a good life. Yet, the very 'goodness' of the Pharisees was phoney. Jesus said to them: 'On the outside you appear good to everybody, but inside you are full of hypocrisy and sins' (Matthew 23.28). With devastating directness, Jesus exposed their fallacious beliefs. Worldly wealth was no indication of virtue, and their virtue was itself a deception.

Human nature does not change. How widespread today is the love of money! It preoccupies people's minds, and is still regarded as a sign of successful living, if not of virtue.

Yet today's reading makes two things crystal clear:

- God is concerned far more about the state of our character than the size of our bank balance.

- We should be concerned more about the values of God's kingdom than the gaining of wealth and the good opinion of others.

✱ *'God has chosen poor people to be rich in faith, and the kingdom of heaven is theirs.' (James 2.5, LB)*

Thursday November 9   Luke 16.19 – 31

The rich man's sin was not that he was rich, but that he did nothing. After all, 'father Abraham', a model of faith and obedience, had also been very rich. This searching parable has both global and personal indications.

The evidence that some nations live in plenty and affluence, while others lack the essentials of life, is abundant – at times, horrifying. Some countries have vast stocks of unwanted food and resources, while in others the bare necessities of life are desperately scarce. How much do the prosperous nations care about their poor neighbours? Helping agencies and concerned individuals do magnificent work, but it is left to the few to take real action.

There is also the personal challenge. The poor man was 'brought to the rich man's door' (verse 20), but still the rich man did nothing to help. What about the poor people at our door? Our neighbours may not lack material goods, but perhaps they are in need of friendship and love. It has been said, 'If everybody cared enough and everybody shared enough, everybody would have enough.' How true!

✱ *Think about Jesus' words; 'Whenever you refused to help one of these least important ones, you refused to help me.' (Matthew 25.45)*

Friday November 10   Luke 17.1 – 10

'Watch what you do!' Jesus used these words after declaring what a terrible thing it was to cause someone else to sin (verses 1 – 3a). It is remarkable that they were addressed, not to the obvious perpetrators of evil, but to his closest followers.

It is always easy to blame someone else. We readily condemn the drug pusher, the dealer in pornography, the racketeer – or even the system – for situations which invite people to do wrong and commit crime. Too often, the 'respectable' of this world, including many who claim to be

Christian, consider themselves to be apart from the evils of society.

Yet Jesus said to his disciples: 'Keep watch on **yourselves**!' (verse 3, NEB). The critical, aloof, superior attitude of some 'good' people also contributes to social wrong. Many of those who are tempted by sinful situations would escape the entanglements of wickedness, if more Christians understood and befriended them. One of the great contributions to the progress of Christianity is the Salvation Army's willingness to be involved in the real needs of desperate people.

✳ *Lord, may I ever be alert, guarding against anything which would cause another to stumble.*

Saturday November 11   Luke 17.11–19

This well-known incident highlights two essentials of the Christian life – **obedience** and **gratitude**.

All ten men listened to the voice of Jesus and did what he told them to – all were healed **as they obeyed**. It is as we obey that miracles take place and our needs are met.

However, only one man 'came back to **give thanks** to God' (verse 18). Ten men cried, 'Take pity on us!'; but only one gave thanks when pity was taken. Shakespeare wrote:

> Blow, blow, thou winter wind,
> Thou art not so unkind
>   As man's ingratitude.

On the human level, ingratitude can inflict great hurt, and perhaps none of us is entirely guiltless of it.

In our life with God, in our sickness and distress, we pray to the One who alone can heal and save us. We are never disappointed – the needed blessing is given. Yet, can we identify with the 'one who came back' – or are we among the nine?

✳ *'We should spend as much time in thanking God for his benefits as we do in asking for them.' (Vincent de Paul)*

For group discussion and personal thought

Read **Luke 15.11–32**, looking particularly at the part about the elder brother (verses 25–32). What can we learn from these verses? In what circumstances are **we** in danger of being like the elder brother?

Remembrance Sunday, November 12   Luke 17.20 – 37

Let us look at three truths which are made plain in this
reading:

- **The kingdom of God requires inward change.** It is a
  new world of inward experience, comprising people of
  every race whose lives are changed by Christ and directed
  by the Holy Spirit.
- **Because of everyday concerns, God's warnings go
  unheeded.** People like Noah and Lot provided exceptions
  to this statement. They heeded God's warnings and did not
  perish. When Christ returns in glory, many will still be
  unprepared; but those who have responded to the gospel
  message 'will go to eternal life' (Matthew 25.46).
- **No one can predict when and how the Day of the Lord
  will come.** At various intervals in history, individuals and
  sects have announced a specific time for our Lord's return.
  All these dates have come – and gone. The words of Jesus
  in verse 23, 'Don't go out looking for it', have been
  disregarded. However, Jesus also declared that when that
  Day does come, it will be quite unmistakable. The question
  that matters is, 'Are we ready for it?'

✷ *Lord, help us to remember with gratitude, and live to build
a world of peace.*

Monday November 13   Luke 18.1 – 8

In every field of endeavour, **persistence** is essential for
success: only after years of laborious research did Marie and
Pierre Curie discover the new element radium, from the
mineral ore pitchblende; many great writers received
countless rejection slips before their works were accepted for
publication; a marathon race demands 'stickability' as well as
speed.

The parable of the unjust judge in today's reading teaches
persistence in the practice of prayer. God, our loving Father,
unlike the selfish judge, readily answers the prayers of those
who, in spite of all discouragements, continue to call upon
him.

In a Scottish church, numbers were steadily decreasing. The
weekly prayer meeting also diminished until, one evening,
only two people turned up. One of them said there was no
point in continuing; the other asked for the key of the room.
The next week he went, as usual, and prayed – alone. From

that evening, attendance at both prayer meeting and church began to grow.

Tennyson was right when he wrote, 'More things are wrought by prayer than this world dreams of.'

✴ *Think of a situation about which you feel discouraged, but remember Paul's words: 'Keep on praying'.*

(1 Thessalonians 5.17, LB)

Tuesday November 14   Luke 18.9 – 17

The story is told of a man who died and went to heaven. When he had become accustomed to the brightness, he recognised many people. Some he had not expected to see there; others, surprisingly, were missing. Yet the greatest shock came when old acquaintances greeted him with the words, 'I never thought I would see you here!' It was a blow to his pride – he had been 'sure of (his) own goodness' (verse 9).

It is said that there are four kinds of pride – pride of face, place, race and grace. No doubt we all suffer, in varying degrees, from the first three, according to our physical attributes, social position and where we happen to have been born. The fourth, spiritual pride, is the most dangerous – destructive of all that is truly good and beautiful. It is the hardest problem for the Christian to overcome.

Jesus pointed to children for the answer. Do we have the naturalness, openness, dependence, trust, and sense of fun, of a child? Or, do we still try to be good and important – not so much for God, but to impress our fellows? The answer to these questions may be a guide as to whether we are – or are not yet – in the kingdom.

✴ *Lord, help me to be grown-up and mature, and yet be willing to receive your kingdom like a child.*

Wednesday November 15   Luke 18.18 – 30

Jesus summarised the ten commandments in the two great injunctions: 'Love the Lord your God with all your heart . . . soul . . . mind and . . . strength; . . . and love your neighbour as you love yourself' (Mark 12.30–31). But here we find Jesus quoting five of the commandments in detail.

This is a timely reminder that the life of every disciple must be regulated by the highest standards of morality.

Certain modern movements have advocated a life of love

and peace, making few, if any, moral demands. However, the love has easily degenerated into a 'free love' and the peace into a spineless acquiescence in corrupt living.

Yet, for the rich man in today's reading, a high morality did not of itself ensure his entry into the kingdom of God. There was still one more thing he needed to do. He had to let go his love of, and dependence upon, material wealth.

What is the 'one more thing' we need to do, in order to become more fit for God's service? In the spiritual life, there is always the next step, and the Holy Spirit will show us what that 'next step' should be.

✳ *Lord, may your Holy Spirit show me the next step I should take, and give me the courage to take it.*

Thursday November 16   Luke 18.31–43

O dark, dark, dark, amid the blaze of noon,
Irrecoverably dark, total eclipse
Without all hope of day!
O first created Beam, and thou great Word,
Let there be light, and light was over all.

These lines from the epic poem, *Samson Agonistes*, by John Milton, aptly reflect the contrasting darkness and light of today's reading. Milton is describing the blindness and captivity of Samson, taken prisoner by the Philistines. He writes all the more poignantly, as he himself was blind.

In similar desperation, the blind beggar of Jericho cried out in his darkness to Jesus, 'the light of the world'. More fortunate than Samson, his sight was restored. He opened his eyes to see and to follow his healer and Saviour.

Jesus had just announced his imminent suffering and death, when, on a cosmic scale, there would be 'total eclipse, without all hope of day'. Yet miraculously day came – Christ rose, 'and light was over all'.

In our own lesser 'Calvaries', when all seems dark we, too, can call upon Jesus. He will give us the light we need.

✳ *For thou hast made the blind to see,*
    The deaf to hear, the dumb to speak,
    The dead to live; and lo, I break
The chains of my captivity.   William T. Matson

The story of Zacchaeus teaches us an essential lesson – the supreme importance of friendship in winning men and women for the kingdom of God. Although Zacchaeus, a dishonest rogue, was very rich and at the top of his profession, he was rejected and despised. In Jesus, he found the understanding and friendship for which he craved.

In the most natural way, Jesus befriended Zacchaeus and shared a meal with him. He did not condemn, criticise or even rebuke him; yet Zacchaeus changed. The impact of God upon his life worked the miracle. He saw where he had been wrong and did something about it. Salvation came to his house through the love of God mediated by the friendship of Jesus.

It is usually through people that the love of God reaches other lives. These people may be preachers, writers or teachers but, more often, they are friends – friends who are themselves friends of Jesus. It is said of David Livingstone, the well-known missionary and explorer, that no one could spend a day in his company and remain the same person.

✷ *Am I winning others for God through the quality of my friendship? Think and pray about this.*

The parable of the gold coins (pounds) resembles the parable of the three servants in Matthew 25.14 – 30. In the latter, varying large sums of money were given, according to the ability of each servant. In today's reading, the same, much smaller, amount is distributed to each. This suggests that to every person is entrusted the same task of living out the life of faith. Prominent among the valuable truths in this parable is the necessity of doing the small thing well.

We learn that anyone who discharges a small duty well may – and probably will – be assigned more important work. This is the way that promotion operates in almost every sphere of life and, not least, in the work of the kingdom of God.

In the 14th century, Pope Benedict XI sought an able artist for a special commission. He despatched a messenger to the Italian painter, Giotto, asking for a sample of his work. Giotto, with a deft sweep of the brush, drew a simple O and sent it back. So perfect was this O that the Pope immediately engaged Giotto, for a large salary, to decorate with frescoes his residence at Avignon.

What small thing is God asking me to do supremely well, that he may entrust me with some greater responsibility?

✷ *'Whatever your hand finds to do, do it with all your might.'*
(Ecclesiastes 9.10, NIV)

For group discussion and personal thought
Look closely at the story of Zacchaeus in **Luke 19.1–10**. In what ways did his meeting with Jesus have practical consequences for him? How should the fact that we have 'met' Jesus affect our relationships with the people among whom we work and live?

MALACHI

Notes by the Revd Michael Townsend, BA, MPhil, BD

Michael Townsend is a Methodist minister in the Halifax Circuit, Yorkshire, England. He is the author of 'Our Tradition of Faith' (Epworth Press) and has contributed articles on biblical, theological and homiletical subjects to various periodicals.

The notes in this section are based on the New International Version.

Malachi was one of the last prophetic books of the Old Testament to be written. Unlike many of the other prophets, Malachi came from a period of relative quiet in the history of God's people. The name 'Malachi' simply means 'my messenger', and we cannot be certain whether this was the prophet's name or an editorial title for the collection of prophetic sayings in this book.

Malachi was deeply concerned with the relationship between God and his people. This relationship, enshrined in the various covenants which God had made with Israel over the years, involved responsibilities and obligations. The prophet aimed to help God's people fulfil these worthily.

Suggestion for further reading

Haggai, Zechariah and Malachi by Joyce G. Baldwin, Tyndale Old Testament Commentaries (Inter-Varsity Press).

Sunday November 19   **Malachi 1.1–5**

'God is love' is one of the great truths of the Bible. It is taught and demonstrated in the Old Testament, but shown most fully in the life, death and resurrection of Jesus, God's only Son. Yet so great a truth can easily become just a religious cliché. It is possible for us to hear those words so often that they lose their meaning. Something like that seems to have been the experience of people in the time of Malachi. God declared his love, but the people responded, 'How have you loved us?'

The reply to that question points to the practical demonstration of God's love in Israel's past: God **chose** them in a way he did not choose other nations. He chose Jacob rather than Esau (see Genesis 25.21 – 34). Also to show that such loving choice continued into the present, the prophet pointed to the continuing failure of the nation of Edom (the descendants of Esau) to achieve victory over the Israelites (the descendants of Jacob).

If 'God is love' is in danger of becoming a religious cliché for us, we need to learn the lessons Malachi taught: to recall his great love for us, and to count our blessings by seeing what God is doing in our lives now.

✷ *Lord, we thank you that you are loving and that you are always at work in our lives.*

Monday November 20   Malachi 1.6–14

A schoolteacher, so the story goes, asked her class to bring items to decorate the school hall for their Harvest Festival service. One girl offered to bring some flowers, but on the day of the Harvest Festival, she came to school without any. 'Where are the flowers you promised to bring?' asked the teacher, and received the reply, 'Mummy says I can't bring them – they aren't dead enough yet'!

Malachi was deeply concerned that the worship being offered to God was unworthy, and that the priests were among those most guilty of this offence. It was, for example, an important principle of the Jewish law that only unblemished animals could be offered in sacrifice. Yet some people were bringing animals which would not even have been acceptable to the civil governor! Malachi knew that unless the worship offered by God's people was their best, the whole foundation of the covenant relationship would be undermined.

It is fatally easy for us to slip into the habit of thinking that worship is routine – anything will do for God. Quite the contrary is in fact the case. Worship honours God's name, so nothing but our best is good enough.

✷ *Help us to worship you, Lord, with our whole hearts, bringing you the best of our lives.*

Tuesday November 21   Malachi 2.1–9

'From the one who has been entrusted with much, much more will be asked' (Luke 12.48b) is an abiding spiritual principle. It is as true today as it was in the days of Jesus, or Malachi.

The prophet realised that the people were being given a very bad example in the matter of worship. It was the priests' solemn responsibility to offer worship but they did it merely as a duty. Their hearts did not honour God and neither did their lives. God's word to them was of judgement. Because their teaching had caused many to stumble and because their example had led others astray, theirs would be the greater condemnation.

Two reflections arise out of this reading for us;

● We need to support with love, prayer and encouragement, those whose work is to minister in holy things. Because they bear a great responsibility for what they say and do, they can be vulnerable. Sometimes Christian workers complain that they receive only criticism and opposition. This ought not to be so.

● We need to look at our **own** lives, and ask: 'What has God entrusted me with? What will he require from me?'

✴ *Help us, Lord, in all we do, to give honour to your name. May the way we live reflect your love for us.*

Wednesday November 22   Malachi 2.10–16

In any society, widespread collapse of the institution of marriage poses a grave problem. It is estimated that in some western countries today one in three marriages ends in divorce. Christians are rightly concerned about this, although they do not always agree on what should be done about it. In today's reading there is a condemnation of divorce, but it is important that we recognise the specific basis of Malachi's concern.

The people of Israel were strongly discouraged from marrying outside their own people. At first sight this seems to be objectionably racist, but the reasons are quite different. The biblical comment on King Solomon's foreign wives is that they turned his heart from the Lord (1 Kings 11.1–8). The gods of these foreign spouses demanded less in the way of loyalty and morality than the Lord did, so all too often both marriage partners ended up following them. To divorce an Israelite wife in order to marry a foreign one was, therefore, a double betrayal of God's covenant love. Whatever else Christians today say about marriage and divorce, we must recognise the importance of both partners in a marriage sharing a common faith.

❋ Pray for those whose marriages are under strain.

Thursday November 23   **Malachi 2.17 to 3.5**

One of the most persistent, and difficult, questions for those
who believe in a God of justice is: 'Why do bad people often
prosper?' There are plenty of people who live by exploiting
others. Some grow rich by trading in addictive drugs or
weapons of war; others live off prostitution. In many countries
unscrupulous employers exploit people's need for work by
paying only starvation wages. No doubt some of these people
do receive their just rewards in this life, but in fact many
prosper and in some cases they are regarded as respectable
citizens within their societies. Where is the justice in this?

Malachi reminds us that God is concerned about these
things. To those who behave in this way and do not repent, he
will come as a God of judgement. The wages of sin will be
death. Although Malachi does not explicitly mention it, the
belief in a life after death, where the world's injustices will be
put right, is necessary for those who believe, as Malachi did,
that God is indeed a God of justice.

❋ Pray for the exploited and oppressed. Pray also for the
exploiters and oppressors that they might repent.

Friday November 24

Minorities often have to work hard to preserve their sense of
identity and purpose. It is easy to be swallowed up and lose a
valued sense of distinctiveness. In many societies today the
Christian minority is aware of this problem. It is not a new
one.

▶ Read **Malachi 3.6–18.**

In many ways we live in a world somewhat like that of
Malachi's time: unbelievers do not give God his due (verse 8);
many people ask the utilitarian question 'What benefit is
there to me in being a believer?' (verse 14); the arrogant, the
evildoers and the blasphemers get along well enough (verse
15). In such a world, those who have experienced God's love in
Christ need the support and comfort which comes from
mutual association. They need to know and value each other.

In Malachi's day those who feared the Lord and honoured
his name had their names written on a scroll. Today, some
churches see their membership rolls in the same light.

However, what really matters is that **God** puts those who honour him on **his** scroll of remembrance; or, as the New Testament puts it: 'those whose names are written in the Lamb's book of life' (Revelation 21.27b).

✳ *Inscribe our hearts with your love, O Lord, so that our names may be written in your book of life.*

Saturday November 25   **Malachi 4.1–6**

Most of us like happy endings, whether to stories, plays, or books of the Bible! From earliest times Malachi 4.6 was felt to be a harsh ending, and so when it was read in the synagogue verse 5 was read again after it. Indeed, Hebrew Bibles print verse 5 again, as the conclusion. But we must let the prophet speak for himself! His final word is a warning of judgement. Elijah's task would be to return and try to avert judgement.

Christians read these verses in the light of the New Testament. John the Baptist's calling was to preach repentance (Luke 3.3,8), and at one point Jesus suggested that John was indeed the Elijah who was to come (Matthew 11.14). It appears that John did not entirely understand that (John 1.21), but certainly he tried to avert judgement and prepare for Jesus' preaching of God's love and grace.

Whether there is to be a happy ending still depends on us and our response. For those who put their trust in Jesus the last word lies with grace, not judgement. This is the good news we have to share with others.

✳ *Give thanks for the sun of righteousness, Jesus our Lord. Pray that you may live by the light he brings.*

For group discussion and personal thought

What are some of the pressures on church leaders and ministers? What are their main responsibilities? Read and discuss **Malachi 2.7**. How can we help and support our church leaders and ministers to do their work faithfully and well?

A REMINDER

- Don't forget to order your copy of **Notes on Bible Readings** for **1990**! You will find the year's scheme on page 256.

1, 2 TIMOTHY

Notes by the Revd Eric S. Mattock

Eric Mattock is a minister in the Presbyterian Church of New Zealand, at present serving in the Tawa Union Parish, Wellington. Previously, he was at Richmond, near Nelson. He has also served in the army and been a police officer.

The notes in this section are based on the Good News Bible.

The heading of **1,2 Timothy** in most Bibles, and the content of these letters, would lead us to assume that they were written by Paul. However, this is unlikely as they refer to a church structure of the second-century Church; also the language and style of writing is quite different from that in letters known to have been written by Paul. The practice of ascribing writings to a well-known hero was widespread in New Testament times. In writing under Paul's name, this unknown author was using the example of Paul to inspire confidence and trust.'

1,2 Timothy contain instructions and guidance on the administration of church affairs, and warnings about false teachers.

Suggestion for further reading

The Letters to Timothy, Titus and Philemon by William Barclay, Daily Study Bible (Saint Andrew Press).

Sunday November 26   **1 Timothy 1.1–11**

The writer of **1 Timothy**, deeply concerned about what was happening in the church at Ephesus, was moved to write a letter of instructions to the leader of the Christian community there.

The church at Ephesus was surrounded by pagan religions and was in real danger of allowing the philosophies and ideas of those religions to dilute its testimony and witness to 'the good news from the glorious and blessed God' (verse 11). The Ephesian church faced a crisis—a real challenge. If it failed to respond it would soon be overtaken by false teachings and its uniqueness as a vehicle of God's grace would be lost.

While circumstances have changed, the Church today faces similar crises, and the threat of false teaching is still real. These may appear in the form of secularism, the worship of power, the cult of success or the pursuit of comfort. As Christians we must be prepared to challenge ideas and philosophies that oppose our loyalty to God in Christ.

✷ *Thank you, God, that in spite of false teachings your living word continues to be heard in the world today.*

Monday November 27   1 Timothy 1.12 – 20

In yesterday's reading the purpose of the law was explained (verses 8 –10). In today's verses the author goes on to write of his own experience. Because of the abundant grace that was poured out for him, he was given faith and love through his union with Christ (verse 14). In the light of this, he was so greatly moved that the only response he could make was to become totally committed to Christ.

Laws cannot make people good – they can merely stop people from doing wrong. The only way people can change for the better is to have a **change of heart** and a **change of priorities**. This can only happen when we realise the unconditional nature of the love of God, which can penetrate deeply into our hearts and turn us right around.

For nine years I worked as a police officer. On several successive occasions I arrested a man who had committed many crimes. Years later I met this man again and was amazed at what appeared to be a total transformation of personality.

'What happened?' I asked.

'Christ arrested me!' he replied.

✷ *Amazing grace (how sweet the sound)*
   That saved a wretch like me!   John Newton

Tuesday November 28   1 Timothy 2.1–15

As Christians we are called to be part of a worshipping community. However, many Christians, who are concerned for their fellow human beings, are tempted to replace true worship with social action. This is because they have become frustrated with a church that is more concerned for its own well-being and comfort than with God's mission to the world.

The writer of **1 Timothy** took it for granted that every

church would be a worshipping community where praise, thanksgiving and intercessory prayer had a high priority. As people lift their hearts in adoration to God, he is able to inspire and empower them – giving them new insights as to how social problems may be tackled, and strengthening them to suffer and work for God's righteousness in society.

Although verses 9–15 appear to give definite instructions concerning the place of women in the Church, we must remember that they were written for a particular situation and cannot automatically be used as general rules for the Church today. We must let the Spirit lead us all – men **and** women – as we seek to serve God in the world today.

✳ *Lord, grant us clarity of vision, that our hearts may always be fixed on your truth, where true joys are to be found.*

Wednesday November 29   1 Timothy 3.1–16

There is an old saying, 'The proof of the pudding is in the eating'. Christian leaders must accept responsibility for backing up their authority by living virtuous lives. As a leader in a Christian community, I am painfully aware that I stand under the judgement of these words. Nevertheless, it is both refreshing and exciting that, even in spite of my failure, God's mission does find its roots in people's lives.

In an age where the Church is increasingly treated with indifference, the temptation to assume the standards of the world is hard to resist. That is why we must be very careful to choose church leaders who will help us in our struggle to express in our lives, those virtues which God calls us to embrace. Church leaders should be people whose ordinary, everyday lives speak of Christ's love.

Further, as Christian people we must all endeavour to prove what we proclaim by the lives we live – to practise what we preach.

✳ *When we decline to accept a leadership role in our church, is it because we are convinced of our unsuitability, or because we are afraid of the demands of leadership?*

Thursday November 30   1 Timothy 4.1–16

The writer was under no illusions about the difficult situation that faced Timothy – especially considering his youth (verse 12). There would be those who would embrace their new faith with a great burst of enthusiasm, but would then soon wither. There would also be people who would try to influence others with ideas and teachings which were contrary to Christ's way. It would be difficult for Timothy – failure was a fact he would have to face.

Although Timothy was given instructions to counter the unhelpful teachings in the church, it was the example of his own life which would speak God's message most clearly. The writer also knew that Timothy would not be able to maintain his work for God if he did not look after himself properly. In the Greek culture of Ephesus, everyone knew how important physical exercise was, so Timothy was reminded that he must regularly engage in spiritual exercise. This would enable his conduct to remain true to God and his love and faith to grow.

In our society today there is great emphasis on physical health and exercise, but what spiritual exercise do we engage in?

✳ *'Do not let yourselves become discouraged and give up.'*
(Hebrews 12.3b)

Friday December 1   1 Timothy 5.1–16

This reading is concerned with the responsibilities of Christians towards one another – especially towards the members of their own family and towards widows with no means of support.

In the community where I work, there are both European and Polynesian people. It is interesting to see the different ways in which these two cultures interpret family responsibility. While many young Europeans expect to receive financial support from the older members of their family, in Polynesian communities the opposite is usually the case – to accept financial support from ageing parents is considered to be a disgrace. Polynesian people see it as their rightful duty to do all they can to ensure that the older members of their families have access to sufficient material and spiritual resources.

Care of ageing parents is part of our Christian responsibility. However, this can be very difficult in a society which exults 'youth' and does not value the wisdom of 'age'. Some of the most distressing pastoral situations are those where an elderly parent yearns for a word from a son or a daughter. In the wider family of the Church it is possible for us to give time and support to those who have no relatives to care for them.

✱ *Lord, help us to value and care for those who are elderly or unable to support themselves.*

Saturday December 2   1 Timothy 5.17 to 6.2

Christianity is vitally concerned with our well-being and with every aspect of our everyday lives. In today's reading, the writer raises some matters that can cause distress in many situations. Rather than waiting until problems arise, he offers suggestions as to how we can avoid them.

● It is important to reward people for the work they do. Words of praise and encouragement are important, especially where quiet workers behind the scenes may be taken for granted.

● **Do not judge others** on ill-founded rumours. A little more care and prayer when choosing people for spiritual leadership would avoid many a sad situation.

● **Serve God where you are.** The abolition of slavery makes it difficult for us to see the application of the final two verses in today's reading. However, these words remind us that Christians can serve God wherever they are – especially as they strive for better industrial relations.

✱ *Thank you, Lord, that you provide us with guide-lines for ordinary living. Help us to live according to these.*

For group discussion and personal thought

Study and discuss 1 Timothy 3.1–13. What qualities do you think we should look for in our leaders both in the church and in the community? Why is it important for leaders to have good characters and happy family relationships?

Advent Sunday, December 3

Two policemen were investigating a house fire in which a man had died. Apparently he had been woken by the fire, left his house and telephoned the fire brigade. However, he suddenly re-entered the blazing house and did not return. When his body was found, a valuable painting – miraculously unharmed – was discovered underneath him. Afterwards people asked: 'Did he own the painting, or did the painting own him?'

▶ Read **1 Timothy 6.3 – 21**.

Two things stand out in this reading:

● Wealth in itself is not condemned. Rather, it is the undisciplined pursuit of wealth that is wrong because it brings its own destructive reward.

● Following on from this, is the call to set our sights on things that really matter – on things that bring true life.

As Christians we must set our hearts and minds on the kingdom of God, not on the vain pursuits of this world. By doing so we shall be liberated to enjoy the riches and freedom which God promises.

✳ *Redeemer Lord, on this Advent Sunday, help us to remember that you left your riches in glory and came to us, so that we might share in your eternal kingdom.*

Monday December 4   2 Timothy 1.1 – 18

Today's reading is both a message of comfort and inspiration. The author, assuming the role of Paul in prison, wrote to encourage Timothy. Timothy was expected to persevere with his work for Christ, even to the point of suffering, knowing that God would give him the strength and grace to continue.

It is difficult to remain faithful to our Christian responsibility in the face of criticism and opposition. Many Christians feel, at times, that the burden laid upon them is too much to carry and the temptation to throw it all away is almost irresistible. However, it is always heartening to learn that other Christians face similar problems. Perhaps we should share our disappointments and doubts with one another more freely, thereby encouraging each other.

The greatest encouragement that God gives us is the example of Jesus. His victory at Calvary reminds us that the power of God at work in us, is truly undefeatable. We, too, can be full of confidence as we **know** and **trust** Jesus Christ, our Saviour and Lord.

✳ *'In all things we have complete victory through him who loved us! Nothing can separate us from his love, which is ours through Christ Jesus our Lord.' (part of Romans 8.37 – 39).*

Tuesday December 5   2 Timothy 2.1 – 13

Timothy had been taught the message of Christ in a very clear

way, and yet he still needed examples from everyday life to
encourage him to persevere in his ministry:

- **The lesson of the soldier.** Throughout the Roman empire
  soldiers were a common sight. Their stamina, obedience
  and loyalty were examples for Christians to follow as they
  sought to serve their commander-in-chief, Jesus.
- **The lesson of the athlete.** The original Greek phrase used
  here suggests that the athlete was a professional –
  someone whose whole life was given to disciplined training
  and observance of the rules of racing.
- **The lesson of the farmer.** The farmer must be content to
  work hard and then wait patiently for the fruits of his
  labour. Through this illustration, Timothy was reminded
  that he would be rewarded for his effort.

Timothy was never told that his task would be easy, but
only assured that if he remained faithful to God, God would be
faithful to him. God will also be faithful to us – his enabling
strength and promises do not change.

✳   *May I run the race before me,*
    Strong and brave to face the foe,
  Looking only unto Jesus
    As I onward go.   *Kate B. Wilkinson*

Wednesday December 6   **2 Timothy 2.14 – 26**

In this reading the writer deals with the problems of false
teachers and disputes over church doctrine. In verses 22 – 26,
helpful advice is given on how to meet such situations.

Disputes over doctrine are still problems which exist and
can be very damaging to the Church. People will always
want to debate matters of faith, whether it be a particular
position on the virgin birth or the importance of speaking
in tongues. Most of us can recall incidents in which a mild
debate developed into a heated argument and got out of
hand.

The guidance in verses 22–26 should help us in such
matters. We need to remember that, when it comes to issues
of doctrine concerning our faith, we are all learners – no one
has a monopoly on truth. The writer of **2 Timothy** suggests
that we 'call out to the Lord for help' (verse 22). In the end we
win people for Christ, not by our eloquence and presentation
of ideas, but by the way we love them – allowing Christ's
Spirit to work through us.

Thursday December 7   2 Timothy 3.1–9

Like other New Testament writers, the author of **2 Timothy**
expected the return of Christ to be close at hand and warned
Timothy what society would be like prior to this great event.
Every area of life would appear to be godless and even people
who held an outward form of religion would exploit weaker
members of the community. In this case, it was women who
would be exploited – the emancipation they had experienced
by the advent of Christianity meant that they were no longer
sheltered by old customs.

While these verses describe the days immediately preceding
the return of Christ, they also describe the state of many great
societies in history in the period of their decline. As the
twenty-first century is approaching we, too, may think that
the end of the age is at hand. Certainly we are living in an age
in which many people are selfish, greedy, proud and violent,
exploiting whom they can.

However, as Christians, it is essential that we do not
become anxious about our future; rather, we are to bring hope
and confidence into the world as we witness to the saving
power of Christ.

* *God is on my side –*
  In him I trust, and I will not be afraid.
                              (part of Psalm 56.9–11)

Friday December 8   2 Timothy 3.10–17

Timothy had the good fortune to be taught the Scriptures
from his earliest years (verse 15). His knowledge of them
enabled him to grow spiritually, to help others and to face
opposition. Both his mother and grandmother had kindled in
him a strong faith (2 Timothy 1.5), which enabled him to
minister to churches even though he was still quite young
(1 Timothy 4.12).

As we read the Scriptures and think about them, God will
often speak to us and there is built up within ourselves a store
of knowledge, truths and lessons by which we are able to trace
the working of God in our own lives. Even though we may

have read the Bible regularly for many years, we can still learn something new and fresh each time we turn to it. Then, when we are faced with difficulties, words we have read will spring to life.

While Timothy only had the Old Testament, we are extremely fortunate to have the treasures of the New Testament and also a wealth of other great Christian literature. Let us always be grateful to God and do what we can to promote the reading of the Bible throughout the world.

✳ *Pray for all people – adults and children – who have not had the opportunity to read God's word.*

Saturday December 9

In a relay race, the baton is passed from one runner to the next. In a sense it is similar in the Christian life. The ministry of Paul was coming to an end, but Timothy was expected to pick up the baton and carry on from where Paul left off.

▶ Read **2 Timothy 4.1 – 22.**

Timothy was encouraged to keep up the good fight and was given words of advice, again reminding him that there would be many difficulties. In the face of this he should remain steadfast and true, and do the best he could.

During the past two weeks, we may have been surprised to read of the constant reminders that Timothy was given to encourage him in his ministry. We sometimes have the mistaken idea that New Testament characters were men and women who faced opposition fearlessly and did not need reminders to do so. However, as we read about the difficulties they faced we can find inspiration to continue in the 'relay race'. The 'baton' we receive is the good news of Jesus Christ. We too, like Timothy and Paul, will receive the victory prize when we have run the full distance of our race.

✳ *'Those who trust in the Lord for help . . . will run and not get weary.' (part of Isaiah 40.31)*

For group discussion and personal thought

Read **2 Timothy 3.1 – 7.** What injustices exist in our own society as a result of people's self-centredness and selfishness? What can we contribute to make our world a better place and one in which the signs of God's kingdom abound?

ISAIAH 55–66

Notes by the Revd Michael Townsend, BA, MPhil, BD

The notes in this section are based on the Jerusalem Bible.

The collection of prophecies in this last part of the book of **Isaiah** comes from a fairly settled period in Israel's history. God's people had been through the trauma of invasion and the most able citizens had been deported to Babylon. The years of exile had been hard, but God had called his people back to their homeland. The prophecies in **Isaiah 40–55** reflect the joy and confidence this gave them. As the books of **Haggai** and **Zechariah** show, the rebuilding of their community was no easy task. By the time the prophecies of **Isaiah 56–66** were written, much Israelite religion had again lapsed into formal observance and there were many social sins. The prophet's message combines hope and judgement to help bring the people back to God.

Suggestion for further reading

Isaiah Volume II by John F. A. Sawyer, Daily Study Bible (Saint Andrew Press).

2nd Sunday in Advent, December 10 (Bible Sunday)

From time to time British supermarkets run a competition where the prize is free food and drink – the winner can take from the shelves whatever they like in a specified short space of time. It is astonishing how much some people can collect in two minutes!

▶ Read **Isaiah 55.1–5**.

In a land where water is scarce and precious, it is sometimes sold in the streets. So it was in Isaiah's day. Of course, people expected to pay for such items as corn and milk and wine, but God's startling invitation to those who want such things is 'though you have no money, come!' (verse 1).

This picture of free food and water shows us that we can come to God, not just for our physical needs, but for the 'richer food than this' (Henry W. Baker), which he also provides. 'Listen', says God, 'and your soul will live' (verse 3). And what payment does God require for the spiritual goods he provides day by day? Nothing at all! All is of grace – his free, generous and wholly undeserved love. What a wonderful invitation, and what a wonderful God! How foolish we would be to ignore it!

Father, on this Bible Sunday, we thank you for your word of grace which feeds us. Bless all who translate, interpret and preach it.

Monday December 11 Isaiah 55.6–13

There are many people for whom God is remote. They say: 'How can the Creator of all the earth be bothered with us?' It is as if they interpret the words, 'the heavens are as high above earth as my ways are above your ways' (verse 9), to affirm their ideas. Yet, for the prophet, the majesty and glory of God are anything but a cause for despair or unbelief. On the contrary, the wonder is that such a God **does** care and has made himself known to us. It is **because** God does not think as human beings do, because he is not unforgiving as they are, that there is hope. Those who truly repent of their sins and turn back to him will discover the quality of his pity and that he is 'rich in forgiving' (verse 7).

This might have remained a truth difficult to grasp and apply, if God had not at a later time given it 'flesh'. In saying that the Word of God 'was made flesh', John's Gospel shows us God's rich, forgiving love in action (John 1.14).

In the weeks leading up to Christmas we prepare ourselves to celebrate the birth of Christ. He is the one who came not to judge the world, but to save it (John 3.17). At this season can we help others to see the God who is not remote, but very near in forgiving love?

Pray for those who acknowledge that there is a God, but do not know his love in Christ personally.

Tuesday December 12 Isaiah 56.1–8

One of the less attractive features of some forms of religion is **exclusiveness**. Feeling that we belong to an exclusive club seems to appeal to our human vanity and pride. It can also be symptomatic of a fear of change. Sad to say, some Christian groups fall into these errors.

Exclusiveness was an attitude among the people of Old Testament times, and the prophets often had occasion to

speak against it. Certainly, those who belonged to Israel were
expected to follow only the ways of the Lord, but they were
also to welcome those who wished to join them – even if they
were 'different' – Israel had no need to fear the influx of new
people into their society. The ancient rule of Israel was that
eunuchs could not even share in public worship (Deuteronomy
23.1); also foreigners were frequently objects of suspicion and
hostility. In God's new order, however, there was room for
both.

If Christian groups are firmly established in the ways of
God, they too need not fear the newcomer or the person who
appears to be 'different'. Where God invites and calls, his
people must not exclude.

* *But we make his love too narrow*
   By false limits of our own;
  And we magnify his strictness
   With a zeal he will not own.   · *Frederick W. Faber*

Wednesday December 13   Isaiah 57.6–15

Why does the Bible so often castigate idolatry? Why is the
prophet in today's reading so scornful of it? After all, we are
frail human beings; we need things we can see and touch. Yes,
indeed – we need symbols in our faith and worship. The
prophets knew that and employed much vivid symbolism in
their teaching; but idolatry is different. It goes further – it
ascribes to the symbol the power, the honour and the worship
which rightly belong to the Creator. That is why idolatry is so
dangerous.

Our idols are unlikely to be 'the smooth stones of the wadis'
(verse 6) or even 'obscene idols' (verse 8, GNB), but they are
very real, nonetheless. Our society idolises all kinds of things
including material possessions, success, achievement and
influence. The trouble with idols is that they do not challenge
us to change our way of life, or to repent. They deceive us into
thinking that we can manipulate them. Those who have idols
for their god, have a **god** who is far too small – a god who
certainly cannot save them. The God in **Isaiah** is quite
different: he is holy and can 'give the humbled spirit new life'
(verse 15). No idol can do that.

* *Thank you, Lord, that you alone are God. Save us from
putting anyone or anything in your place.*

It is reported that, in a few places in South America, local Christian communities have decided not to celebrate the Holy Communion again until their society becomes just and all their citizens are free. 'How', they ask, 'can we break bread together when some of our brothers and sisters have no bread at all? How can we celebrate a sacrament of unity when our community is torn asunder by injustice?' Possibly we may feel that such a reaction is extreme, and that it is better to continue celebrating the Holy Communion as a sign of God's invitation to justice. However, we must not miss the pain or the point.

The Bible repeatedly tells us that unless our worship is accompanied by integrity of life-style it is utterly worthless. In Israel it was considered virtuous to fast. Such fasting, the prophet proclaimed, was useless when accompanied by oppression and violence and bitterness (verse 4). Instead, the sort of fasting God really wants is concerned with social justice (verse 7). Can we take this to heart as a lesson for today's work and worship?

✳ *Pray that your worship may have the integrity of life behind it which God requires.*

Many people are under the impression that the Old Testament tells of a God of wrath, while the New Testament tells of a God of love. This is quite untrue. Both Testaments tell us – although with different emphases and styles – of a God of truth and righteousness whose love and wrath are two sides of the same coin.

In today's reading, the prophet portrays God as looking for justice but not finding it. Therefore, God determines to intervene in human affairs directly. Although the prophet does not specify how this is to happen, he says that God's coming will be as a reprisal to his enemies (verse 18), but it will be as redemption for those who turn from their faults to become his friends (verse 20).

God's intervention has come most fully in his Son Jesus Christ. This brought judgement for those who refused to accept him, but as salvation for those who did accept him. God continues to come to us through the circumstances of our everyday lives, and we are faced with accepting or rejecting him. Sometimes he intervenes to point out our faults, but whatever he does we can be assured that he always acts in love.

✳ *Love was born at Christmas,*
   Love all lovely, Love divine.   *Christina G. Rossetti*

Saturday December 16   Isaiah 60.1–10

When we talk about a city, we sometimes refer to the 'bright lights' even though we know that cities are often places where social problems are at their worst.

In biblical times, cities were – like ours today – a mixture of good and bad. But one city above all stood for something special – that was Jerusalem. King David established it as his capital in the golden age of Israel's prosperity. God promised that his blessing would rest upon it and flow from it. Whenever Jerusalem was invaded the people mourned; the promise of restoration brought great joy.

In today's reading, the prophet looks forward to the time when Jerusalem will be the envy of the earth and others will come to pay homage. That promise has never been entirely fulfilled. When the crux came, Jerusalem rejected God's chosen One (Luke 19.41–44). Yet the Bible still offers us the vision of a holy city – a new Jerusalem – where one day we shall live, and in which there will be no more death, mourning or sadness (Revelation 21.1–4).

✳ *Lord, may your blessing rest upon our homes and communities, and may we look forward in faith to being citizens of heaven.*

For group discussion and personal thought

Last Sunday was Bible Sunday. What verses from this week's readings have been particularly helpful to you? In what ways has the Bible spoken to you during this year, and how has this affected your life? How can we help others in the church fellowship to find Bible study more meaningful and enjoyable?

● Have you remembered to order your copy of **Notes on Bible Readings** for 1990?

God cares for his people and loves them. Despair need never
be the last word for God's people. They had known defeat and
exile, and then later the joy of being restored to their own
land. Yet the somewhat dispirited community life which
followed the restoration hardly seemed like a 'year of favour'
(verse 2).

In today's reading the prophet announces that God still has
good things in store for his people. He compares it to the Year
of Jubilee (Leviticus 25.8–13) which was intended to
celebrate Israel's being set free from slavery in Egypt. God's
future will include liberty and freedom (verse 1), the reversal
of their despondency and mourning (verse 3) and the
restoration of what had been destroyed (verse 4).

When Jesus began his ministry in Galilee, he chose this
passage from **Isaiah** as a kind of manifesto for his own
ministry (Luke 4.16–20). Through his life, death and
resurrection God's promises have been widened from Israel to
the whole world. In the deepest sense, those who have trust in
Christ know liberty even when they are captives, sight even
if they are blind, and freedom even if they are oppressed. For
Christians, despair is indeed never the last word.

✳ *Pray for those who are poor, oppressed or in prison, that they
may know the liberty Christ brings.*

Monday December 18   Isaiah 62.1–12

The future is always God's gift. We spend much of our lives
thinking and planning, working and praying, so that the
future for ourselves, our family and our nation will be a good
one. There is nothing wrong with that; God wants us to be
positive and forward-looking. But we are reminded in today's
reading, that even when human endeavour has done its very
best, the future is still God's gift.

No doubt those who lived in Jerusalem at that time eagerly
wanted a good future. In this poem they are reminded that it
is God who brings things about. He will not give up
Jerusalem, but will confer a 'new name' upon her (verse 2).
People will rejoice when God 'takes delight' in them (verse 4);
the restoration of the city will be God's work (verse 7), and the
reason for hope is that the Lord will come to save them (verses
11–12).

There is no good future for any of us unless we submit our

plans, hopes and fears to God and allow him to do his work with us. When that is done we can have every confidence in what God has in store for us.

✳ *Pray for those who are anxious about the future.*

Tuesday December 19

Do we really want God enough? We say we do, but is it true? Our faith and worship can easily become lip-service, but it is often in times of adversity and trouble that we come to know how deeply we desire God, and how wonderful he is.

▶ Read **Isaiah 63.15 to 64.4**.

It was when the people of Israel came to realise how far they had travelled from God, how deep their sin and failure were, how they had become like people who did not bear God's name (verse 19), that the impassioned cry could go up to God, 'Oh, that you would tear the heavens open and come down' (verse 1). God always hears that kind of cry. He is able to do something when it is acknowledged that he alone has power to save those who trust him.

This cry for God's presence is a universal human longing. It has been answered in his wonderful sending of Jesus his Son. In these days leading up to Christmas, as we reflect on the coming of Christ to our world, and on the salvation he brought, we know that this above all else is what no eye has seen and no ear has heard (compare verse 4 with 1 Corinthians 2.9). Yet it is the world's greatest open secret. If we want God enough we can find him, for he has found us first, through Jesus.

✳ *Lord, there are many who have deep spiritual needs yet do not know you. Show them your love in Christ.*

Wednesday December 20

There has been much discussion in Christian circles in recent years about whether we can call the disease AIDS the 'wrath of God'. Such an idea has been possible because, in Western societies at least, AIDS has been most common among those who follow a life-style which many Christians would judge to be wrong. How **does** God's anger – wrath – make itself known to us?

▶ Read **Isaiah 64.5–12**.

In this reading there is a clear indication of the sinfulness of the nation and a plea that God's anger against their sins should not go too far (verse 9). This anger is seen in terms of God's silence (verse 12) and the way in which, as the prophet puts it, God 'gave us up to the power of our sins' (verse 7). This thought is strikingly similar to the way Paul describes the anger of God. Three times in Romans 1.24 – 28 he describes how God 'left' or 'abandoned' people to the consequences of their deeds. What those consequences are depends, of course, on the nature of the sin.

Although we have all sinned, we are not left without hope. The answer to the plea that God should not remain unmoved by his people's plight is found in the compassion of Christ our Saviour.

✷ *Praise God, for he has visited and redeemed his people.*

Thursday December 21   **Isaiah 65.8 – 10, 17 – 25**

The proverb 'one bad apple infects the barrel' is only a half-truth when applied to the spiritual life; for where there is good, however little it may be, God can take and use it.

In the Old Testament this is frequently expressed in terms of the 'remnant' – the best-known story probably being the one in which Abraham secured God's agreement not to destroy Sodom even if only ten righteous people could be found within it (Genesis 18.16 – 32).

In today's reading God promises that there will not be destruction for the whole of Israel, because there are some who serve him (verses 8 – 9). For those who are saved there is rich promise of an idyllic future. The picture the prophet draws of this might seem to us to be somewhat exaggerated. However, we must understand that he is not making a literal promise that, for example, all true believers will live to be a hundred (verse 20)! This idyllic picture of life is often used by the prophets to stress that God will be good to his faithful people (see Zechariah 8.4 – 5).

✷ *As our Christmas celebrations draw near, think about the ways in which God has been good to you, and give thanks.*

Friday December 22   **Isaiah 66.1 – 2, 5 – 16**

We are prone to think that God needs our offerings. If we have done a piece of work for God there is a temptation to think

247

'God will be grateful for that'. Today's reading puts all our work for God into proper perspective. He is the Creator of everything that is; he is the good and perfect giver of every gift we receive and everything we possess. How then, could we possibly imagine – except through human vanity – that by doing work for God, we have done him a favour? As God says, 'all of this is mine' (verse 2).

However, there is one thing we can offer God, and it is the most precious thing of all – it is a 'humbled and contrite spirit' (verse 2). God will not compel us to offer that, but he does invite it. When he invited Mary to co-operate with him in his purposes for the saving of the world, she replied, 'I am the handmaid of the Lord' (Luke 1.38). In Mary's response there is the pattern for all Christian response. Those who are willing to offer a humble spirit to God allow him to do great things through them. May that be true for us.

✷ *Accept the gifts we offer*
  For all thy love imparts,
  And, what thou most desirest,
  Our humble, thankful hearts.   *Matthias Claudius*

Saturday December 23   Isaiah 66.18 – 24

At times, we make God too small. We speak and behave as if he is only concerned about Christians. The Bible offers many correctives to this lack of vision, by making it plain that he is God of the whole earth (Psalm 24.1). In today's reading we are told about the time when the Lord says that 'all mankind will come to bow down in my presence' (verse 23). It is a wonderful picture – the glorious diversity of the nations gathered in worship of the one true God.

Jesus came to this world in order to make this possible. He was named **Jesus** precisely because he would save his people from their sins (Matthew 1.21) – his death on the cross would make salvation available to all (John 12.32). Those of us who are privileged to know God's love in Christ cannot rest content until others have had the opportunity to know it too. The Christmas season draws near, and offers us the opportunity to tell others about the baby in the manger who became for us the Man on the cross. We can play our small part in hastening the time when Isaiah's vision will become reality.

✷ *Gather your people together, Lord, in worship and praise.*
May the whole earth be filled with your glory and peace.

For group discussion and personal thought

Think about the star of Bethlehem as a sign of hope. One of the main themes of the prophecies in **Isaiah 55 – 66** is **hope**. Look particularly at **Isaiah 60.1 – 2; 61.1 – 4; 62.10 – 11** and **65.17 – 19**. What are your hopes this Christmas – for yourself and for the world?

Prayer for Christmas

Jesus,
new-born child of all time,
we greet your birth
with wide-eyed delight.
You are precious beyond words
for our world needs your presence more than ever.

Let the angels' promise of your good news
offering joy and peace to all the world
be heard by those who lead and guide.
Let kings bow down
and all creation greet this holy moment
as we seek to grasp its magnitude.

For you are God's gift
silently delivered
to every human heart.

LOVE COMES DOWN AT CHRISTMAS

Selected Christmas readings

Notes by the Revd Lesley Husselbee, MSc, PhD

Lesley Husselbee (nee Beale) is minister of Cores End United Reformed Church, Bourne End, Buckinghamshire. She has previously taught in primary and secondary schools in London, was a senior lecturer at the Roehampton Institute, and held a pastorate in Coventry.

The notes in this section are based on the New English Bible.

We can never fully appreciate all the implications of God's love for us, but we are given some very special insights into this love in the story of the birth of Jesus. Love was present with Mary when a messenger told her that she was to give birth to the Son of God. It was there when Joseph took her to Bethlehem and Jesus was born in a stable. The glory of it was revealed to shepherds, and later to Simeon who saw the universal meaning of it. The writer of **John's Gospel** proclaimed it as the Word of God – God's very self come to us in a human being. This divine love – as declared in **1 John** – is seen, heard and handled in the life of the Church. Love is where God is and where men and women respond with faith to Jesus his Son, the Saviour of the world.

4th Sunday in Advent, December 24   **Luke 1.26 – 38**

'There is nothing love cannot face.' (1 Corinthians 13.7)

In the story of the angel and Mary it may seem that God's love is present only in a gentle, humble reception of him. It is tempting to see Mary as a quiet, passive girl who acted as a receptacle for God's gift of himself to her. But, although Mary responded in this way, she was greatly disturbed by what she heard.

Later, in her song of praise which we call the *Magnificat*, Mary showed that one of the signs of the presence of the love of God may be in revolutionary change. Read **Luke 1.46 – 55**. These words may be so familiar to us that sometimes we fail to understand their meaning for us today. Would a stranger identify you as one of the poor or one of the rich? One of the powerless or one of the powerful? God does not reject those who have power and material belongings; but, if we have these, we have a responsibility to help others.

If we respond whole-heartedly to God's love — as Mary did — it will make demands on us which may be highly uncomfortable.

✳ *On this Christmas Eve, pray for those who are hungry and homeless, and for governments and others in power that they may enable everyone to obtain dignity and power to control their lives.*

Christmas Day, December 25   Luke 2.1−7

'There is no limit to . . . its (love's) endurance.'
(1 Corinthians 13.7)

How inconvenient it must have been for Joseph and for Mary, who was just about to give birth, to have to uproot from their home and travel to Bethlehem! How desperate they must have been to find shelter that night! And yet, even in the most difficult of circumstances, we see God's love shining through in a harsh world. We see it in Joseph's care for Mary and the child to be born. God's love is present even where governments make harsh and unreasonable demands on people; and wherever people are homeless or hungry. God is there to support us whatever our difficulties.

Whenever we see famine in the world; whenever we see people being killed in wars fought by nations seeking power; whenever we personally encounter anxiety, illness or bereavement, it is tempting to blame God for his neglect. But God's supreme gift of his Son, born in far from ideal conditions, proves that God's love is always surrounding us. Indeed, it is often through trouble, difficulty and suffering that we grow most as people, and learn most about God's will.

✳ *Lord, we praise you that you are always showing us signs of your love, even when life is difficult. We thank you most of all for the self-emptying gift of your Son. Be especially with those who are battling with hardship and despair today.*

> *Joy to the world, the Lord is come!*
> *Let earth receive her King;*
> *Let every heart prepare his room.*   Isaac Watts

'Love is never boastful, nor conceited.'

(1 Corinthians 13.4)

When we have good news that affects us deeply, with whom do we choose to share it first? We do not usually choose rich or influential people to be the first to hear. Rather, we tell the people we love most. We tell our family, we tell people who will listen with sympathy – people who will rejoice with us.

God had great news to share – the greatest there has ever been. His Son had been born in Bethlehem! And who did God choose to be the first ones to share this marvellous news? He did not choose those who had made it their life's work to study his will; nor did he choose rich and influential people; nor even good orators who could proclaim the news in well-chosen words. He chose **shepherds** – ordinary, rough men of the fields and hills.

God is no respecter of persons. His love comes to all of us, even if we feel that we are only ordinary people. It comes to outcasts, to the rejected. The glory of God's love shines in the face of sinners, and upon people who have no standing in the world.

✳ *Lord, thank you for choosing me for the privilege of hearing the good news of the birth of your Son. Help me to respond with love, sympathy and rejoicing, so that my life may be changed and your love known to others.*

'There is no limit . . . to its (love's) hope.'

(1 Corinthians 13.7)

God gave the world the gift of his Son because he loves us. Mary and Joseph wanted to respond to that love by bringing their child Jesus to the temple in loving gratitude for his gift. They came to fulfil the ancient Jewish ceremonies:

● As the first-born son, Jesus was sacred to God and, according to the law (Exodus 13.2), he had to be given back to God.
● They came so that Mary could be purified after childbirth. According to the Jewish law, a woman was unclean for forty days after she had given birth to a boy. At the end of that time she had to bring a lamb offering to be burnt at the altar as a sacrifice to God and as a sin-offering. But a lamb was expensive; Mary and Joseph could only afford two pigeons – the 'offering of the poor'.

Behind these ceremonies is the conviction that a child is a gift of God. How precious is the gift of a child – or of any person for that matter! We can only respond to God's love, in sending us the gift of his Son, by the loving care that we show for all people.

✳ *Pray for parents, that they may create a loving home for their children.*

Thursday December 28   Luke 2.25 – 35

'Love is patient.' (1 Corinthians 13.4)

'Lord, where are you? Why don't you **do** something?' How anxious we often become when we pray to God and nothing seems to happen! We like to be in control of our lives and to see instant results. If nothing happens when we pray, it is tempting to assume that God has deserted us.

Simeon can teach us a great deal about patient love. Most Jews of his time regarded themselves as God's chosen people. They constantly expected that some great champion, or even God himself, would break into history by some spectacular means, and they waited impatiently for that day. But Simeon was one of a few people who were known as 'the quiet in the land'. They believed, not in violence and force, but in a life of constant prayer and quiet watchfulness, until God should come.

This quiet, patient openness enabled Simeon to recognise God's love at work in the baby Jesus, when he was brought into the temple that day. In his great hymn which we call the *Nunc Dimittis* (verses 29 – 32), Simeon praised God for enabling him to witness his promise. He was also given the insight to recognise that God's loving gift of his Son was not just for Jewish people, but for **all** people in the world.

✳ *Lord, help me to be still and know that you are God. Take away my anxiety and my desire for instant results. Instead, in your loving-kindness, grant me the insight to discern your will.*

Friday December 29   John 1.1 – 14

'Love will never come to an end.' (1 Corinthians 13.8)

How hard we find it to go on loving and caring for a person or a group of people when they do not respond! It is even harder when they throw our love and care back in our face. It is very difficult to go on telling others about God's love for us when they do not want to listen – and even worse, when they become abusive. It is very tempting to give up.

But God did not give up. When people refused to recognise him, even though he had spoken to them through the prophets, he sent his most precious gift – the fullest expression of his love – his Son. This was not an easy thing for him to do for it entailed giving all of himself, and involved suffering and death.

God's love never ends. It has always been available for us and always will be. Jesus Christ – the **'Word'** – is the embodiment of God's love, wisdom and reason. Through Christ God offers us light and life – the opposite to rejection, destruction, condemnation and death, and all the dark things of our world.

✴ *Lord, help us not to be bitter if things have not turned out as we would have wished: if we have tried to be helpful and no one has thanked us; if we have put ourselves out and no one has noticed; if we have done our best but were told we had failed. Help us to remember your constant love for us.*

Saturday December 30   1 John 1.1–10

'But the greatest of all is love.' (1 Corinthians 13.13) When copper was discovered in Northern Rhodesia in the 1920s, the people came from miles around to work in the mines. The area had not previously been visited by western missionaries, and there were no churches, so Christian miners set up their own church in Ndola. Christianity grew and spread. In Ndola (now in Zambia), there are churches in every suburb, and each has over 1,000 members. The church has grown because Christians there have a personal knowledge of the love of Christ. That knowledge and love of God has so lit up their lives that it is contagious. They want to pass on what they have seen and heard.

The community of the Church should be a place where we can see, hear and touch the love of God; a place where we can experience his love for ourselves, so that it becomes a tangible thing – not least when we take part in Holy Communion, and when we are assured of God's forgiveness. As we move into a new year, can we resolve to pass on our personal experience of the love of God to others, like the Christians of Ndola?

✳ *Lord, help me to share my personal experience of Christ with others. May there come a time when everyone in the world has a deep, personal knowledge of your love.*

For group discussion and personal thought

Reflect on what has happened to you in 1989. What do you regret? What do you remember with most joy? This week's readings tell us about several people who recognised God's love as shown in Jesus. What can we learn from them? In the light of this, what resolutions will you make for 1990?

Sunday December 31　　　　　　　　　**1 John 4.7 – 21**

'If God thus loved us . . . we in turn are bound to love one another.' (1 John 4.11)

A mother was distressed when her baby was diagnosed as being mentally-handicapped. At first, she was angry with God for causing this to happen, and found it difficult to love the baby. Later, Christian friends helped her to understand that God had not caused the handicap and, as time went on, a very special love grew up between her and her son. This was made stronger because he needed her in a very special way, and had an especially loving personality. The child, in fact, taught her to love in a way that she never would have done had the boy been 'normal'.

We are never nearer to God than when we love. It is only by knowing God that we learn to love, and only by loving that we learn to know God. God loved us so much that he sent his Son into the world, so that by his example we can have a special insight into God's love for us.

As we enter a new year and indeed, a new decade – we may be thinking of making resolutions. What a difference it would make to our lives, and to the lives of other people, if we could grow more and more loving in all our relationships as the decade advances!

✳ *Lord, we offer to you the past year, its joys and regrets. We ask your blessing on the year to come and pray that you will help us to love you and other people more each day.*

SCHEME OF READINGS for 1990